60 Minute
Guide to Shockwave™

60 Minute
Guide to Shockwave™

William W. Hurley II
T. Preston Gregg
Sebastian Hassinger

IDG Books Worldwide, Inc.

Foster City, CA • Chicago, IL • Indianapolis, IN • Braintree, MA • Southlake, TX

60 Minute Guide to Shockwave™

Published by
IDG Books Worldwide, Inc.
An International Data Group Company
919 E. Hillsdale Blvd.
Suite 400
Foster City, CA 94404

Library of Congress Catalog Card No.: 96-75772

ISBN: 0-7645-8002-7

Printed in the United States of America

10 9 8 7 6 5 4 3 2 1

1A/QS/QU/ZW/BR

Distributed in the United States by IDG Books Worldwide, Inc.

Distributed by Macmillan Canada for Canada; by Computer and Technical Books for the Caribbean Basin; by Contemporanea de Ediciones for Venezuela; by Distribuidora Cuspide for Argentina; by CITEC for Brazil; by Ediciones ZETA S.C.R. Ltda. for Peru; by Editorial Limusa SA for Mexico; by Transworld Publishers Limited in the United Kingdom and Europe; by Al-Maiman Publishers & Distributors for Saudi Arabia; by Simron Pty. Ltd. for South Africa; by IDG Communications (HK) Ltd. for Hong Kong; by Toppan Company Ltd. for Japan; by Addison Wesley Publishing Company for Korea; by Longman Singapore Publishers Ltd. for Singapore, Malaysia, Thailand, and Indonesia; by Unalis Corporation for Taiwan; by WS Computer Publishing Company, Inc. for the Philippines; by WoodsLane Pty. Ltd. for Australia; by WoodsLane Enterprises Ltd. for New Zealand.

For general information on IDG Books Worldwide's books in the U.S., please call our Consumer Customer Service department at 800-762-2974. For reseller information, including discounts and premium sales, please call our Reseller Customer Service department at 800-434-3422.

For information on where to purchase IDG Books Worldwide's books outside the U.S., contact IDG Books Worldwide at 415-655-3021 or fax 415-655-3295.

For information on translations, contact Marc Jeffrey Mikulich, Director, Foreign & Subsidiary Rights, at IDG Books Worldwide, 415-655-3018 or fax 415-655-3295.

For sales inquiries and special prices for bulk quantities, write to the address above or call IDG Books Worldwide at 415-655-3200.

For information on using IDG Books Worldwide's books in the classroom, or ordering examination copies, contact the Education Office at 800-434-2086 or fax 817-251-8174.

For authorization to photocopy items for corporate, personal, or educational use, please contact Copyright Clearance Center, 222 Rosewood Drive, Danvers, MA 01923, or fax 508-750-4470.

 is a trademark under exclusive license to IDG Books Worldwide, Inc., from International Data Group, Inc.

ABOUT IDG BOOKS WORLDWIDE

WINNER
Eighth Annual
Computer Press
Awards 1992

WINNER
Ninth Annual
Computer Press
Awards 1993

IDG BOOKS WORLDWIDE

Welcome to the world of IDG Books Worldwide.

IDG Books Worldwide, Inc., is a subsidiary of International Data Group, the world's largest publisher of computer-related information and the leading global provider of information services on information technology. IDG was founded more than 25 years ago and now employs more than 7,700 people worldwide. IDG publishes more than 250 computer publications in 67 countries (see listing below). More than 70 million people read one or more IDG publications each month.

Launched in 1990, IDG Books Worldwide is today the #1 publisher of best-selling computer books in the United States. We are proud to have received 8 awards from the Computer Press Association in recognition of editorial excellence and three from Computer Currents' First Annual Readers' Choice Awards, and our best-selling ...*For Dummies*® series has more than 19 million copies in print with translations in 28 languages. IDG Books Worldwide, through a joint venture with IDG's Hi-Tech Beijing, became the first U.S. publisher to publish a computer book in the People's Republic of China. In record time, IDG Books Worldwide has become the first choice for millions of readers around the world who want to learn how to better manage their businesses.

Our mission is simple: Every IDG and Compaq press book is designed to bring extra value and skill-building instructions to the reader. Our books are written by experts who understand and care about our readers. The knowledge base of our editorial staff comes from years of experience in publishing, education, and journalism — experience which we use to produce books for the '90s. In short, we care about books, so we attract the best people. We devote special attention to details such as audience, interior design, use of icons, and illustrations. And because we use an efficient process of authoring, editing, and desktop publishing our books electronically, we can spend more time ensuring superior content and spend less time on the technicalities of making books.

You can count on our commitment to deliver high-quality books at competitive prices on topics you want to read about. At IDG Books Worldwide, we're continuing in IDG's 25 year tradition of delivery quality. You'll find no better book on a subject than one from IDG Books Worldwide.

John Kilcullen
President and CEO
IDG Books Worldwide, Inc.

IDG Books Worldwide, Inc., is a subsidiary of International Data Group, the world's largest publisher of computer-related information and the leading global provider of information services on information technology. International Data Group publishes over 250 computer publications in 67 countries. Seventy million people read one or more International Data Group publications each month. International Data Group's publications include: **ARGENTINA:** Computerworld Argentina, GamePro, Infoworld, PC World Argentina; **AUSTRALIA:** Australian Macworld, Client/Server Journal, Computer Living, Computerworld, Digital News, Network World, PC World, Publishing Essentials, Reseller; **AUSTRIA:** Computerwelt, PC TEST; **BELARUS:** PC World Belarus; **BELGIUM:** Data News; **BRAZIL:** Annuário de Informática, Computerworld Brazil, Connections, Super Game Power, Macworld, PC World Brazil, Publish Brazil, SUPERGAME; **BULGARIA:** Computerworld Bulgaria, Networkworld/Bulgaria, PC & MacWorld Bulgaria; **CANADA:** CIO Canada, ComputerWorld Canada, InfoCanada, Network World Canada, Reseller World; **CHILE:** Computerworld Chile, GamePro, PC World Chile; **COLUMBIA:** Computerworld Colombia, GamePro, PC World Colombia; **COSTA RICA:** PC World Costa Rica/Nicaragua; **THE CZECH AND SLOVAK REPUBLICS:** Computerworld Czechoslovakia, Elektronika Czechoslovakia, PC World Czechoslovakia; **DENMARK:** Communications World, Computerworld Danmark, Macworld Danmark, PC World Danmark, PC World Danmark Supplements, TECH World; **DOMINICAN REPUBLIC:** PC World Republica Dominicana; **ECUADOR:** PC World Ecuador, GamePro; **EGYPT:** Computerworld Middle East, PC World Middle East; **EL SALVADOR:** PC World Centro America; **FINLAND:** MikroPC, Tietoverkko, Tietoviikko; **FRANCE:** Distributique, Golden, Info PC, Le Guide du Monde Informatique, Le Monde Informatique, Reseaux & Telecoms; **GERMANY:** Computer Business, Computerwoche, Computerwoche Extra, Computerwoche Focus, Electronic Entertainment, GamePro, I/M Information Management, Macwelt, PC Welt; **GREECE:** GamePro, Macworld & Publish; **GUATEMALA:** PC World Centro America; **HONDURAS:** PC World Centro America; **HONG KONG:** Computerworld Hong Kong, PCWorld Hong Kong, Publish in Asia; **HUNGARY:** ABCD CD-ROM, Computerworld Szamitastechnika, PC & Mac World Hungary, PC-X Magazine; **INDIA:** Computerworld India, PC World India, Publish in Asia; **INDONESIA:** InfoKomputer PC World, Komputek Computerworld, Publish in Asia; **IRELAND:** ComputerScope, PC Live!; **ISRAEL:** PC World 32 BIT, People & Computers; **ITALY:** Computerworld Italia, Computerworld Italia Special Editions, Lotus Italia, Macworld Italia, Networking Italia, PC Shopping, PC World Italia, PC World/Walt Disney; **JAPAN:** Macworld Japan, Nikkei Personal Computing, SunWorld Japan, Windows World Japan; **KENYA:** East African Computer News; **KOREA:** Hi-Tech Information/Computerworld, Macworld Korea, PC World Korea; **MACEDONIA:** PC World Macedonia; **MALAYSIA:** Computerworld Malaysia, PC World Malaysia, Publish in Asia; **MEXICO:** Computerworld Mexico, GamePro, Macworld, PC World Mexico; **MYANMAR:** PC World Myanmar; **NETHERLANDS:** Computable, Computer! Totaal, LAN Magazine, Macworld, Net Magazine; **NEW ZEALAND:** Computer Buyer, Computerworld New Zealand, MTB, Network World, PC World New Zealand; **NICARAGUA:** PC World Costa Rica/Nicaragua; **NIGERIA:** PC World Africa; **NORWAY:** Computerworld Norge, Computerworld Privat, CW Rapport Klient/Tjener, CW Rapport Nettverk & Telecom, CW Rapport Offentlig Sektor, IDG's KURSGUIDE, Macworld Norge, Multimedia World, PC World Ekspress, PC World Nettverk, PC World Norge, PC World's Produktguide, Windows Spesial; **PAKISTAN:** Computerworld Pakistan, PC World Pakistan; **PANAMA:** GamePro, PC World Panama; **PARAGUAY:** PC World Paraguay; **P. R. OF CHINA:** China Computerworld, China Infoworld, Computer & Communication, Electronic Product World, Electronics Today, Game Camp, PC World China, Popular Computer Week, Software World, Telecom Product World; **PERU:** Computerworld Peru, GamePro, PC World Profesional Peru, PC World Peru; **POLAND:** Computerworld Poland, Computerworld Special Report, Macworld, Networld, PC World Komputer; **PHILIPPINES:** Computerworld Philippines, PC Digest, Publish in Asia; **PORTUGAL:** Cerebro/PC World, Correio Informático/Computerworld, Mac•In/PC•In Portugal; **PUERTO RICO:** PC World Puerto Rico; **ROMANIA:** Computerworld Romania, PC World Romania, Telecom Romania; **RUSSIA:** Computerworld Rossiya, Network World Russia, PC World Russia; **SINGAPORE:** Computerworld Singapore, PC World Singapore, Publish in Asia; **SLOVENIA:** MONITOR; **SOUTH AFRICA:** Computing S.A., Network World S.A., Software World; **SPAIN:** Computerworld España, COMUNICACIONES WORLD, Dealer World, Macworld España, PC World España; **SWEDEN:** CAP&Design, Computer Sweden, Corporate Computing, MacWorld, Maxi Data, MikroDatorn, Nätverk & Kommunikation, PC/Aktiv, PC World, Windows World; **SWITZERLAND:** Computerworld Schweiz, Macworld Schweiz, PCtip; **TAIWAN:** Computerworld Taiwan, Macworld Taiwan, PC World Taiwan, Publish Taiwan, Windows World; **THAILAND:** Thai Computerworld, Publish in Asia; **TURKEY:** Computerworld Monitör, MACWORLD Türkiye, PC WORLD Türkiye; **UKRAINE:** Computerworld Kiev, Computers & Software Magazine, PC World Ukraine; **UNITED KINGDOM:** Acorn User, Amiga Action, Amiga Computing, Amiga, Appletalk, CD Powerplay, CD-ROM Now, Computing, Connexion, GamePro, Lotus Magazine, Macaction, Macworld, Open Computing, Parents and Computers, PC Home, PC Works, The WEB; **UNITED STATES:** Cable in the Classroom, CD Review, CIO Magazine, Computerworld, Computerworld Client/Server Journal, Digital Video Magazine, DOS World, Electronic, InfoWorld, I-Way, Macworld, Maximize, MULTIMEDIA WORLD, Network World, PC World, PUBLISH, SWATPro Magazine, Video Event, WebMaster; **URUGUAY:** PC World Uruguay; **VENEZUELA:** Computerworld Venezuela, GamePro, PC World Venezuela; and **VIETNAM:** PC World Vietnam

About the Authors

William W. Hurley II is a multimedia producer with experience in all aspects of multimedia, including development, training, and project management. William attended the Texas State Technical College Audio/Video Production program. He has also composed and recorded original soundtracks and sound effects for multimedia productions.

When he's not working on title development, William provides audio engineering and MIDI training, and multimedia production services to producers and development engineers nationwide. William has also conducted beta testing for several software companies and is one of the original alpha and beta testers for Macromedia Director 5.0, Netscape 2.0, and Shockwave. William is a member of the Netscape Development Partners Group and is currently working to advance the presence of multimedia and multimedia training on the Internet.

William W. Hurley II
14300 Tandem Blvd. #168
Austin, TX 78728

Office: (512) 908-8722
E-mail: Mystic@outer.net

T. Preston Gregg is an Internet technology consultant with a focus on commercial content distribution and interactive multimedia. Preston co-manages the content and systems of Apple Computer's http://www.info.apple.com World Wide Web site, Apple's largest Internet-based content presence with a focus on technical- and support-related information. Preston also serves as a content advisor to Tulum Communications, an Austin-based Internet consulting and multimedia development firm.

Preston's technical efforts revolve around Macintosh- and UNIX-based Internet servers, Internet content design, and technology integration. Aside from server development and administration, Preston designs Web-based systems with a flair for automation, navigation, viewer interaction, speed, and usability.

Preston is a graduate of the University of Texas at Austin with a B.S. in Journalism. Aside from computers, Preston enjoys flying small aircraft over the beautiful Texas hill country, the unique and lively Austin music scene, and spending time with his wife, Jodi.

T. Preston Gregg
8217 Shoal Creek Blvd., Suite 106
Austin, TX 78757

Office: (512) 835-8348
E-mail: pgregg@tulum.com

Sebastian Hassinger splits his time among writing, consulting, scripting, messing with multimedia and computer graphics, spending time with his family, occasionally eating—but never, ever sleeping. During the day, he's a partner in OuterNet Connection Strategies, an Internet service provider, and lends a hand in the production of Apple Computer's online and subscription support services.

Sebastian coauthored *The Foundations of WWW Programming with CGI and HTML*, *The 60 Minute Guide to VRML*, and *World Wide Web Programming Secrets*. All are IDG Books Worldwide titles; the first two were published in 1995, the third in 1996. Sebastian wants to be a fireman when he grows up!

Sebastian Hassinger
2215 Post Rd., Apt. 2012
Austin, TX 78704

Office: (512) 908-8517
Fax: (512) 206-0345
E-mail: singe@outer.net

Acknowledgments

William W. Hurley II: I want to start by thanking my family: Mom, Dad, and Charlie. They have always shown support for everything I have done. I would also like to thank everyone who helped to make this project a reality: my coauthors, Sebastian Hassinger and T. Preston Gregg, as well as Ed Tittel and everyone at IDG Books. This book was a team effort, and I would like to thank the Macromedia part of our team, John C. "Bud" Colligan, Rachel Schindler, Carrie Myers, and everyone else at Macromedia who helped. A special thanks goes to a special friend who has always been supportive, even when that friend doesn't know it. Above all, I would like to thank God and my loving wife. Both are constants in my life, and neither could I live without. Trish, your love and support during this project were unparalleled, and I can't begin to tell you how much you mean to me.

T. Preston Gregg: Writing books takes much more than just getting words to paper. This book wouldn't have happened without the dedicated efforts of many individuals. First, I would like to thank my coauthors, William and Sebastian, as well as Ed Tittel, who managed the author team while busy with numerous other projects. Your time and dedication are appreciated.

Thank you to my wife, Jodi. Without your patience and support I could not do any of this. You have been wonderful throughout this effort. A special thank you to my parents, Tom and Frances. Without your support from day one, none of this would be possible. Thank you for hanging in there. Also, acknowledgments to Michael and Nathan for keeping me going throughout this project.

Sebastian Hassinger: This book has been a rocket ride! I had the privilege to work with some of the most enthusiastic, dedicated, nonstop individuals I know, and I feel indebted to all of them. In particular, I want to thank my coauthors, William Hurley and Preston Gregg, for trusting me when the waters were murky. Thanks also to Ed Tittel and everyone at IDG for keeping it all together. Special thanks to Nina, Eyre, and Haefen, without whom none of this would be possible.

Finally, all of us would like to thank the whole IDG production team—including Ralph Moore, project editor extraordinaire; Michael Stewart, our favorite technical editor; Jerry Olsen, our wonderful manuscript editor; and Ronnie Bucci and Dusty Parsons, our favorite compositors—for all of their help in putting this book together. Last, but by no means least, we'd also like to thank our old friends and partners, Anne Marie Walker and Amy Pedersen, for giving us another chance to work together.

The publisher would like to give special thanks to Patrick McGovern, without whom this book would not have been possible.

Credits

IDG Books Worldwide, Inc.

Vice President and Publisher
Christopher J. Williams

Publishing Director
John Osborn

Senior Acquisitions Manager
Amorette Pedersen

Managing Editor
Kim Field

Editorial Director
Anne Marie Walker

Editorial Assistant
Tracy J. Brown

Creative Services
Julia Stasio

Project Editor
Ralph E. Moore

Manuscript Editor
J. W. Olsen

Technical Editor
James Michael Stewart

Composition and Layout
Ronnie K. Bucci
Dusty Parsons
Andrew Stachiewicz

Proofreader
Mildred Rosenzweig

Indexer
Liz Cunningham

Cover Design
Liew Design

Contents

CHAPTER 1

Foreword

*t*rue multimedia on the Internet is here! What was once only a dream is now a reality: With Shockwave for Director, you can easily integrate full-blown multimedia into your Web pages. This new technology empowers every multimedia producer, designer, and artist to create and deliver multimedia content on the Internet. The tools to build such Web publications have never before been available to mere mortals. But with Shockwave, you don't have to know complex programming languages to wow your audience with outstanding interactive multimedia content.

Shockwave combines the enormous popularity and capabilities of Internet communications with the high-level interactivity of multimedia and Macromedia Director's broad developer base. Shockwave draws on Director's outstanding content creation capabilities to provide a vast source of material that will be available on the Internet. Shockwave also provides state-of-the-art compression technology in its Afterburner module to deliver large amounts of information "across the wire" in a reasonable amount of time. Finally, the Shockwave plug-in, which has already been adopted by Netscape Communications, Inc. for Navigator 2.0, provides users with the ability to play multimedia content right from their own Web browsers.

Shockwave's combination of content, compression, and broad availability will be hard to beat. On behalf of Macromedia and the whole Director development community, I'd like to say: Welcome to the multimedia revolution, and enjoy using this new technology on the Internet! I think you'll find this book a useful tool to help you get started.

Best Wishes,
John "Bud" Colligan
President and CEO
Macromedia, Inc.
http://www.macromedia.com

Introduction

*W*elcome to Shockwave, your key to delivering multimedia through the World Wide Web! Shockwave is the first technology your authors have ever encountered whose creator, Macromedia, Inc., delivered a complete package to the marketplace the same day they announced their intentions to do so. Thus, rather than dealing with alpha or beta code prior to an official release, we've had the rare good fortune to work with a reasonably complete and polished environment. For once, this has been a case where a new technology has led those developers who seek to use it. Rather than being prodded into features and functions by its unruly developers, Shockwave has sprung much more fully formed from its originators than is so often the case with new application technologies.

But even though Shockwave for Director technology is ready to rock 'n' roll, it's still far from mature. Macromedia is already working on numerous extensions and enhancements for future releases. At the same time, many developers are scratching their heads and trying to figure out how to make the best use of Shockwave's exciting possibilities.

By now, you're probably wondering: What is this Shockwave stuff, anyway? In a nutshell, Shockwave provides an Internet delivery mechanism for multimedia projects created using Macromedia Director.

Because Director boasts a large developer base—more than a quarter-million users—and has been in use for some time, this translates into a whopping amount of content that has already been created.

Better still, Shockwave provides a powerful front-end compression tool to squeeze multimedia projects into sizes more suited for Internet delivery. It's not unusual for a typical Director file to exceed two megabytes in size; for CD-ROM or hard-disk based projects, this is no big deal, but for delivery over the Internet, that's a mighty big deal indeed. Shockwave's compression tool is called Afterburner, which can reduce multimegabyte projects to less than 100KB in size! This makes Internet delivery much more tolerable, especially for the majority of users, who connect via modem.

On the receiving end, the main Shockwave ingredient is a plug-in module. Prosaically enough, this module is called *the Shockwave plug-in*. Basically, this plug-in extends a Shockwave-enabled Web browser by handling and displaying incoming Shockwave projects, which are recognized by their unique file extensions. At present, Netscape 2.0 is the only Shockwave-enabled Web browser, but with more than 70 percent market share, this guarantees broad, immediate exposure for Shockwave on the Web.

By the time you read this, things should have settled down quite a bit. Other browser vendors who have announced support for the Shockwave plug-in will probably have working beta versions, if not commercial releases, of that code. That should help to reduce any uncertainty about Shockwave, as will more widespread design and development experience. We can only hope that, by pointing out good usage techniques, alerting you to our own mistakes, and steering you around the hazards we encountered, our experiences can be your guide and help you master this fascinating technology quickly and easily.

About This Book

There are two fundamental ways to think of this book:

1. It is built to be approached as a series of three, 60-minute tutorials on Shockwave in which each tutorial delivers a specific lesson or set of information on the subject.

2. It is meant to be an overview of the current state of Shockwave technology, but also to provide sign posts to more current information, because Shockwave is a moving target right now.

In neither case is this book meant to be an exhaustive reference work on Shockwave. Rather, it should serve you as an introduction to the technology's key concepts and capabilities, and provide an entry point to the collection of information about, tools for, and examples of Shockwave content available on the Internet.

What Is Shockwave for Director?

Shockwave is a packaging technique and a delivery mechanism for multimedia content created using Macromedia's Director software. It provides a mechanism for taking completed Director projects, or movies as they're often called, and wrapping them for delivery via the Internet. Shockwave also includes a display handler plug-in for Web browsers that is capable of understanding the file formats used to deliver Director movies and of rendering their contents on a variety of desktop platforms. Today, these platforms include the Macintosh OS and numerous flavors of Microsoft Windows for the PC (Windows 95, Windows NT, and Windows 3.x).

In typical WWW browsers, data rendered in the browser is limited to text, low-quality audio and video, and images. With Shockwave, the types of data that can be rendered are endless. Shockwave makes it possible to add interactive multimedia capabilities to Web pages, as well as more traditional (and passive) collections of moving pictures and sounds. Either way, it promises to enliven the Web considerably.

Part I: Introducing Shockwave

The first tutorial (Chapters 1 through 3) covers the basics of Shockwave, including the company behind its motivation and design, and its operation. More important, it also covers how to plan and execute a multimedia project, and arranges an introduction to Director for those who may be unfamiliar with the program. In Chapter 1, you learn the Shockwave basics with some simple examples and a technology overview. In Chapter 2, you learn how to plan a multimedia project from start to finish, including design, client relations, budgeting, and working with outside contractors. In Chapter 3, you tackle your first real multimedia assignment as you build two simple Director multimedia projects.

At the end of this tutorial, you should understand Shockwave's basic structure and the essentials of its operation and runtime behavior. You'll also have an appreciation for Macromedia Director's power and flexibility as a multimedia authoring environment.

Part II: Applying Shockwave Technology

The second tutorial (Chapters 4 through 6) covers the ins and outs of using Shockwave technology to package Director movies for Internet delivery. It also covers the basics of Director content, including file formats, save commands, and the built-in Lingo scripting language. Likewise, we review the installation and using of Shockwave's Afterburner compression utility, and explore how to maximize the benefits it can provide. Then, in Chapter 6, we give you a brain dump of useful tips and tricks for authoring Director movies to get the best performance from Shockwave. At the end of this tutorial, you will understand what's involved in installing and using Shockwave, and how to extract the best possible performance and capability from it.

Part III: Internet Shockwave Delivery

The final tutorial (Chapters 7 through 9) takes an in-depth look at integrating Shockwave content into Web pages and at what's involved in making this work on the server side. This part of the book begins with step-by-step instructions to incorporate Shockwave content in a Web document. It then discusses design issues that can crop up when you integrate multimedia content into your Web pages. It also discusses how to accommodate visitors to your pages who may not be using Shockwave-enabled browsers—without necessarily running them off. Next, we examine real-world examples to show how they handle their Shockwave content.

Next, we examine the issues inherent in serving up Shockwave content on the Internet, including a detailed discussion of selecting, locating, configuring, and tuning your Web server. This tutorial concludes with a comprehensive overview of content testing and maintenance techniques, with a heavy emphasis on keeping your site current, fresh, and fully operational.

After a look at these delivery-focused issues, we turn speculative and discuss Shockwave's potential, along with recommended applications, its shortcomings, and future research and implementation directions. Throughout, we try to use concrete examples and to point to readily accessible Web sites wherever possible.

How to Use This Book

This book tells you what Shockwave is all about and how it works, including the technology's keywords, operation, and construction. Then it tells you what's involved in rendering and using Shockwave-based content. After that, you explore authoring and using Director content in detail to get a flavor of what Shockwave can do, and how it can be used to extend HTML documents or to make Web-based environments more dynamic and visually interesting.

When you type in the Lingo fragments or whole scripts found in this book, be sure to copy the information exactly as you see it. We've tested all of this code to make sure it works properly, and would like to protect you from the frustration of having to fix other people's mistakes—especially ours.

We also recommend that you obtain the right set of Shockwave components before you try to start creating too much content for Shockwave delivery. Wherever appropriate, we point out sources for tools and inspiration, and share our experiences using them and their results.

Remember, this book is intended more as an overview of Shockwave and a discussion of its present capabilities and future potential than as a full-blown programming reference. You'll find no shortage of references to on-line resources for programming information in this book. But you won't find the comprehensive manual, complete Lingo syntax diagrams, comprehensive coverage of all Director menus and features, or other tools found in detailed training materials. You'll see us refer to the Director manuals frequently, as they're the best places to start looking for comprehensive information or the lowest level of detail.

Finally, as you read along, you'll occasionally see the following icons, which have been strategically placed to draw your attention to useful information.

Tip: This information will save you (and possibly your intended audience) time and aggravation.

Note: This denotes a special point of interest that you may want to keep in mind when creating your project.

Where to Go from Here

Like all of the *60 Minute Guides*, each part of this book on Shockwave builds on what comes before it. Therefore, we strongly recommend that you set about three hours aside and spend one of those hours on each part of this book. This book will make a great deal more sense if you read its parts in their order of occurrence.

After your initial pass through the material, we expect that you'll find the on-line resources particularly useful. Our Appendix therefore provides a chapter-by-chapter listing of all of the URLs in the book. To help you deal with any specialized terms we use, you'll find a comprehensive Glossary at the back of the book as well. The Glossary should help you figure out what words like *sprite* and *cast* mean within Director's context. You'll not only find yourself revisiting a nice chunk of multimedia programming terminology, you'll probably even expand your vocabulary along the way—at least we did!

Note: Please note that, while there are several instructions in this book to save your work for further use, you will not be able to do so without the commercial version of Macromedia Director. The version included on the accompanying CD-ROM is save-disabled and is meant purely as a tutorial tool.

The CD-ROM that accompanies this book is filled with useful materials. In addition to a complete set of Windows and Macintosh Shockwave components, you'll find a save-disabled demo of Director and many widgets and examples, including tutorials we put together expressly for this book.

But whatever you do, please enjoy this book and the material it covers. Feel free to share your comments and criticisms with us. Our addresses and other contact information are provided in About the Authors.

Part I

Introducing Shockwave

*t*his part, which includes Chapters 1 through 3, represents the first of three 60-minute tutorials. This first tutorial covers the basics of Shockwave, including the company behind its motivation and design, and its operation. More important, it also covers how to plan and execute a multimedia project and arranges an introduction to Director for those who may be unfamiliar with the program.

In Chapter 1, The Wave of the Future, you learn the Shockwave basics with some simple examples and a technology overview. We introduce Macromedia, the company behind the Shockwave technology and its Director multimedia authoring software. We also cover the background requirements you'll want to master to get the best use from this book and review some of the most frequently asked questions about Shockwave technology.

In Chapter 2, Planning Your Project, you learn how to plan a multimedia project from start to finish, including design, client relations, budgeting, and working with outside contractors. You start off by following the steps to a successful project, beginning by defining your audience. Next, you establish project goals and a timeline, then create its underlying concept. Finally, you define the content that your users will ultimately see.

In Chapter 3, Assembling and Authoring Your Project in Director, you tackle your first real multimedia assignment as you build two simple Director multimedia projects. You begin with an overview of Director's authoring environment and its key components and menus. From there, it's on to the sample projects, which should let you see your name in lights—plus other interesting special effects!

At the end of this tutorial, you'll understand Shockwave's basic structure and the essentials of its operation and runtime behavior. You'll also develop an appreciation for Macromedia's power and flexibility as a multimedia authoring environment.

The "Wave" of the Future

*W*elcome to your first step toward using the new and exciting technology called Shockwave. In this chapter, we discuss Shockwave technology, its functionality, its uses on the Internet, and the impact it will have on the Net—today and in the future.

What Is Shockwave?

Shockwave allows true multimedia and interactivity over the Internet. This new technology will change the face of the Internet as more and more static Web sites become fully interactive. Shockwave also helps developers offer numerous types of multimedia that have never before been seen on the Internet.

The Company behind Shockwave

Let's take a brief look at the company behind Shockwave, Macromedia. Macromedia is the virtually undisputed leader in multimedia and digital arts software tools. It offers a full range of products for both Microsoft Windows and Macintosh platforms.

Among the company's flagship products is Macromedia Director, an animation and authoring tool for multimedia production. Director has become an unofficial industry standard and is the platform upon which

Shockwave is based. This gives Shockwave a tremendous advantage because Macromedia has already established a sizable base of users who can instantly take advantage of this new technology.

Shockwave is not a new authoring environment for the Internet. It is simply a new way to adapt multimedia titles authored in Director for use in an Internet setting. Because of this, more than one-quarter million multimedia professionals who already use Director now can use existing skills and even existing projects on the Internet.

In this way, they can change static Web sites that consist only of text and graphics into interactive masterpieces. Interactive advertising, promotion, entertainment, and educational titles developed using Director will now be available via the Internet to a much larger audience than more traditional CD-ROM offerings could ever reach.

Historically, multimedia titles have been constrained to large-capacity delivery mechanisms, primarily because of the amount of data involved. Dedicated kiosks, business presentations, and especially CD-ROMs have been used to deliver these offerings to their audiences.

However, all three have their limitations. Obviously, kiosks and presentations can reach only a limited audience at any one time because viewers must come to the Director project and not the other way around. The industry has turned to CD-ROMs as a way to mass-market multimedia projects, but problems with mass production and distribution continue to pose obstacles to success. As a delivery mechanism, the Internet has none of the pitfalls of these other systems and is a logical and, in fact, an ideal vehicle to deliver multimedia projects to the largest possible audience.

The World Wide Web, with its component technologies of HTTP and HTML, represents the first real attempt to create a means to deliver multimedia to internetworked computers anywhere in the world. As a first step, the Web has achieved remarkable things; however, it is limited by being primarily text-based, as well as static and stationary. Multimedia is characterized by tremendous kineticism, with the marriage of audio, video, animation, and text to deliver large amounts of information efficiently and even entertainingly.

Shockwave represents a revolutionary attempt to bring cutting-edge multimedia to the Internet by building on the foundation supplied by the Web. It is likely that any attempt to create such a compelling synthesis of technologies will impact the Internet and its users no matter what the outcome. With that in mind, let's look at the features and the opportunities that this new technology offers you in authoring interactive Web sites.

From the Macromedia news release for Shockwave:

Macromedia Brings Multimedia to World Wide Web

San Francisco, CA—October 30, 1995—Today at the Macromedia International User Conference, Macromedia (NASDAQ: MACR), the leader in multimedia and digital arts software, demonstrated Shockwave for Director content from several of the new media industry's leading companies including Netscape, CKS Interactive, 2-Lane Media, Organic Online, and Canter Technology. Shockwave for Director delivers high-impact, interactive multimedia productions to the World Wide Web by bringing optimized Director productions—with interactive graphics, sounds, and animation—to the Internet. . . . "More than 250,000 creative professionals who already use Director are now able to transform static Web pages into compelling interactive advertising, promotions,

entertainment, and educational experiences like those we saw today," said Bud Colligan, president and CEO of Macromedia. "Shockwave technology and our partnerships with Microsoft, Netscape, Navisoft, Silicon Graphics, and others are enabling Macromedia's customers to bring the highest level of multimedia to the web."

"The Web is very hot in the entertainment and advertising industry; everybody wants to get online and have the newest, most innovative and cutting-edge compelling content," states Jonathan Paijon, executive vice president of 2-Lane Media, which is showcasing the concentration-style game it developed for Disney's *Toy Story* Web site. He continues,

Continued

San Francisco, CA—October 30, 1995—Today at the Macromedia International User Conference, Macromedia (NASDAQ: MACR), the leader in multimedia and digital arts software, demonstrated Shockwave for Director content from several of the new media industry's leading companies including Netscape, CKS Interactive, 2-Lane Media, Organic Online, and Canter Technology. Shockwave for Director delivers high-impact, interactive multimedia productions to the World Wide Web by bringing optimized Director productions—with interactive graphics, sounds, and animation—to the Internet. . . . "More than 250,000 creative professionals who already use Director are now able to transform static Web pages into compelling interactive advertising, promotions, entertainment, and educational experiences like those we saw today," said Bud Colligan, president and CEO of Macromedia. "Shockwave technology and our partnerships with Microsoft, Netscape, Navisoft, Silicon Graphics, and others are enabling Macromedia's customers to bring the highest level of multimedia to the web."

"The Web is very hot in the entertainment and advertising industry; everybody wants to get online and have the newest, most innovative and cutting-edge compelling content," states Jonathan Paijon, executive vice president of 2-Lane Media, which is showcasing the concentration-style game it developed for Disney's *Toy Story* Web site. He continues, "Shockwave opens exciting new doors for everything from original online entertainment to interactive product demos, and press kits for major studio

Who Stands behind this New Technology?

The first thing that all of us want to know with any new technology is: Will it be around for a reasonable amount of time, or is it just the buzzword of the day? Judging from recent events, Shockwave is here to stay. Macromedia has already formed partnerships with some of the biggest names in the computer industry to ensure that this new Internet technology will continue to be available to the public so long as demand remains strong.

Such companies as Netscape, Navisoft, Silicon Graphics, and Microsoft have joined in an effort to bring true interactivity and multimedia to the Internet. By their participation and support, these companies are tacitly endorsing the notion that Macromedia's Shockwave will be a front-running technology for some time to come.

These companies also have plans to integrate Shockwave technology and supporting elements into their Internet browsers, authoring tools, and related products. Using Netscape Navigator 2.0 or later, Navisoft NaviPress, Silicon Graphics, WebForce, or Microsoft's Internet Explorer or Internet Studio, users will be able to run Director movies embedded in Web documents, seamlessly and with the full power of Director-based multimedia on the user's local desktop.

This industry-wide support is one of the many reasons that Shockwave is changing, and will continue to change, the face of the Internet. With this technology, users can create content on Web sites previously only seen in CD-ROM titles.

Netscape holds the lion's share of the Internet browser market and has released a Windows version of the Shockwave plug-in. It also will soon release Macintosh and Power Macintosh versions. This kind of support for Shockwave ensures its looming status as an industry standard for multimedia and as the delivery vehicle of choice for multimedia over the Internet.

How Will Shockwave Keep Pace with the Internet?

As with any new technology, people are bound to question where Shockwave will be in a few years. A common question is: How can Shockwave keep pace with the ever-growing, ever-changing phenomenon we call the Internet? There are several ways in which this can happen.

The first of these ways leverages Macromedia Director's established developer base. Most multimedia professionals already use Director as their primary authoring tool. This gives Shockwave a definite advantage because it is based on an existing authoring tool. Unlike other recently introduced Internet technologies such as Java or the Virtual Reality Modeling Language (VRML), Shockwave doesn't require its users to learn a complex programming language to add multimedia capabilities to their Web sites.

Director also provides developers at almost every level with an ability to base and create their content within a powerful, friendly authoring environment. Most of the interactivity that Web sites need can be created using Director, without requiring any programming whatsoever. Nevertheless, Director includes a compact and useful scripting language, Lingo, that can be employed to create stunning multimedia sequences and effects, "Principles of Shockwave Conversion and Lingo Usage."

Lingo allows Director users to add custom functionality and control to their projects. It also lets users add features not found in Macromedia Director through incorporation of external entities called X-Objects. X-Objects are custom files that may be programmed in high-level languages such as C or C++. Examples of the functionality that X-Objects can add to a project include text-to-speech conversion and a custom database. (We cover Lingo in more detail in Chapter 4.)

All of us have experienced the birth and death of some technology or other in our professional lives. Nevertheless, we believe that Shockwave has the industry support necessary to remain an Internet standard well into the foreseeable future.

Shockwave also has the vast resources of the Macromedia development community, which includes Director programmers, commercial and graphic artists, Lingo programmers, audio-video producers, and other industry professionals. It's easy to see that with this kind of support Shockwave is a technology that can evolve into the multimedia Internet standard we've all awaited.

What Comprises Shockwave Technology?

Shockwave is composed of three distinct parts that work together to create interactive multimedia Web sites: a development platform, a compression engine, and a runtime environment. Let's examine each of them in turn:

1. *Macromedia Director* is a multimedia authoring environment that enables creation of a wide range of multimedia projects, including kiosk shows, CD-ROM titles, and interactive presentations. It allows users to create files on one platform and play them back on a variety of industry-standard platforms such as Apple's Macintosh and Microsoft Windows. All Shockwave projects destined for Internet delivery must be created using Director.

14

2. *Afterburner* is a tool created for Director that takes movies authored in Director and compresses them by an average of 60 percent. This makes the movies ready to post on an HTTP server, from whence they are available to Internet users around the world. Director movies compressed through Afterburner can be identified by their .DCR file extension.

3. The *Shockwave plug-in* contains a runtime environment with all the resources and code needed to play Shockwave projects. This allows .DCR files to be incorporated into the HTML documents that make up your Web site. The plug-in also recognizes Director movies with a .DIR or .DXR file extension.

Netscape 2.0 is the first Web browser to use this plug-in, but other browsers and on-line services also are gearing up their next releases for this plug-in support.

Together, these three pieces form the basis for a multimedia technology that defines a new direction for the Internet. With the exception of Macromedia Director, which is required to create the movies for your Web sites, all of the other elements needed to create and view content will be provided at no additional cost.

Afterburner will be distributed via the Internet itself, at no cost to individuals wanting to create content for the Internet. The plug-in will soon be a standard inclusion in nearly every popular Web browser. All in all, this combination makes Shockwave a viable technological advance that should shape multimedia technology and content on the Internet in the years to come.

Shockwave's Advantages over Other Technologies

The main reason Shockwave has created such excitement in the Internet and multimedia communities is that it rivals or surpasses every technology of its kind, including proposed standards that haven't even been developed yet. To better understand the advantages that the Director-Shockwave combination offers, let's look at each of these products individually and list a few of its major benefits.

Advantages of Macromedia Director

Overall, Director gives Shockwave several unique advantages. Director is an incredibly powerful authoring tool, virtually unmatched by any other product in the multimedia industry. We could list many advantages that Director provides you in creating content for the Internet, but we will only focus on the main ones. So, let's look now at how each such advantage can help you design and produce your own multimedia Web sites.

- *Director is an industry standard.* Director is already used by most of the top multimedia designers and producers in the industry. This industry acceptance gives Director a wealth of support information and technical tools, and a developer base to create all the tools you are likely to need in the future.

- *Director is platform independent.* Director is already a multiplatform authoring environment. This translates well into the world of the Internet, where such standards as TCP/IP already exist for multiple platforms.

- *Director is based on ease of use, not programming skill.* Director supports the creation of highly interactive multimedia content without requiring mastery of complex programming languages. With Director, users can easily create multimedia projects with a professional look and feel using a package that is relatively quick and easy to learn.

- *Director is highly expandable.* Director's functionality can be expanded through the use of Lingo and X-Objects. Its extensibility is almost boundless, which translates into seemingly endless opportunities for use on the Internet.

What should be apparent from these advantages is that Director forms a powerful, easy-to-use foundation for the technology known as Shockwave. However, it should also be obvious what Shockwave and Director are *not*: namely, a general-purpose programming language. Shockwave and Director provide powerful animation and interactivity; but this is not the same as delivering a general platform for everything from databases to circuit modeling.

Advantages of Macromedia's Shockwave

Shockwave represents a "second coming" for Internet use and enthusiasm. This technology allows the creation of previously unheard of things. This helps explain why Web site creators around the globe are already making Shockwave versions of their home pages. There are many advantages to using Shockwave, so let's look at some of its major contributions to the delivery of highly interactive multimedia content over the Internet.

- ***Shockwave is quickly becoming an industry standard.***
  Shockwave already is widely accepted by the Internet development community. That's because Shockwave's ability to leverage existing Director content and expertise makes it by far the best technology for delivering multimedia content on the Internet.

- ***Shockwave uses simple HTML commands for integration.***
  Shockwave .DCR files are integrated seamlessly into your existing HTML documents through simple HTML tags. You can add .DCR files to your Web pages as easily as you might add any static graphic image today. The Shockwave-specific HTML tags are discussed later in this chapter, as well as in Chapter 8.

- ***Shockwave will incorporate the Java programming language.*** Sun Microsystems is working with Macromedia to integrate Java with Shockwave. Java and Shockwave will be a combination that other technologies will be hard pressed to beat.

- ***Shockwave will be incorporated into most Web browsers.***
  Almost every major Internet browser vendor has announced plans for Shockwave support. This will accelerate the delivery of necessary viewing capability to Internet users. Because Netscape is the first such browser to incorporate a Shockwave plug-in, it's safe to assume that numerous others can't be far behind.

These benefits only scratch the surface of the advantages that those Web sites that utilize Shockwave technology will have over traditional, static Web sites. The bottom line is that Shockwave offers Internet multimedia developers an industry-standard authoring environment that supports quick and easy development of interactive multimedia. Shockwave also has advantages in other areas, such as performance and functionality, as you'll discover while reading this book and working through the tutorials and samples in later chapters.

Linked Media with Shockwave

The first release of Shockwave doesn't allow linked media over the Internet. Linked media is a problem in a networked environment, because after successfully downloading a movie, network traffic or other considerations could prevent retrieval of the linked materials. Macromedia and Netscape are investigating a solution that bundles linked media with the movie, but this capability is not available in the Shockwave 1.0 release.

Although Netscape 2.0 has a QuickTime plug-in, Shockwave doesn't yet support QuickTime—a direct result of Shockwave's current lack of support for linked media. Macromedia hopes to support QuickTime in a future release.

What about "Competing" Technologies Such as Java?

Java is another emerging Internet technology. Like Shockwave, it allows developers to do some highly interactive things. However, many people do not understand what Java does and try to compare it to Shockwave in a Shockwave versus Java face-off.

It is misleading to compare Shockwave with Java in an adversarial way. The companies behind these two technologies (Macromedia and Sun Microsystems, respectively) don't compete for the same markets, and the two technologies they make are quite different in both their intent and their capabilities. These two technologies are aimed at two very different types of users, as the following comparison demonstrates.

- *Shockwave for Director by Macromedia:* Shockwave is optimized for creative professionals with little or no programming experience (e.g., graphic artists, animators, videographers, sound specialists, imaging professionals, writers, trainers, educators, and 3-D developers). These creative professionals can now create multimedia content for the Internet without recourse to any programming language.

  Director is available today for Power Macintosh, Macintosh, Windows 3.1, and Windows 95. Director playback is available on

3DO, and players have been announced (and should ship in mid-to-late 1996) for OS/2, OS/9, and Online Media. The Director authoring environment and Shockwave delivery technology are also easy enough for relative novices to master.

- *Java by Sun Microsystems:* Java is aimed at programmers and engineers who want to create secure, multiplatform, distributed applications and systems. Java requires its users to be familiar with an object-oriented (C++-like) syntax that makes it useful to programmers and engineers, but adds a significant learning curve for users with little or no programming experience.

  The Java programming language is available in beta form only on Solaris, Windows NT, and Windows 95. Versions have been announced but are not yet available for Power Macintosh and Windows 3.1.

  Additionally, as a technology Java is not as mature as Director and Shockwave. What this means is that there will be some time lag between the wide introduction of Java and wide availability of the code and object libraries and resources necessary to develop Java-based solutions quickly and easily.

It is easy to understand the advantages that Shockwave has over Java for delivering high-speed, interactive multimedia across the Internet. However, there's a small twist to consider: Macromedia has licensed Java and it plans to incorporate Java with Shockwave technology.

This move may seem odd at first, but in fact there is excellent reasoning behind it. Macromedia licensed Java because it is an excellent system-level language. They can use Java as a foundation for network-based multimedia tools and applications. Because Java will be an important Internet standard with much to offer, Macromedia will initially support the user community by providing playback of Java applets in future versions of both Director and Authorware.

At the same time, Macromedia will use its own Shockwave technology and the strength of Java as a system development language to create a new continuous-publishing tool for high-bandwidth Internet applications of the future. This tool will be aimed at Web authors who require constantly updated multimedia and typographically rich content.

This licensing arrangement demonstrates that these two technologies aren't in direct competition. The most likely scenario for their joint deployment will see Shockwave providing a front-end to Java-based custom Internet applications.

What Do I Need to Start Using Shockwave?

You will need a small list of things to begin using Macromedia's Shockwave. We'll assume that you have either a Power Macintosh, a regular Macintosh, or a PC running Windows. Let's take a look at a few of the other items you will need to begin working with this new technology:

1. A basic understanding of HTML
2. Macromedia Director
3. Afterburner
4. A Web server to deliver your content
5. The server configuration/information for Shockwave
6. A Web browser that supports the Shockwave plug-in
7. A well-written guide to Shockwave—that is, this book!

Please note that, in some capacity or other, items 2 through 6 in this list can be found in item 7 or on the accompanying CD-ROM. In all seriousness, this book will help you regardless of your knowledge of any of the topics listed above. After reading this book and applying the techniques from the following chapters, you will be able to use Shockwave to enhance the design and capability of your Web site.

Next, we briefly discuss these items. We provide an overview of each item here, as a big-picture rendition of the essential details found in later chapters.

Macromedia Director

Shockwave is an exciting new technology for the Internet, based on the multimedia authoring standard of Macromedia Director. To create original multimedia content for Shockwave, you need a licensed copy of Director. You can purchase this application through normal software channels.

However, for the exercises in this book, we provide you with the Director movie files you need. You can use Afterburner, which is also included with this book, to burn the files we have provided and post them to your Web server. If you already own a copy of Director, you can also create your own files and replace our example files with your own personal multimedia content.

Afterburner

Afterburner is the application that converts Director movies into .DCR files that can then be embedded into your HTML documents and played back via the Internet. You take several steps when converting a Director movie with Afterburner. Here's a list of the basic steps in this process. (You'll get all the details you can stand in subsequent chapters!)

1. Create a Director movie.
2. Test the movie on your local file system and on any other available platforms.
3. Post-process the title through Afterburner.
4. Place the compressed file on an HTTP server configured for Shockwave for Internet delivery.

Converting a movie file with Afterburner doesn't change the Director movie or the appearance of the movie. Afterburner simply uses a proprietary compression scheme to significantly reduce the movie file's size to make it transmit more quickly over the Internet.

Basic HTML Knowledge

We say that a basic understanding is required because HTML is a formatting language that normally requires mastery of a vast array of written documentation. Several places in this book you'll find the necessary information about HTML to post multimedia content to your Web server and to embed .DCR files into your Web pages.

Tip: If you've never seen HTML or want to learn more about this topic, see the following title from IDG Books Worldwide: *HTML for Dummies*, 2nd Ed., by Ed Tittel and Steve James, 1996.

Basic Web Terminology

The basic elements of HTTP that Macromedia suggests you should be acquainted with to deploy Shockwave projects on the Internet are covered next. This text is also available on Macromedia's Web site at:

```
http://www.macromedia.com
```

A *URL*, or Universal Resource Locator, is the standard address format for anything on the Internet. A URL has three parts:

- The name of the Internet protocol (e.g., FTP, gopher, or HTTP)

- The name of the Internet host (e.g., www.macromedia.com, ftp.macromedia.com)

- The directory structure within which the file you're seeking resides

An *HTTP server* is a computer that delivers World Wide Web data across the Internet. HTTP stands for HyperText Transport Protocol. In response to a request for a specific URL, the HTTP server returns a block of data plus that data's MIME type.

A *MIME type* names the type of content associated with a block of data. MIME stands for Multipurpose Internet Mail Extensions. It was originally proposed and used for enriching e-mail content. In the context of the World Wide Web and HTTP, a MIME type specifies the type of data returned from a server. MIME types can include text, graphics of various types (.GIF, JPEG, .PNG, and so on), sound, or Director movies.

A MIME type consists of two parts, the content type and the content subtype. The content type specifies a major category, such as image, audio, or application. The subtype specifies a particular data type within that category, such as image/JPEG. For a Director movie, the MIME type is application/x-director, where the *x* indicates the need for an external, or helper, application to play that data (e.g., the Shockwave plug-in).

A Web Server on Which to Post Your Content

To host your new Shockwave content, you must post it to a Web server. You may own a Web server or pay an Internet service provider (ISP) to post the content on their Web server. An Internet presence from an ISP usually provides connections and servers that are faster than what you can afford on your own. (For more information about this crucial issue, please consult Chapter 8.)

An HTTP server (also known as a Web server) is a computer that delivers data across the Internet to a browser when a Web page is requested. This server could be any of a number of computers running any of several operating systems, such as UNIX, Mac O/S, Windows NT, or OS/2. Be sure to ask for this information when using an ISP for your Internet presence.

Server Configuration/Information for Shockwave

Virtually any server that hosts Web sites today can be configured to post Shockwave files. It only takes the correct configuration for the .DCR MIME type. This allows the server to properly serve .DCR files to Shockwave-compatible browsers.

All of the most popular and commonly used HTTP servers can be configured to post Shockwave files. Whether you configure your own server or provide configuration information to an ISP, you'll find the necessary information in Chapter 7.

Configuration information is available on the Internet as well. Go to Macromedia's home page at http://www.macromedia.com, then locate the Getting Started section in the Shockwave pages.

A Shockwave-Compatible Web Browser

Although Netscape is currently the only browser that supports Shockwave sites, many other browsers will soon be similarly equipped. It is important to remember that the Shockwave plug-in is required to view sites even if you already have Netscape 2.0 installed on your computer. It is also a good idea to keep an eye on the Macromedia home page for news releases and information about other software companies that will soon be offering Shockwave-compatible versions of their Web browsers, especially if Netscape isn't your browser of choice.

> ## Shockwave Pricing and Availability
>
> Information regarding Shockwave technology, sample movies, and related files are available at Macromedia's Web site:
>
> `http://www.macromedia.com`
>
> The Shockwave for Director kit should be available free to registered Director 4.0 users at Macromedia's Web site by the time you read this. This kit includes Afterburner, documentation on tips and techniques for the Internet, sample movies, and the Shockwave player, which plugs into the Netscape Navigator 2.0 browser.

Frequently Asked Questions about Shockwave

Many questions about Shockwave will be answered in this book. Also, many basic questions are usually brought up in discussions of this new technology. We'll take a moment now to discuss two of them in a concise format. As you begin to generate your own questions, check the glossary and the index in this book to see if you can find some useful information on your own.

What about Bandwidth and Movie Size on the Internet?

Bandwidth can be a problem with any network. Many people find that their first concern about Shockwave is file size. When viewing a Shockwave Web site, end users download .DCR file as part of HTML pages, much as if they were downloading HTML pages that contain .GIF or JPEG images. This raises the concern of not being able to access a Shockwave site because of the speed of the Internet connection in use. As always, users connected to the Internet via a 14.4 Kbps or 28.8 Kbps modem have different download times than someone using an ISDN or a T1 connection.

It is also important to remember that you are not posting the Director movies you save to your hard drive onto the Web server. Before you post a project, you use Afterburner to reduce file sizes dramatically. In most cases, you realize about a 60 percent reduction.

Through advanced techniques, it is possible to reduce file sizes of 2–4MB to around 50–100K. This reduction is the main reason that Shockwave works so well on the Internet. In some cases, you may include a graphic into a Shockwave project, burn the movie file with Afterburner, and find that the .DCR file is smaller than the original, static graphic you imported into your Director movie!

We address this concern in greater detail in the second tutorial. In particular, Chapter 6 provides numerous tips and tricks to minimize Shockwave file sizes. As with all Web page content, size and transmission time greatly affect the user's experience of your site. For this reason, this aspect of Shockwave should be of great importance when you develop your own projects.

Can I Have More than One Movie in a Web Page?

HTML documents can include more than one movie per page. The user can scroll through the HTML page that contains a movie while that movie, or multiple movies, are playing. The user can interact with the movie and enter text from the keyboard into text fields programmed into the movie. The movie itself can access information from the network and open additional URLs—or even call other movies—using Lingo commands we discuss later.

Technically, there's no limit to the number of movies you can incorporate into a Web page. However, each Shockwave movie consumes an additional 50–100K of RAM beyond the size of the actual movie. Users with low amounts of RAM may have problems viewing pages that contain several Shockwave movies.

For example, if a user has only 8MB of RAM and views a page that contains four movies, RAM constraints may limit him or her to viewing only two or three movies at one time. Other problems can occur if you provide the user with too much information on one page, as we discuss in detail in Chapter 9.

Note: When a user views a page on your Web site and jumps to another page, Shockwave frees the RAM it no longer needs to display the movies from the previous page. Thus, if the first page contains a movie that requires 100K and the second page's movie only needs 50K, when a user leaves the first page, the 100K for its movie is freed. When the second page is loaded, only the 50K its movie needs is consumed.

What Are People Saying about Shockwave?

Of course, the companies spearheading this technology are also excited about its prospects. As you saw, the Macromedia Shockwave news release earlier in this chapter includes quotes from some of these organizations. You can also view comments from the public about Shockwave in a discussion on Shockwave technology on Macromedia's Web site. Visit their threaded discussion main page at:

```
http://www.macromedia.com/Local/Bin/Threads/index.html
```

The Shockwave thread also provides a venue where you can discuss questions and issues. Keep in mind that this is a technical discussion area for Macromedia's users, not a technical support forum officially supported by Macromedia. Even so, you'll find plenty of valuable information.

Macromedia's Web site is probably the best place to catch the latest buzz on Shockwave and related technology topics. We suggest that you add a bookmark in your Web browser so you can easily check back to find the latest news.

By using Internet search features in your browser, you can also search on the term, Shockwave. As this technology develops, more and more registered sites will offer Shockwave content produced by, and information about, Shockwave. In other words, we expect the amount of Shockwave material on the Internet to grow substantially in the next year or so.

Note: Try a search on Shockwave to see what you find. The Internet will remain the best place to find information on Shockwave technology. To begin, try the following URLs:

```
http://www.yahoo.com
http://www.excite.com
http://www.lycos.com
http://www.webcrawler.com
http://www.opentext.com
http://www.infoseek.com
```

Summary

With this chapter's Shockwave overview, you are ready to learn more about how to create multimedia Web content. The most important thing to remember when you begin using Director and Shockwave is the so-called arc of development.

Arc of development describes the process of creating a project in the multimedia world. Planning is the glue that holds everything together when you develop content with Shockwave. Many things are included in the arc of development. In Chapter 2, we discuss the proper planning procedures to follow to achieve your goals and keep your project and timelines on schedule.

CHAPTER 2

Planning Your Project

n ow that we've established Shockwave's basic concepts, it's time to lay down the initial stages of creating a project. Macromedia Director is a multifaceted tool that can be used to create content for many media, including CD-ROM, interactive television, and now the Internet. Regardless of the versatility of your development tools, however, successful projects cannot be carried through completion without strong project planning, organization, and management direction. A foundation based on research, time management, resource organization, and project planning is critical to the success of your project.

In this chapter, we examine the building blocks of successful project management, with an emphasis on multimedia projects. These fundamentals actually apply to virtually any creative project, including video, film, radio, and writing endeavors. Without strong leadership and organization, projects of this type have a particular tendency to go astray. For this reason, this topic is especially relevant to any discussion of interactive multimedia on the Internet.

As the name suggests, multimedia is a multifaceted collection of media. As such, it tends to have many elements and variables to juggle. Therefore, it is vital to understand how to manage these multifarious aspects of the "arc of development" before leaping straight into the development fray.

Defining the Steps to a Successful Project

For your project to achieve successful completion, you must first define the steps that will take you to that goal. Unfortunately, failure to lay out a detailed plan of your project often leads to problems that cause unnecessary pain and agony down the road. It is important to note that not all projects will follow the same steps. Therefore, you may want to list the steps in project development for each project before you begin, to identify the phases that are relevant to your particular project.

It's equally important to understand that, while what we discuss in this chapter is only one way of managing projects, it represents a complete set of instructions. In presenting this information, our goal is to allow you to form your own project outline and to give you a foundation that you can either adapt or use outright to create your own outlines to fit the projects you work with on a day-to-day basis. To illustrate how these principles can be applied to your own projects, we present an example project. As we discuss each step of this guide to project planning, we apply our recommended process to this example.

To set the stage for our example, presume that we, as Internet multimedia producers, have been hired by a retail music CD store to create an on-line presence. They want to sell their wares on the Internet through what they want to call SoundNet. As we accept this task, the principles of project planning immediately come into play. To help us better understand the planning concepts and their relation to SoundNet, we discuss each topic in general first, then relate it to the SoundNet project. The following are the project planning concepts we will employ:

- *Establish your audience*—who you want to see your project.

- *Establish your goals*—what you would like to achieve with your audience.

- *Establish your timeline*—define not only when your project should be complete, but also establish intermediate milestones.

- *Create your concept*—develop a concept that applies to your audience, your goals, and your timeline. Analyze and compare your concept in depth, and research other concepts that may help your design.

- *Define your content*—establish those items needed to complete your project. This may include elements such as text, graphics, movies, and sound. Include all items you will produce internally and those that come from external sources. Catalog those processes that create the content. Finally, determine how the entire project will be assembled.

Establishing Your Audience

The first step in project planning is to define your audience. The importance of this part of the process cannot be overstated, for without a good understanding of the type of person or group that you're targeting, it's difficult to achieve useful results. Without an audience in mind during the entire creative process, a project will lack clarity and focus. The end product will portray this lack by its inability to capture viewers' attention or their imagination. The project will be a waste of time, and the end product a flop. To avoid this catastrophe, strive to define exactly for whom your project is designed.

In the case of our example, because SoundNet offers all kinds of music, there's no single target audience at which we must focus our efforts. Here, it's important to note that with SoundNet anyone who uses the Internet is a potential customer. In fact, because the demographics of the Internet are so strongly slanted toward people with disposable income and better than average education, we can tell our client that it provides a prime audience for their wares.

You may want to further refine a profile of your target audience by asking yourself the questions that follow.

Who Will Access This Information?

The Internet is accessed by millions of people in more than 80 countries worldwide. By publishing on the Internet, it's possible to reach people from every social, economic, ethnic, and political background. The Internet empowers every publisher by leveling the field of entry and by eliminating traditional barriers that inhibit widespread communication.

With millions of avid Internet viewers, few barriers exist to reach vast numbers of people. The question is: Who do we *want* to reach? Faced with a huge potential audience, too many Web developers adopt an attitude that can best be stated as: Build it and they will come. Although this can sometimes be effective, publishers often find that their sites don't achieve the intended results and slowly fade into oblivion after the novelty wears off. This isn't what you want when you spend your budget and time on a Web project!

This lackadaisical attitude is actually a symptom of not truly understanding the "why" behind a project. The path to tightening the focus on your intended audience leads to a series of introspective questions. Answered properly, the answers should tell you more about your own motives as well as about the people you want to reach.

- Am I selling a product or a service?
- Am I promoting?
- Am I supplying specific information?
- Is my content open to the public or restricted to a smaller group of people?
- Does the audience seek the information I'm publishing, or am I simply enticing viewers to visit my site?

The sole intention of SoundNet is to use the Internet to promote business and expand a customer base by offering compact discs for sale. SoundNet would also like to supply visitors to their Web site with information on the company, its products, and its people. The motivation is the hope that Internet visitors will generate publicity for the company, and perhaps more traffic at the physical store.

Because SoundNet does not intend to publish any information to the Internet that is not public, security concerns are not extreme. However, the site will also support commercial transactions, so purchase and credit data will need to be protected. This is an important distinction—namely, between limiting access to the server and protecting data submitted by your users.

In this case, SoundNet doesn't offer information that is essential to the audience. However, its audience may or may not be seeking the information the company places on their Web site. Because the site will not instantly attract people with unique and sought-after data, it instead needs to attract users the old-fashioned way—through packaging and promotion.

Ask yourself many questions when defining the content for your audience. Then, when you're finished, ask some more. The questions we've presented here should give you ideas about the information you should seek, and should also suggest what types of questions are appropriate for your project.

What Are Your Audience's Expectations?

It is crucial to deliver information to your audience effectively. After all, they're spending valuable time at your site when they could be exploring any number of Internet wonders elsewhere. Whether you work for a mega-corporation or publish a personal home page, you must represent your interests to the Internet community.

When viewers visit a Web site, they have a personal interaction with that site's publisher. In the viewers' eyes, the information contained within a site represents the publisher's core identity, be it an individual or a business.

From this perspective, it should be clear that the better the publisher's understanding of the viewers' expectations, the more effectively the publisher can speak to them. If users come to your Web site expecting entertainment and find sober statistics and political analysis, they will leave disappointed.

On the other hand, if they come to a site looking for hard data on poplar trees and find a vast database of tree information with a powerful search engine and an intuitive interface, they will probably be pleasantly surprised. More important, they will be more likely to make return visits to that site.

The look of a site, the ease of finding information, and the content's usefulness can all make a significant impact on viewers' feelings about its publisher. The element of personal interaction separates Web publishing from all other media. When developed and implemented wisely, the results can be tremendous. Unfortunately, far too many Web sites are little more than virtual billboards that lack creativity, usefulness, and some real reason for their existence.

Because SoundNet is a retail establishment, users will expect some kind of on-line catalog, or perhaps an on-line ordering system. If that's all the site offers, however, you may find few return visits or little traffic overall. To create a stir with a Web site—even with the allure of exotic media such as Shockwave movies—designers must strive to differentiate their content.

If you merely reproduce what consumers get from any number of snail-mail CD catalogs, you've missed the point and your efforts will fail. Exploit the vast potential of the Internet to make the site unlike anything your customers have seen or even imagined, and you are more likely to reap rewards from your efforts.

For SoundNet, some ideas for Internet-specific content could include audio samples of CDs or searchable catalogs. Perhaps a software agent could query customers about what kinds of music they like and provide suggestions for other titles and artists that might suit their tastes.

Tip: It is relatively easy to draw people into a Web site by pandering to their expectations with a flashy, come-hither facade. However, to satisfy your viewers and make them want to return repeatedly, you must have a deep understanding of their expectations.

What Is Your Client's Role in the Project's Creation?

The vast majority of Web sites are created by contract developers on their clients' behalf. In such cases, the relationship between developers and their clients must be carefully explored to avoid complications. In many ways, your client is your primary audience, much in the same way that advertising campaigns must first sell themselves to the company that writes the checks. However, there are dangers hidden in focusing too much on the client and not enough on their customers, who comprise the project's ultimate target audience.

The question you must consider most carefully to avoid this pitfall is: Who owns the information that you publish, and do they have a say in how the content is presented? Often, the answer to the second part of this question is a resounding "Yes!" This can be either bane or boon, depending on the circumstances.

Another question to consider is: Has your client published on-line before? Understand the personality of your client and their content. Find out if the client has a style guide for published content. Most style guides are designed around print media and don't lend themselves well to on-line presentations. But such guides can give you a feel for the client's published image. Regardless of the availability of other style guides, develop a style guide specifically for your project and agree upon its elements with your client early in the project development cycle.

With SoundNet, imagine that we work directly with one of the company's principals. While the company may not have previously published content on-line, the principal has played a major role in all of his or her company's other publishing efforts. If we work our relationship with the principal to the project's advantage, we can use the client's extra resources.

An overriding concern in the early stages of the working relationship is to impress upon the client that the Net and the Web are not print, radio, television, telemarketing, or any other promotional medium they already know. Too often, companies approach the on-line world as an extension of existing marketing and advertising strategies, and their efforts are often met with scorn and derision by the on-line audience.

We must impress this difference upon our client by stressing the importance of speed and efficiency in every aspect of the content and its delivery. We stress small filesizes in every section of this book, and that obsession is a direct result of on-line marketing tenets. Unlike other electronic media, the reins are in the users' hands; if they feel that their time is being wasted, they turn away and never return. This may sound daunting, but the upside is that we can promise our clients that our on-line experience and creativity will deliver their message imaginatively and effectively.

If we properly educate our client early on, the lines of responsibility for SoundNet can be clearly drawn. The client should apply the company agenda and philosophy to the project, while we adapt that message to the Web, with punctuation provided by Shockwave movies.

How Will Your Audience View Your Project?

Does your content appear on a compact disc or a local "intranet," or will it be presented globally on the Internet? Different media lend themselves to different implementations, each with its own benefits and problems. Research your chosen medium carefully, and base your content decisions on its particular characteristics.

Bandwidth is the weakest link of the Internet. The vast majority of the Internet community accesses the Web via modem connections. If you intend to reach the average Internet user, consider that they will download your content at a rate of one to three kilobytes per second. If a graphic or movie on your page is 60K, it could take a full minute to download. The content of a single high-density floppy disk (1.44MB) takes approximately 10–15 minutes to download over a 28.8 Kbps modem. Remember the impact of download times when planning the scope and complexity of your project's content!

The more complex and involved your graphics and effects are, the more difficult and time-consuming it is to access your Web content. Choose an average connection profile for your target customer, and design your graphics to fit those capabilities.

Tip: A good way to get an idea of your viewers' experience is to access your site with a 14.4 Kbps modem rather than a high-speed network connection when testing new ideas. If it's too slow to for you to bear, it'll be too slow for your audience too.

Because SoundNet aspires to sell compact discs to the Internet community at large, the site should be developed with the lowest common denominator in mind. However, the client is adamant that we shouldn't limit our efforts or cripple the end results by designing the site specifically for a 14.4 Kbps modem and a text-only browser. This kind of "push-me, pull-you" directive will become hauntingly familiar as you develop your own clientele. To get the best of both worlds, SoundNet will be designed with Netscape and a fast modem as the vehicle of choice, but will offer "lite" versions of its pages for those not so well equipped. Judicious use of links to force users to download longer, more complex files and formats will also give them a choice about whether or not they want to wait two minutes to hear the latest clip from Hootie and the Blowfish.

Which Browser Does Your Audience Use?

Do your viewers arrive via commercial on-line services such as America Online, CompuServe, Prodigy, or eWorld, or are they directly connected to the Internet through ISPs? Many commercial services require that customers use a specific Web browser. Often, these browsers aren't as sophisticated as commercial browsers and don't always support more advanced markup.

Despite Netscape's pre-eminence, there are many flavors of Web browsers that offer a wide variety of features and abilities. Browsers can range from text only, to fully graphical, to Netscape enhanced. Obviously, Shockwave-enabled browsers are what should interest you. Nevertheless, it's important to remember that your viewers come to visit your site from a variety of computer platforms, and from an equally wide range of browsers. So, it's wise to plan ways to handle visitors who may not be properly equipped to view all of your content.

Some Web sites employ a variety of document formats and designs, but many of these work correctly only with Netscape. If you target a wide audience and want to ensure that your content looks good on many different browsers, it's important to design your content around published HTML standards rather than proprietary HTML tags.

This isn't possible when developing Shockwave sites, because this capability is only available from selected browsers. In fact, at the time of this writing only the 2.0 version of Netscape supports the Shockwave plug-in. This will change rapidly, but there will always be a segment of the intended audience that simply cannot view your Shockwave content.

The way to work around this, should you so desire, is the same workaround as for any Netscape-specific HTML extension: Design a parallel site with generic browsers in mind. That way, if a user's browser can't handle proprietary tags and features, the user can switch to the generic pages and look at a version of your site *sans* bells and whistles.

Given our design decision to make SoundNet palatable to users with 14.4 Kbps modems and graphical browsers of just about any kind, it should come as no surprise that we will design the low-bandwidth, or lite, version of the pages for generic HTML 2.0 browsers. Given the focus of this book, it should also come as no surprise that the high-tech version of the pages will feature audio clips and Shockwave movies galore!

What Are Your Audience's Limitations?

Parallel development of multiple versions of a Web site may seem like a lot of effort, especially in the name of supporting odd-ball browsers. However, such efforts may be necessary to accommodate your intended audience's limitations. Although the overriding consideration is users' bandwidth, other variables may also be involved.

After you've considered the bandwidth issue, it's important to continue to ask what your target audience's limitations are. In other words, is your target audience even on the Internet? It's possible that the type of customer you need for your product or service has not yet made the leap to the Infobahn. (You may be building an enormous site for people who can't even see it!) If this is true, you'll need to rethink your concept or consider delivery mechanisms other than the Internet.

In addition to the questions of connection speed and browser type, other potential limitations must be addressed. Do potential language barriers need to be addressed? Given the Internet's global reach, some percentage of the people interested in what you have to offer won't speak English. If so, you may want to consider translating some or all of the text on your site to eliminate such barriers.

Should age restrictions be imposed upon your audience? If your content isn't suitable for minors, you must address the possibility that children might stumble upon your site. Publishers must do what they can to make sure minors aren't exposed to inappropriate materials. This is both a moral and a legal responsibility.

Who Is the Competition?

The final factor to consider when defining your audience stems from your project's context. The primary question here is: "Does your project compete with other, similar offerings?" If so, what can you do to make your project more compelling than these other sites?

An excellent approach to answering this question involves subjecting the competition to the questions we've asked here. If you can identify ways in which competitors have failed to identify the common audience, you can offer what they do not and, we hope, attract more users.

In the larger scheme of things, consider what you're doing to lure viewers to your content. Offering incentives, such as giveaways and contests, or designing entertaining games on your site, are some examples of the kinds of hooks you can use to capture your audience.

Your choice of enticements is dependent on the original purpose of your site. Are you attempting to increase awareness of a product, service, or technology with your Web site? If so, contests and giveaways can help excite your audience about the possibility of owning your product.

Is your content inherently boring? This can be a difficult question to answer honestly, especially when the data in question belongs to a client. However, an honest answer can lead to strategies for making the site and the data "sexier," and can ultimately mean the difference between a thriving Web site and a ghost town.

For SoundNet, while other sites are run by music CD retailers, our client feels they have content and a corporate image that are exciting enough to differentiate their site. As the site's designers, it's up to us to ensure that the image and the content are communicated effectively.

Note: The two essential questions to consider when establishing content for your Web site are:

- How does your project fit into the existing World Wide Web?
- What can you do to make your site stand out?

If you know what your competition is doing and how you will make yourself stand out from the pack, you're well on your way to building the kind of content that can help to draw users into your site.

Now that you have a better understanding of your audience, it's time to move to the next stage, planning your project, which is when you seek to define its ultimate *raison d'être*.

Establishing Project Goals

Any successful project must have well-defined, measurable goals. If you establish such goals, they'll provide you with a yardstick to measure progress. Too often, projects based on excellent ideas aren't completed or never reach their intended audience, because their creators failed to establish objective ways to determine when a project goes off track or the means to correct deviations from the path to success.

Your ideas only remain yours until an audience experiences and is moved by your work. You may have great ideas, wonderful content, and the best possible packaging, but if no one experiences that work, none of the benefits of success accrues. Therefore, the ultimate goal of any project must be to reach the intended audience with the end product. This single goal is actually composed of a multitude of lesser goals, many of which speak specifically to your particular project.

After you define and establish these particular goals for your project, you create the foundation upon which the entire undertaking rests. Along the way, we continue the SoundNet example and build on what we covered earlier. Although precise goals depend on your project's specific characteristics, it is critical to consider the following guideposts while establishing project goals.

What Do You Want to Achieve?

It may sound silly to state this question so baldly, because you must have had some idea of what you wanted to achieve to embark on this project. However, the question bears asking—and answering—seriously, because it's the prime motivator for your project.

Is the goal to educate, to entertain, to inform, or to sell? Do you want your audience to learn, enjoy, understand, or buy? Does your effort have a specific goal, such as informing a large number of Internet viewers about a product or service? Or perhaps to sell a product using the interactive marketing that Shockwave can deliver over the Internet?

Whether you're attempting to generate income, transform beliefs, or entertain viewers, you must clearly visualize an end result from your efforts. It will be much easier to achieve this result if you take a hard look at what you seek to accomplish, document that notion at the very beginning of your project, and revisit it right through the project's completion.

A well-defined and well-documented set of results supplies a useful framework upon which to base decisions as you progress through your project from start to finish. In addition, with the desired results defined you have the key to answering another crucial developmental question—how to measure your success.

If you're under contract to a client, how can they measure your success in fulfilling your end of the deal? Depending on the specific project, it may make sense to rely on server statistics, goods sold, e-mail or calls generated, or other concrete statistics to measure results.

Whatever the means, it is essential to build an accurate measurement of the success into your project. This approach means that you won't only have a clear vision of what you want to achieve, but you'll also have a way to determine how well you reach your goals.

In the SoundNet example, the client has set the following goals for the Web site:

- To establish a presence that incorporates an interactive Web site for their retail chain

- To establish a lead in Web marketing for their products that can be easily maintained

- To aid in worldwide marketing and advertising of their physical stores through the Web

These are only some of the goals that the client has established, but they are the top three that will be used to judge the success of the project. We need to return to these basic goals again and again when designing our project, but building methods to measure accomplishment of these goals is equally important. To that end, we should establish a metric to determine how well the final project meets these three primary goals.

Exploring Additional Goals

Once you establish your basic motivation for a project, branch out and explore secondary and tertiary goals that emerge from the primary theme. These are usually defined as aspects of a project that aid attainment of the project's primary goals. Another way to look at such additional aspects is as the feature set for your Web site.

Your choice of features should be informed both by your desired end results and your intended audience. In effect, features act as a way to gently lead audience members to the desired effect. For example, it is typical to want to build a loyal viewer base who will return to your site repeatedly. You can achieve this goal in numerous ways, but usually by continually updating a site's content so that users find something new each time they visit. This could take the form of promotional offerings, serialized entertainment, or news of interest to your audience.

Another method is to offer a valuable resource that's easily accessible through your site, such as a database of some kind. Again, the specific form such features take depends upon the particular project. Our point is that, after you know what results you want to achieve, you should use the ultimate goals to shape the feature set for the entire site. To realize those goals, you have to develop a host of secondary and tertiary goals for your project.

As a final note, it's absolutely critical to know your target audience and to develop content that appeals to a large percentage of that population. It's also important to remember that it takes more than cool graphics to draw visitors. Intelligent content, reasonable filesizes, appropriate page layouts, and intuitive organization can make your site a resource rather than just another billboard on the Internet.

For SoundNet, our client has set several goals, some of which you can achieve immediately and others that are limited by current bandwidth and technology. It's important to keep these goals in focus as we lay the groundwork for the site. If we deliver a site that doesn't have a built-in evolutionary path, our work will have a short shelf life and our client won't stay satisfied for long.

Now that your goals have been set, let's turn to the development of your project's timeline.

Establishing a Timeline

Your timeline is the single most important aspect of your project. It can make your project a success, or document a disaster. On-line publishing efforts can be highly involved and require the efforts and talents of a variety of people. A timeline helps to orchestrate these efforts, and helps you to understand how the various pieces of your project must fit together to stay on schedule.

On-line media require a mix of artistic talent, business skill, and technical knowledge. You're likely to be involved with different types of people with vastly different work habits. Individual participants will also react to schedules, pressures, problems, and stress differently. The human element in a group project can be a strong asset or a major liability. To accentuate the positive side of this dynamic, it's important to maintain a focus on intergroup communication throughout any project. The dominant theme of such communication should take the form of clear and specific deadlines, and an overall timeline for the entire project.

For SoundNet, the timeline has been dictated to us. The client's representatives want to see "something on the Web" within three weeks after starting the project. They then want to see the rest of the Web site operational within an additional six weeks. This is an intense schedule, but we can honor it if we draw upon the client's resources. Let's look at this timeline starting with our acceptance of the job and covering the schedule dictated by SoundNet.

Week One

The job has been accepted and we must create the SoundNet Web site for their retail chain. We have received the skeleton of a schedule that includes two completion points:

- Have a Web server configured with a page that announces that the Web site will soon be available. This must be done within the first three weeks.

- Have a functional Web site operational within an additional six weeks. This gives us a grand total of nine weeks to complete our project and meet the three goals the client set to judge our success.

We'll use this information to generate a detailed timeline.

Week Two

We have set a goal to meet the preliminary requirement for a "coming-soon" Web page for this week. To meet this goal, we only need to have the company supply us with the artwork for their logo. We must also build a short introduction to add to the artwork and place the resulting page onto their Web site. Note that this presupposes establishing a URL and having a Web server in place.

Week Three

At this point, we meet with our client to show them our ideas, concepts, and timeline for their approval. We also formalize arrangements for subsequent dealings with the company's art and legal departments.

Week Four

We chart the organizational layout of the Web site. We also begin direct contact with the client's art department to obtain the artwork for the Web site. We also obtain the proper releases from the client's legal department to post their company information and artwork on the Web site by this time.

Week Five

By this week, we complete the preliminary Web site, ready to show our customer. We show a basic storyboard of the site "live" on the Internet from a password-protected area of our site.

Week Six

During this week, we meet twice with the client's representatives. The first meeting is on Monday, when we show our initial storyboard. The second meeting is on Thursday, when we show whatever revisions emerged from Monday's discussions.

Week Seven

Development continues. Twice each week we permit the client to log onto the site to view the work in progress. Our primary aim is to solicit feedback on progress and direction to let the client supply any necessary mid-course correction. If any schedule changes must occur, now is the time for us to begin negotiations based on the severity of mid-course correction.

Week Eight

During this week, we hold another series of meetings with the client. This is the last week we can make changes to the SoundNet site. The ninth week is reserved for content checks and beta testing to ensure that all of our CGIs, Shockwave movies, and other additions operate properly.

Week Nine

This is the last week available to finish the site to meet the schedule.

Week Ten

The site goes live!

As our example should demonstrate, a timeline is a detailed chart or table (such as Table 2-1) that is based on dates that state actions and deliverables throughout a project. A timeline must incorporate planning cycles, client meetings, and the delivery of each element on the project's path to completion. A timeline must include a start date, a final delivery date and each major element between. It's also helpful to establish measurable milestones along the way. Milestones are any items of major importance that mark various deliverables that you complete along the timeline.

Consider milestones as individual mini-projects within your meta-project. Always recognize on-time completion of a milestone by rewarding your team accordingly. Milestones can help break a large project into manageable units, make your schedule easier to define, and make completion times easier to estimate. Recognizing on-time completion of each milestone also helps to sustain morale, focus, and energy for your entire working team.

Table 2-1: This is a roughed-out timeline for the example SoundNet project

Week	Actions
Week 1	Meetings with client to determine specifics of project.
	Pay special attention to content required; assign delivery responsibility for all text, graphics, and code.
Week 2	Prepare "coming-soon" page to announce site. Requires functional Web server and preliminary graphics.
	Work should be underway on all required content items.
	Establish contact with client's art department for logo artwork.
Week 3	Meet with client to show progress and get feedback on work to date.
	Focus on overall concept for site.
	Discuss any rough graphic designs or copy text.
	Finalize legal arrangements with client for use of existing content.
Week 4	Kick into high gear.
	Begin collecting all appropriate content from client.
	Create a storyboard for entire site.
	Formalize remaining deadlines and milestones.
	Communicate extensively with creative staff to delegate responsibilities and to ensure common, shared understanding of project.
Week 5	Pull existing content together to create preliminary version of site (Web version of storyboard, with documents for each SoundNet page).
	All links should be functional, with most pages sparsely populated with skeletons of final form.
	Include mock-up of the HTML forms necessary for customer transactions, with beta version of CGI for on-line shopping.
	Entire site must be password protected at this point.
Week 6	**Monday:** Meet with clients to preview skeleton site. Gather feedback and note all requested changes.
	Thursday: Meet again to review revisions.
Week 7	Flesh out entire site with text, graphics, data, and so on.
	Allow client to view progress periodically.
Week 8	Final meetings with client to ensure project is on track as development winds down.
	First beta site fully functional by week's end.

(continued)

Week	Actions
Week 9	**Testing:** 1. Expose site to internal audience. 2. Expose site to client. 3. Expose site to selected external audience. Immediately fix any problems turned up by testing; further testing. Verify completion of all goals set by contract. Establish degree of client satisfaction.
Week 10	**Monday morning:** *Site goes live!*

Note: Pay close attention to the deadlines you set for your project. All too often, managers set arbitrary completion times for projects and their constituent milestones, only to discover later that they made unreasonable estimates. This can result in completion delays.

When undertaking a project on a client's behalf, if practicable it is a good idea to set your internal deadlines a week or two ahead of the client's deadlines. It's even more important to stick to that internal timetable, but it never hurts to add a little padding during the final days of a project when the unexpected so often occurs. If a client decides at the last minute to change some vital project detail, you still have a grace period to deal with the resulting chaos. And if everything goes as planned, nobody has ever been fired for finishing a job ahead of schedule!

Complex projects often require elements such as graphics and content from many sources. Many projects meet their doom because project leaders based their schedules on the assumption that items contracted from outside sources arrive on time. Make sure that you plan for delays, especially when a third party is involved. When a critical element is delayed, make a contingency plan so other elements of the project can proceed even if one or more stalls.

Consider your timeline a living document. It should contain dates and times that are important to meeting your goals, but you should recognize that events can change even the best plans without notice. If you haven't considered the contingencies, unforeseen events can easily spell disaster for your project.

To avoid this downfall, allow your schedule to evolve as your project progresses. Don't look at your timeline with tunnel vision, seeing it only as a view of the final due date. Consider it as a window that displays day-by-day progress, and continue to contemplate all of the hurdles that remain before your project can be called complete.

Finally, communicate with the rest of your production team on a regular basis about the evolving state of the project's timeline. If you keep your schedule to yourself, it loses its value; it will atrophy and become obsolete. This creates a compelling argument for abandoning the timeline and proceeding without a new one. To drop your timeline because you're overwhelmed is never a step toward success.

Here are some starting points to help you create a schedule for your own project:

- Establish a drop-dead date for completion. If this is work for a client, confer with them to determine their desired delivery date. Set an internal deadline a week or two earlier.

- Break your content into internally and externally produced components. From there, map estimated times to completion for all of the various components. Be sure to consider all of the variables for each component, especially human and equipment resources. Often, resource demands will overlap and require two components to be developed serially instead of in parallel.

- Plan for chaos. What happens if the source for an externally produced piece of content fails to deliver? A key piece of equipment fails? A member of your team leaves? It isn't possible to anticipate every contingency, but a little disaster planning goes a long way!

- Schedule milestones, or stages of completion, along the way. Celebrate achieving milestones to maintain or boost morale.

- Communicate timelines as a whole, and each milestone along the way, to the entire project team. Involve each team member in the timeline's evolution.

After you rough out the basics of your project's timeline, you can immediately make decisions that cause it to change. The next stage, for example, should be to decide on your project's encompassing concept. This action can wreak havoc on a newly created timeline by rearranging

Client Relationships

When working with clients, you must develop good channels of communication to avoid working at cross purposes. At the beginning, decide together whether the client needs to approve the project at every stage or just at major milestones. Also, make the lines of authority clear, particularly whether they grant you authority to approve content elements on your own or whether the client must make all decisions.

It is essential to understand your clients and to factor their involvement into your timeline. It's also critical to document client involvement in project processes.

It is common for clients to have only a limited technical understanding of the elements of an on-line project. They may not be accustomed to working with such concepts or with the project's technical side. For this reason, clients may not feel comfortable making decisions or approving stages of the project without discussing it with peers or management. If you're unprepared, this can cause serious delays and significant frustrations.

Expect approvals to be an issue, and explicitly discuss the approval process with your clients. As a rule, expect clients to be slow to approve stages, and plan your timeline accordingly. The most effective way to limit the disruptive potential of this relationship is to foster a single point of client contact. If all communication between a project team and a client passes through one individual on either side, you reduce the chances of miscommunication and misunderstanding. These two contact individuals will develop an increasing understanding of each other over time, and will better be able to convey messages to the rest of their teams.

For the SoundNet project, we have direct contact with a client that sees this Web site as their "baby." In fact, we deal directly with one or more top-level executives from the company. Client relations takes on new meaning when dealing with people at this level, who often see things with a bottom-line attitude.

The CEO at SoundNet may not want an explanation for why something can't be done. They may only see a "No" from you as a red flag. Be sure to use diplomacy with your clients. Remember, your clients wouldn't hire you if they had the skills, knowledge, and time to develop

(continued)

48

their ideas in-house. You may want to provide information about what can and can't be done, and why, at the beginning of your negotiations. This allows them to better appreciate your area of expertise and will help you to see eye-to-eye on issues that may arise during production of their Web site.

priorities for various project features and components. Familiarize yourself with this type of revision, because it is only the beginning of the changes you'll make to the timeline along the path to completion.

Creating the Concept

The foundation for your project is established by the definition of your audience, your goals, and a rough timeline. Now, you should strive to create a central project concept. The concept is the project's overall theme and should represent the embodiment of all previous research and brainstorming.

When creating your concept, evaluate the information you gathered from evaluating your audience, setting your goals, and establishing your timeline. Then, develop a concept that unifies all these elements into a cohesive whole. Think of the concept as a narrative that encompasses all elements of the project. This is a grandiose goal, but it is imperative to scrutinize the concept to ensure that it is both reasonable and realistic based on established resources, requirements, time restrictions, and the intended audience.

Your concept need not be dictated only by resources you have available, but it can be drastically affected by resources you don't have at your disposal. The resources you take into consideration should include those time constraints that you instituted with your first stab at a timeline, as well as the budgetary, technological, and human resources at your disposal. It makes no sense to create a TV show motif with original video content on a Web site if you have no facilities to produce original digital video footage and no financial resources to seek them externally.

Although you should develop your concept based on your customer's and your own constraints, strive to push the envelope on what is practical with your technology and budget. Use the results of your initial investigation to build the right concept for the job.

For SoundNet, the client's top management established the basic concept for us. Their needs are relativly simple now, but they may be asking for impossible concepts six months down the road.

When the basics of your concept start to coalesce, you can also start on another method of documenting and planning your project, a storyboard. Derived from the film industry, a storyboard is a series of sketches or illustrations that represent the various views or scenes that will be sewn together to create the entire flow of a project.

Because the conceptual theme of the site correlates with a type of narrative, it makes sense for you to draw pictures of your story as you begin to formulate it. If you keep working at this storyboard, it will prove invaluable in determining the precise elements you need to pull together to achieve your vision.

After established, your driving concept—like your timeline—shouldn't be considered engraved in stone. Always strive to improve your project by re-evaluating your concept and second-guessing your decisions. As the project evolves, its guiding ideas must evolve too.

Analyzing and Comparing Your Concept

If you don't test and revise your initial concept, your viewers will. But by then, it may be too late to make critical changes when you become aware of problems. Therefore, it is necessary to examine your project's theme from your audience's perspective as well as your own. This is difficult, since your intimate involvement with the content can hamper your objectivity. But there are some techniques that can help.

When you think your concept is bullet-proof, turn around and try to smash it to pieces. It's difficult for any publishing effort to cover all areas of content on a given subject. But find and isolate those areas in which the project is weakest. By isolating problem areas and evaluating their significance, you can build a better solution.

Test your concept with individuals who aren't close to your project. In some situations, it may be possible to contract test viewers in focus groups to evaluate the project at predetermined intervals along your timeline. Listen carefully to their feedback and watch their reactions. Avoid becoming blinded to outside ideas and thoughts. It is important to keep an open mind and objectively accept criticism.

Finally, stack your plan against products already in existence. Careful examination of the competition can expose weaknesses in your own scheme as well as in theirs. Your own weaknesses can be fixed, while theirs can be exploited to produce competitive advantages.

After you're comfortable with a project's concept, it is time to involve your clients. Be wary of showing thoughts or examples to clients too early in the concept development phase. Changing gears midway through that phase for the wrong reasons can cause serious schedule setbacks.

If your customer sees a half-baked concept and forms a negative opinion, it can be difficult to overcome. When presenting critical elements to the client, like the concept, always treat it as a full-blown business presentation. Present the client with a well-balanced and developed concept. Spend the time to help the client understand the concept in depth. Understand and address each question or concern.

After you're satisfied that both you and your client fully understand the concept, it's time to begin development. Don't be shy about trying to "sell" the client on your idea, because spending the extra time working to excite your client about the concept is time well spent.

With a firm handle on the conceptual theme for the project, you can return to the feature set you developed when setting goals. With the concept as the motivating force, define exactly what will be required to realize each of those elements that will be incorporated into the end product.

Defining Your Content

A thorough understanding of the elements necessary to complete a project is enormously important. Without full knowledge of these elements, it's impossible to make accurate time and cost estimates.

Now that your goals and the project's concept are defined, you have also gained an abundance of features to be translated into component parts. These parts can all be defined as pieces of content, whether they are textual, audio, or graphical.

Different types of content have unique aspects that require attention, but also share common characteristics. Some of these shared facets are:

- Who's responsible for delivery?
- Does the team possess the necessary skills to create the content in-house?
- Will the responsible team member require training to complete the task?

- Is an external source for the content more convenient?
- Do materials exist that can be adapted to the project's needs?
- Must licensing fees be paid, or permission granted, to use certain content? (This is pertinent to SoundNet, where playback of copyrighted audio will occur.)
- What software tools are required for each particular piece of content?
- Is additional hardware required for the content, and are funds available for its purchase?
- Are any service bureaus needed for the content, such as photographic digitization or digital video, or audio production?

These questions can be asked of nearly any piece of content. In addition, these questions can be asked on a macro- or microcosmic scale. What that means is that they apply to individual pieces of content—for example, a piece of text that welcomes the user to the site or a .gif image of a product shot—as well as to complex pieces of content, such as a Shockwave project.

For example, if you want to create an interactive guide to your site, you need to break this complex piece of content into its component parts. Then, each component is examined and classified using the questions just discussed.

For SoundNet, we presume that the client has an active, in-house source for corporate identity materials such as marketing copy and art. In that case, the client can assume responsibility for delivering content in a timely fashion to you for the Web site production.

Furthermore, we presume that we have all of the necessary skills to complete the SoundNet project. However, we want to formulate a backup plan to increase our head count on the project because of the tight development schedule. Most important, we have the expertise and experience to learn any necessary skills quickly enough to give the appearance that we already had them at the onset of the project!

We'll work with the client's legal department to make sure we have adequate permission to use the art they provide. In addition, we'll pay close attention to the sources for any collateral artwork that makes its way onto the SoundNet pages, such as CD cover art.

Since we presume a closed circuit exists between us and our client's internal resources, we can forego the extra precautions necessary when using an outside contractor to provide content. If you have the chance to work this way, jump at the opportunity because the introduction of third parties into a project can be a source for chaos. However, we should add that some of the most enriching, cost-effective materials often come from contractors and other outside sources.

With your content understood, how can you carry through from planning to completion? Defining the production process is yet another key ingredient to your project's success.

Defining Your Process

When defining the processes necessary to deliver a project on time, first develop a detailed checklist of due dates, content, structure, and the time necessary to complete each stage of the checklist. A detailed checklist is an invaluable item to help you keep your project under control. The checklist model can also be applied to the content list developed earlier in this chapter. Each element of the project can be listed, along with all the pertinent data produced by answering our list of questions in the preceding section.

A checklist also gives you an at-a-glance view of all of the items that comprise your project and their current stages of development. This can also be helpful if your client needs an unanticipated update on project status, or if you need to make decisions based on time or resources.

Often, clients won't understand what must be done to complete a project. A detailed checklist can help you and your client understand the many elements of the production process. Checklists also provide a simple reference guide to the details necessary for project completion.

It's a good idea to create a process document that summarizes the goals of your project, its timeline, the items needed for the project, and all of your checklists. This document should be updated throughout the course of the project. Then, it may be used at any time as a reference to information on the project's progress, along with its documented goals, responsibilities, and requirements.

It's not at all uncommon for misunderstandings about the services provided, timelines, and expenses to occur. This type of document can help to protect you. Documenting processes during the early stages of a project forces all parties involved to think through many of the elements in the project before making decisions that could affect a positive outcome.

Defining your overall process should be the final step in planning your project, before you embark on gathering your content, completing your project, and releasing it to the audience. With the SoundNet project, other people are involved in this decision-making process. Thus, when entering the final stage of planning, we must also make sure to involve the client in defining the project's processes.

The definitions for your processes can vary significantly, depending on the types of projects you undertake and the quantity of resources at your disposal. Delve as deeply as you can into the details of any and all processes, whenever possible involving those people who will be directly creating project elements.

Beyond a certain level of detail, however, you will find you need to implement the project to understand its processes further. Creation is always a discovery process, and it's valuable to take what is learned on the job and incorporate it into whatever you came up with before the project began.

Not Quite a 12-Step Program!

The final ingredient to add to the various project development stages we've described consists of a reverse perspective on the work as a whole. This is a concept called *backward planning*. Applied to the stages of project planning we've been discussing, this simply means that you start at the end of the project with an idea of the finished product, then work backward, detailing the steps necessary to reach that destination.

This actually is a natural way to work, because you and your client would normally launch an entire project with some vision of the final results. The rest of the details of the project can spring from that vision, including defined goals, the timeline, the feature set, the necessary resources, and the like. When your backward planning is complete, you'll have arrived at the very first steps of the project, and will be ready to begin work, moving forward.

All of the steps we have discussed require significant investments of time and energy, but we feel strongly that it is time well spent. We've already stated our belief that strong project planning leads to tight project management, which in turn leads to successful results. As an added incentive, consider how valuable all of the documentation you generate on one job can be when you begin another. With your map of multimedia development drawn through experience and careful thought, your next venture will be much easier.

To illustrate, let's study an example of the ideas, concepts, and project management techniques used to create a Shockwave-based Web site. We've mentioned the basics behind the SoundNet project throughout the chapter. Now that you have a firm understanding of how the ideas discussed in this chapter coexist with the SoundNet project, let's examine SoundNet in more detail. This not only serves as a review of what has been covered throughout the chapter, but as we proceed, other ideas will emerge.

SoundNet: A Project Planning Example

We continue our discussion of a fictional project to create SoundNet, an on-line music retail store for an outside client, at our development company. We use the creation of a timeline for the project to illustrate the principles covered in this chapter.

Using the process of backward planning, the first item to examine is the final item that appears on the timeline. For the SoundNet project, this is the release date when the public will actually be able to view the content we place on the Web site. With the last item on the timeline established, we can determine and add to the chart those items needed to bring the project to its final stage.

Our timeline begins with the final scheduled event. We record all milestones leading up to the end result as separate points under this item on our list. Keep in mind that a timeline can be envisioned by different people in different ways. Feel free to use whatever approach makes most sense to you, and what works best in your organization when working on your own projects.

Project Timeline

Moving backward from the date of September 12, the next item should be some kind of final buy-off, or approval, of the site by the client. This suggests that we should have someone check over the content, the site's look and feel, and other aspects at least once before the client looks at it for a final time. Let's add both of these items to our list.

- SoundNet available on the Internet: September 12
- Final client approval before release: September 5
- Final project evaluation by developers: August 29

Continuing backward, the next phase adds a considerable amount of information to our timeline, encompassing alpha and beta tests, initial posting of content, and establishing the site's Web server and its Internet connection.

First, we add the final beta test. This is different from the final project evaluation by the development team. In the previous step, we evaluated the content and its interface for a last time ourselves, before the customer gives the project the go-ahead. In the beta test phase, we check for technical errors in the programming of the HTML and the Shockwave movies that make up our site, as well as review the content for currency, accuracy, and correctness. Beta tests usually involve third parties outside the development organization, so we need to recruit and communicate with these testers.

Beta testing usually follows alpha testing. In an alpha test, you catch most of the errors in the site's programming and content. The alpha test phase involves testing by a limited number of people within the ranks of the development team. It's crucial that you test your project whenever you make changes, before you show it to anyone who represents the client. Alpha test cycles are meant to catch glaring errors that slip through the development process, while beta tests are more like semipublic trials meant to test the overall concept, interface, and flow of a site.

Before alpha testing, we add an item for posting our content. This is the point at which all of the content for the Web site is finished, at least in preliminary form, and ready to be tested in the context of the Internet. At this point, we post the content onto the Web servers that will soon serve our creation to the public. Placing the content on our servers obviously requires that these machines be prepared by the time you get to this stage. Therefore, the next item in our list is to establish our servers and their connection to the Internet.

- Beta testing phase: August 21
- Alpha testing phase: August 14
- Content posted on the Internet: August 1
- Servers established on the Internet: August 1
- Connection to the Internet established: July 28

Remember that this is only an example project, and your future projects could involve pre-established servers and content.

Prior to posting our content to our Internet servers, we must finish our content development, including receiving materials from any outside vendors. To commemorate this event, we add a step to our timeline that represents the completion of the project development that occurs right before we post content on the Internet.

Now, we near the project's beginning. Several of these last bullet points could be expanded further—in fact, the same can be said for each of our bullet items. But we'll keep this example simple, so that the process doesn't become overwhelming.

As we enter the home stretch, we add the approval of the project materials, the collection of those materials, and the analysis and creation of a storyboard for the project:

- Completion of project development: August 13
- Approval of project materials: July 28
- Collection of materials: July 24
- Analysis of the storyboard: July 19
- Creation of the storyboard: July 17

At this point, 13 items make up our list of bullet points. Based on our prior discussion of project planning, the items that should precede our list are:

- Analysis of the project concept: July 14
- Creation of the project concept: July 12
- Establishment of goals: July 10
- Establishment of intended audience: July 9
- Planning meeting with customer: July 7

To recap: The analysis of the concept is when we look at the concept in greater detail before presenting it to the client for approval to continue. This is an important step because it's critical that the client understand the shape of the project in its entirety.

The item that reads "creation of the project concept" is the stage that follows the preliminary planning stages. At this point, we analyze the concept that we have created for weaknesses using similar, existing projects and outside opinions.

Establishing the project's goals and audience are two rather abstract steps that are intertwined with one another. In practice, both points can probably be accomplished by a good brainstorming session or two. Nonetheless, they deserve separate billing because it is important that each one is concretely defined as we proceed.

Finally comes the point of departure for the entire project—the initial meeting with the client. This is the first step after the client hires you. At this stage, you sit down with the client and any other groups involved with the project to discuss their goals and expectations. It is from notes taken during this meeting that all of the raw material for the early stages of development come. To meet the timeline we've presented, this must occur during the first week of July.

Where to Now?

With the top level of our timeline complete, you can proceed with the actual grunt work of creating the project. As you move from action item to action item, you fill in the details of each milestone as it approaches. The simple list you create evolves, grows, and serves many purposes— resource management, task delegation, a focus for team communication, and much more. It's up to you to keep it current, and to make it work!

Summary

At this point, you've gained a basis for approaching your own projects. Staying organized is the best way to stay afloat in the turbulent waters of multimedia development. If there's one lesson we want to impart, it is that simple Web projects and Web projects that revolve around Shockwave elements are two entirely distinct endeavors. Even a seasoned Web development team encounters new challenges when the element of true interactive multimedia production is added to the mix.

With a foundation of the theory behind Shockwave and preparation for multimedia development, you're ready to leap into the world of hands-on experience. In the next chapter, you learn the basics of the Shockwave development platform and create a complete multimedia project!

CHAPTER 3

Assembling and Authoring Your Project in Director

*n*ow that you've established a plan for the initial stages of your project, we walk you through building two sample projects in Macromedia Director. Because Director is the development platform for Shockwave projects, it's the application you'll be most involved with when creating your projects. We build the first example without any supporting materials. The second example uses graphic and sound files from the CD-ROM included with this book. We use Macromedia Director to build both projects from the ground up, then prepare them for conversion to Shockwave documents.

We concentrate on Director basics and what you need to know to successfully create, save, and modify a Director project. In later chapters, you'll work further with our projects, convert them into Shockwave files, and upload and install them on a Web server.

Note: Remember that, while there are several instructions in this book to save your work for further use, you will not be able to do so without the commercial version of Macromedia Director. The version included on the accompanying CD is save-disabled and is meant purely as a tutorial tool.

What we don't provide in this book is a comprehensive survey of all of Director's many features and capabilities. This is a deep software product, the kind that takes years to learn completely. It's therefore beyond the scope of this book to turn you into a Macromedia Master.

Project One

In this section, you establish a basic understanding of Macromedia Director's authoring environment as you build your first project. In Chapter 4, "Principles of Shockwave Conversion and Lingo Usage," you convert it to Shockwave format for Internet use.

This first project involves simple Director sprite animation and imported, external files. The second project is a little more complex and involves several simple Lingo commands that enable you to build a more interactive project. (Lingo is Director's built-in scripting language.) For both projects, you create your content inside Director. However, you have an opportunity to import graphics, sounds, and other files from external sources into both projects after you have completed these two examples. This first project involves building simple text and graphics within Director, then manipulating the content to make it animated and interactive.

Though this project is not a full-scale multimedia production, the project planning steps we laid out in Chapter 2 still apply. No matter how large or small your project may be, it's always valuable to keep formal organizational factors and planning techniques in mind. That way, as you proceed, you have a toolbox open and ready to apply wherever appropriate.

Step 1: Open Director's Windows

Start by opening Macromedia Director and then opening the Stage, Cast, and Score windows, as well as the Control Panel. If you don't know the shortcuts for opening these windows, use the Windows menu. To do this, select Windows from the menu commands and then open all of the windows just mentioned.

After you've opened these windows, resize them (if necessary) so that you can work with each window comfortably. The Stage is where you place items imported into, or created for, your Director project. It's the "visible area" in which all of the events you create for your cast members are seen by end users.

Additional Resources for Learning and Using Director

Macromedia offers an extensive list of complementary multimedia products and services. This list is printed regularly in *Macromedia Connections*, the company's monthly newsletter, and includes organizations and individuals that teach classes on how to use Macromedia Director.

Macromedia also offers information on *Macromedia Connections* on-line at the URL provided below. This is one of the best places to look if you've perused your manuals and still have questions about the application.

Macromedia's Authorized Training Program is designed to train businesses and institutions that want to provide training on Macromedia products. Information on this program may be found on-line at:

```
http://www.macromedia.com
```

Or, you can find information in *Macromedia Connections*. Check out this resource if you want to learn more about Director or if you'd like to train others to use the program.

Additionally, if you run a Mac, check out IDG Book's *Macromedia Director 4 For Macs For Dummies*, authored by Lauren Steinhauer, for a clear, concise reference to the many features of Director. Keep your eyes open for future Director books from IDG too.

Director's Major Windows Explored and Explained

Before we continue with the second step of Project One, we take a major detour to talk about each of the Director windows that we just mentioned—the Stage, Cast, and Score windows. (We do this because these Windows define the program's fundamental capabilities, not to make you hold your breath until step 2!)

Director is based on a theater metaphor, the main components of which are a stage, a cast, and a score. You use the cast to store items, or actors, for your project. The score controls the actions of the members of your cast on the stage. Finally, you use the stage to play your multimedia project for viewers.

The main interface that's used when building and testing projects is the Control Panel window, which can start, stop, rewind, and advance a project. At this point, let's examine each of these windows in detail.

The Stage Window

The stage is where you place items imported into, or created for, your Director project. It's the visible area in which all of the events you create for your cast members are seen by end users.

One of the most important things to determine about the stage when creating content for your Web site is its size. The stage's default size is 640 (width) by 480 (height), measured in pixels. Because this is the standard size for a VGA computer monitor and the actual viewing window for your movie will be much smaller, it doesn't lend itself for use in a Shockwave document.

Most Web browsers default their window size to a viewable area that's anywhere from 450 to 480 pixels wide. Take this into account when creating movies in Director.

The Stage window in Director can be modified to fit the default size of most Web browsers by adjusting the width and height of the stage. Figure 3-1 depicts the Preferences window for Director. This window is where you must set the stage size to fit the width we mentioned. (We'll cover this topic in more detail later in the chapter.)

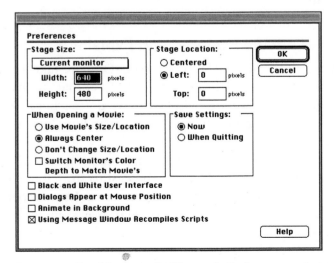

Figure 3-1: Use Macromedia Director's Preferences window to make the width suitable for a Shockwave project.

The Cast Window

The Cast window is where you store all of the members of your project's cast. This is the window in which you import cast members created in other applications into your project. The Cast window also allows you to organize your cast members in one place.

While a cast member is selected in your Cast window, its name and number are displayed in the window's top section. Figure 3-2 shows what this window looks like.

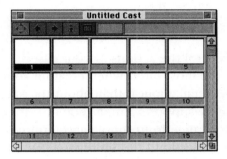

Figure 3-2: This is Director's Cast window, where a cast member's name and number are displayed.

The Cast window allows you to rearrange your cast members by selecting them and using drag-and-drop operations to move them to other slots.

Note: You can move cast members into slots that are already occupied by other cast members. If you do this, the cast member who previously occupied that slot will be replaced.

The Cast window has numerous options, including the maximum number of cast members visible in the Cast window, the number of cast members in one row, the size of cast member slots, the cast member ID style, and the types of cast member icons. These options help to customize the Cast window and can help you to better organize your project. Figure 3-3 shows the starting point that we suggest you use when working with Director.

After you become more familiar with the Cast window, you'll probably want to experiment with Director's many related options to find those settings that best fit your working style.

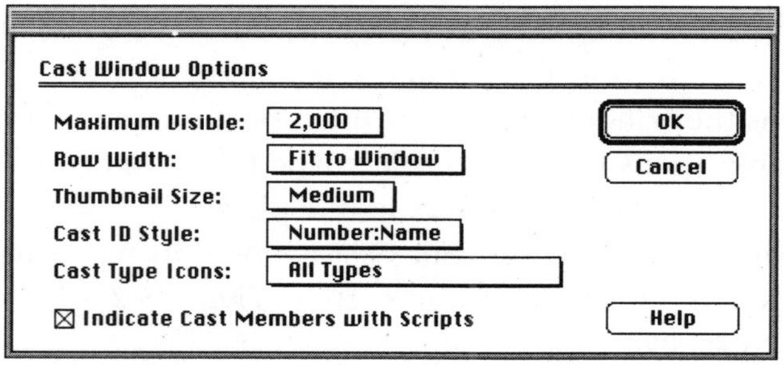

Figure 3-3: These are recommended Cast window options.

The Score Window

The Score window is where you control the actions of your cast members. This is the window you use most often when creating your project, so we provide a little more detail about it than about the Stage and Cast windows. The Score window supports a multitude of features for creating Director projects, which range from simple and intuitive to subtle and complex. To adequately understand the Score window, we start with a general overview, then look at a few of its main features.

Figure 3-4 shows the Score window's main symbols and other items. You should also notice the series of numbers. The set that runs vertically contains the numbers 1 through 48 in increments of one. Each of these numbers represents a channel in your score. To better understand this, let each number represent a cast member. If you think of it this way, you recognize that you're limited to a total of 48 cast members in the project score at any given moment.

The next set of numbers, which runs across the top of the window, represents the frames in your score. Notice that these numbers occur in increments of five, starting with 1 on the left-hand side of the window and continuing to the far right-hand side. As your project grows and you use more frames, notice that the application provides additional frames at the end of the Score window. These additional frames may be viewed by using the horizontal scroll bar to move the window's display area further into the score.

At this point, you should understand that you can place up to 48 cast members on the stage at once (or in a single frame). Of course, in a project destined for Shockwave delivery, you wouldn't want to have that many elements simultaneously active on the stage because of the large filesize and Internet downloading time that would result.

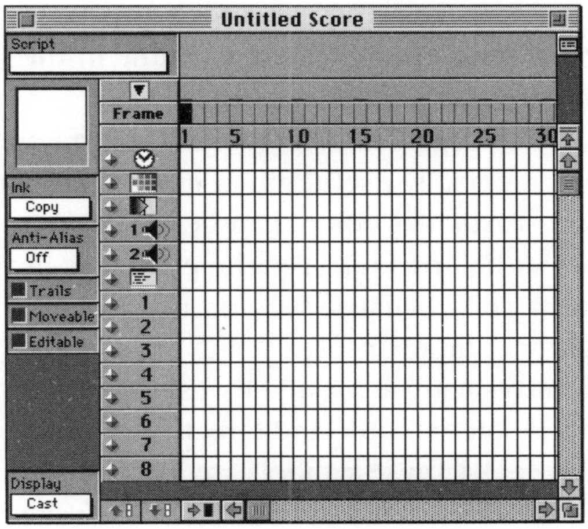

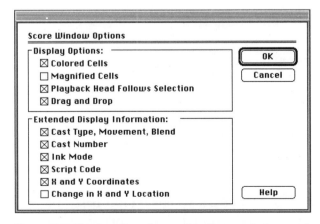

Figure 3-4: Director's Score window offers many features.

Also, note that another window is dedicated to the options you can control in the Score window. Figure 3-5 shows the Score window options and what we suggest it should resemble as you begin using Director to author your Shockwave project.

Score Window Options

Display Options:
- ☒ Colored Cells
- ☐ Magnified Cells
- ☒ Playback Head Follows Selection
- ☒ Drag and Drop

Extended Display Information:
- ☒ Cast Type, Movement, Blend
- ☒ Cast Number
- ☒ Ink Mode
- ☒ Script Code
- ☒ H and Y Coordinates
- ☐ Change in H and Y Location

OK
Cancel
Help

Figure 3-5: The interface for setting Score window options is presented here with recommended settings.

Notice that, in Figure 3-5, the first checkbox handles Colored Cells. We check this option so that we can use the five extra cell colors that Director provides to better organize your project while working in the Score window. When this box is checked, you can assign any of the five extra colors (yellow, green, blue, pink, and red) to any frame in the Score window regardless of its number or the symbol beside it.

Experiment with using colors to organize your score when building your project. Colored cells are especially useful when more than one person is working on a project. Particular colors can be assigned to individuals so that changes are easily marked. (For the examples in this chapter, we won't apply colored cells, because we don't use a large number of frames or particularly complex scores.)

Additional Score window controls may be located by using the six symbols near the left side of the Score window and directly under the word "Frame." As you saw in Figure 3-4, these symbols are located between the line of frame numbers and the first track number. By default, the Score window opens with these symbols scrolled off the top, so you may have to scroll down to see them after loading a project file.

Tempo Control. Starting from the top, the first symbol in the Score window looks like a clock. This symbol represents the project's tempo for a particular frame. Double-clicking any frame in this channel brings up the window shown in Figure 3-6.

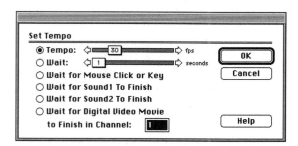

Figure 3-6: The Set Tempo window lets you control the timing for the selected frame.

The first option that appears in Figure 3-6 is Tempo, based on frames per second. Changing the tempo setting in frames per second changes the tempo for the rest of the score until another tempo is set.

The second option is Wait. This option pauses playback of the score for a specific number of seconds at a particular frame.

There are four more options in the Set Tempo window. These options are all event based; that is, some event must occur for playback of the score to continue. We examine these remaining options in more detail than the options just discussed because they must be used properly in your score to obtain the proper results.

The first of these four options is Wait for Mouse Click or Key. This option pauses the playback of the score until a key on the keyboard is pressed or the input device sends a signal, usually represented by a mouse click. When this option is checked, a mouse symbol appears in place of the mouse at the frame where the Wait for Mouse Click or Key has been assigned.

Use of the Wait options means that playback of the score remains paused until a keyboard or mouse signal is sent. There is no time-out if a signal isn't sent. If you choose to use this option in a movie, users must click the mouse button or press a key for your movie to continue.

In a Shockwave document, this command could cause trouble for your users. If users fail to move the mouse over your movie, the pointer symbol for the mouse may not change to the wait symbol. This means your users could continue viewing the text or other items on your page—or fail to view your entire movie—because they don't understand what's expected of them. If you use this option, try to include some form of instruction—preferably, outside the Shockwave document—so that users understand what this symbol means and what to do when they see it.

The second, third, and fourth options are similar in that, when used, they wait for a sound or movie to finish playing before continuing playback of the score. There are only two sound channels in the Score window. The Wait for Sound1 and Wait for Sound2 options pause playback until the sound in the specified channel finishes playing.

The final option in the Set Tempo window is the Wait for Digital Video Movie. This pauses playback of the score at a frame until the movie on a certain channel finishes playing, as determined by the number in To Finish in Channel input. This option can also be controlled by Lingo and, as in most cases, Lingo is the preferred method of control because it provides more precision and flexibility.

> **Note:** The first release of Shockwave does not support linked media, such as movies. In Chapter 6, "Shockwave Tips & Tricks," we discuss several ways to work around this lack of linked media.

Palette Control. Directly under the clock symbol in the Score window is the symbol for palette control. When a frame in this channel is double-clicked, a window appears with several options that affect your project's color palette. As depicted in Figure 3-7, the available options create palette effects and change palettes during the score's playback.

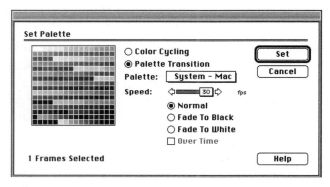

Figure 3-7: The Set Palette window provides multiple options to control your project's color palette.

Among the available options are nine preset color palettes and the following, additional choices:

- Color Cycling
- Speed
- Fade to Black
- Fade to White

Though you won't use these controls in our examples, experiment to observe their effects.

Transitions. The next symbol represents a transition at a certain frame. If you double-click a frame in this channel, the Set Transition

window opens with several options related to transitions as depicted in
Figure 3-8.

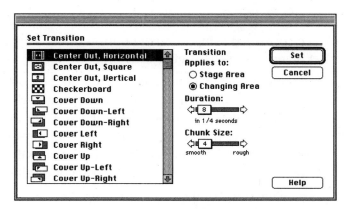

Figure 3-8: The Set Transition window offers 52 frame transition effects.

Fifty-two frame transition effects are available for our Director projects.
We have picked a simple transition to illustrate how to use the Set
Transition window.

After you pick a frame in the Transition Channel and double-click, the
Set Transition window appears. When the window is open, pick the
first transition in the list at the left of the window, which should be
labeled Center Out, Horizontal.

To the right of the scrollable window within the Set Transition
window, you find several options for this transition. The first option lets
you choose the area of the stage where the transition will apply. The two
choices are Stage Area and Changing Area. This means that the transition
can affect the entire Stage window or just the area that is changing on
the stage as the playback of the score moves to the next frame.

The second option is the transition's duration, measured in quarter-
second increments. The third option sets the chunk size for the transition,
which basically controls how smoothly or roughly the transition occurs.

To set a transition, follow these six steps:

1. Pick a frame for which you want the transition to occur. The
   transition occurs from the selected frame to the next frame in the
   score's playback sequence. This means that if you want a
   transition to be complete by frame 10, you set the transition at
   frame 9. Double-click that frame's transition channel.

2. Select the transition you want to apply. To do this, scroll through the transition choices in the scrollable window at the left of the Set Transition window, then click the transition you want.

3. Set the area in which you want the transition to occur. Select one of the two choices provided using the radio button beside it; that is, choose either Stage Area or Changing Area.

4. Set the transition's duration by clicking and holding the box on top of the timeline. Drag the box forward or backward until the number inside the box reflects the amount of time you want the transition to take. Remember that the number in the box must be multiplied by four to calculate the number of seconds that will elapse, because the number in the box is a quarter-second value.

5. Set the chunk size, which determines how smoothly the transition affects the stage. Use the same techniques to adjust the chunk size that you used to set the duration.

6. Click the Set button. Your transition is now complete.

Sound Channels. The next two symbols under the transition symbol in the Score window represent the two sound channels that you can use to add audio to your score. Please note that you need not place a sound in the sound channel to make it play during the playback of your score. Sounds can also be associated with events in the score at particular frames, or with cast members.

Like almost every other part of Director, sound can be played, stopped, faded in, and faded out with Lingo. Double-clicking a frame in the sound channels brings up a window that only allows the selection of a sound from your cast and no additional options. This is because most sound features are controlled using Lingo.

Script Channel. Finally, the last symbol in the Score window represents the score script channel. This channel is located between sound channel two and the first cast member channel, channel number One. Double-clicking a frame in this channel opens a window for creating a score script. Figure 3-9 shows this window with Director's default script stub. The stub comprises the On ExitFrame and End segments of the score script already placed with your script.

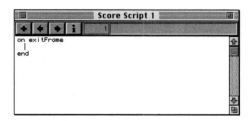

Figure 3-9: The Score Script window opens containing Director's default script stub.

With the Score Script window open, you can also view other scripts by clicking the left or right arrows. Clicking these arrows moves your viewpoint to those scripts that precede or follow the present script in the Cast window.

The Control Panel Window

The Control Panel window is the last window we cover before explaining the menu commands. The Control Panel window is that collection of tools used to manipulate score playback. As Figure 3-10 reveals, the Control Panel controls are similar to playback controls on an audio cassette player or a VCR.

Figure 3-10: The Control Panel window resembles a VCR.

The Control Panel contains several controls in addition to these familiar-looking VCR or cassette player controls. Here again, we only explain the Control Panel as much as is needed to complete our projects. The control functions that aren't covered in this section are explained well in the Director manuals.

The first Control Panel control that we cover is the Mute button. Normally, this button looks like a speaker with a sound wave emanating from it. But when clicked, it changes to a speaker without sound waves. This controls sound during playback of the score.

The second control you need to understand is the icon that looks like an arrow pointing at a line or wall. You may have seen similar icons if you've used a music sequencer or video editing software. This control instructs the playback head either to play through to the end, or to loop back to the beginning after the last frame of the score has played. This is a toggle, so single clicks alternate the icon between play-through and play-loop symbols. For the projects you create here, you must understand both modes.

The last two Control Panel symbols handle the position of the playback head and the frame rate during playback. The first of these controls is located in the bottom left-hand corner of the Control Panel window. This is the control that moves the playback head—a kind of cursor that indicates your current position in the score. Click the up or down arrow to increase or decrease the frame number.

The second control is located directly to the right of the playback head control, directly at the bottom center of the Control Panel window. This control changes the frame rate of playback when the play button is pressed. The project's frame rate can be manipulated by the controls in the Set Tempo window, but it can also be manipulated by Lingo. To change the current frame rate, simply use the up and down arrows in much the same fashion that you did with the playback head position control.

Note: You should observe a feature that many new Director users miss. If you click the mouse once on the section of this control that contains the letters FPS, the letters change to SPF. FPS stands for *frames per second,* as we have already discussed, while SPF stands for *seconds per frame.* (You won't use the SPF setting for the projects in this chapter.)

This concludes our look at the windows in Macromedia's Director. For the purposes of this chapter, these are the only windows you need to understand to start work on your projects. This means that we now can resume coverage of your first sample project!

Note: You can find information beyond that covered in this chapter in the manuals that accompany the Macromedia Director software.

About Fonts and Director

Macromedia Director doesn't build the fonts you choose for text into any of its files. This means that if we provide you with a *film strip* file or *projector* that uses a font that isn't resident on your system, font substitution occurs.

You have several options to resolve this problem. If exact reproduction of typography is important, you may have to purchase the exact font that's required. Otherwise, you can substitute the missing font with the local font that best matches the missing font's metrics—how much space it takes up on the page—or looks. Overall, the best source for information about fonts and Director is the manual that accompanies the application.

Step 2: Set the Stage

From the File menu, choose Preferences (Figure 3-1); under Stage Size, set the width to 448 pixels and the height to 100 pixels. We set the width to 448 to get as close to our maximum of 450 as possible within Director's limits. (It increases size in 16-pixel increments.) This lets the resulting project fit comfortably within an average Web browser window.

Next, if you're on a Macintosh, set the Stage Location to Centered. (This the default in Windows.) Once your Preferences are set, click the OK button to close the window.

Step 3: Your Name, Please

Open a Text window by using the Window Text command from the menu bar. Type your name; then highlight it. Use the Text pull-down menu on the menu bar to change its font, size, and style for a more distinctive look. Since it's your name, you might as well personalize it!

Step 4: Casting Call

Soon after you type your name into the Text window, it appears in the window for cast member number 1. In the Cast window, cut and paste this cast member (the name you typed) three times into cast members 2, 3, and 4 using keyboard shortcuts or the Edit menu. You now have the same name in slots 1, 2, 3, and 4 of the Cast window.

Remember, the Cast window is where you store all the members of your project's cast. If you had materials created in other applications, you would import them as cast members. For this project, you've simply created four copies of the same text element (your name) as cast members 1 through 4.

The Cast window allows you to rearrange your cast members by selecting them and using drag-and-drop operations to move them to other cast member slots.

Step 5: Personalize Your Cast Members

Open the Tools window from the Windows menu. After it's open, click once on cast member number 1 and choose Edit Cast Member from the Cast menu. Cast member 1 opens in the Text window. (You can also open a cast member for editing by double-clicking its window within the Cast window.) Select your text by dragging your cursor over it in the Text window, then select a color by clicking and holding the black box inside the Tools window. This brings up a color palette from which you can choose a text color.

Repeat the steps you used to color cast member 1 for cast members 2, 3, and 4. Use any colors, but make sure that each of the four cast members has a different color.

Step 6: Going in Circles

Open the Paint window by choosing it from the Windows menu. After it's open, select a color by clicking and holding the black box on the left side of the Paint window.

After choosing a color, select the Ellipse tool from the left-hand side of the window. When selecting the Ellipse tool, make sure you select the side that's filled, on the right side of the tool's button. This tool drag-draws hollow or filled ellipses and circles in the Paint window using the currently selected color as a fill. If you hold down the shift key while you drag the mouse, the tool draws perfect circles. Drag-draw a circle about a quarter-inch in diameter, then close the Paint window.

Step 7: Assemble Your Cast

Place the five members of your cast onto the stage so you can use some simple techniques to animate them. To place each cast member on the stage, use the simple drag-and-drop technique. Here's how: First, make sure that you can see both the Score window and the Cast window at the same time. Then, click and hold cast member 1 while dragging it into the Score window and over the second channel position in the first frame.

Repeat this process to place the remaining cast members in the score, as follows:

- Move cast member 2 into channel 3, frame 1
- Move cast member 3 into channel 4, frame 1
- Move cast member 4 into channel 5, frame 1
- Move cast member 5 into channel 6, frame 1

We purposely left channel 1 free because you'll use it in the second project.

Step 8: Give Your Cast an Encore

Now that you've positioned each cast member in its initial place, insert a second copy of each cast member in its respective channel. To do this, drag each cast member from the Cast window to the following positions in the score:

- Move cast member 1 to channel 2, frame 10
- Move cast member 2 to channel 3, frame 5
- Move cast member 3 to channel 4, frame 15
- Move cast member 4 to channel 5, frame 30
- Move cast member 5 to channel 6, frame 30.

We will make the circle clickable later in the lesson, so we want it present throughout the project.

Step 9: Prepare to Animate

We now implement some simple animation techniques. To do this, you first need to rearrange some of the cast members on your stage.

Specifically, you want to grab the four copies of your name and move them to the points of an imaginary compass centered in the middle of the stage.

To make sure you're editing the correct cast member, click on the frame cell in each channel before changing the position. Move cast member 1 in channel 2, frame 10 to North; move cast member 2 in channel 3, frame 5 to South; move cast member 3 in channel 4, frame 15 to East; and finally, move cast member 4 in channel 5, frame 30 to West. (Note that this action takes place on the stage, not in the Cast or Score window.) As you position each of these cast members, leave just its barest edge showing on the stage.

Note: The small box on the right side of the thick selection bar is a resize handle, which allows you to resize the area enclosed by the selection bar. Don't grab this. Because all that you want to do is move this selection, you can grab the selection bar anyplace, hold down the mouse button, and drag the cast member where you want to put it on the screen.

Step 10: Lights, Camera, Action!

After you've moved the cast members into the positions specified in step 9, you use the In-Between Linear command from the Score menu to animate each cast member's movements.

To establish an animation sequence for a cast member, sometimes called sprite animation, select each cast member's initial frame. Then, holding down the shift key, select its last frame. For example, to perform this action on cast member 1, first click on frame 1 of channel 2. Then, hold down the shift key and click on the same cast member again, this time at frame 10. After you click, release the shift key.

Now, select In-Between Linear from the Score menu. This generates the appropriate information needed to make the cast member in this channel move smoothly from its initial frame to its final frame while simultaneously placing the data into the score. Repeat the process for the other three cast members. After you complete this sequence of commands, your Score window should resemble the one shown in Figure 3-11.

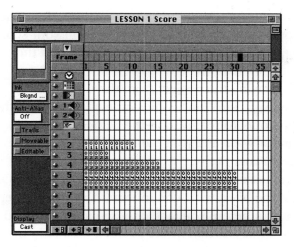

Figure 3-11: The Score window should look like this after step 10.

Note: You may notice that the white blocks that represent text fields cover the area behind them as they fly across the stage. To resolve this, select all of the cast members at all of the positions on the stage by clicking the mouse down in frame 1 of channel 1. Continue to hold the button down while dragging the mouse to frame 30 of channel 6. This selects all of the frames in the score. Then, choose Background Transparent from the Ink menu in the Score window. This makes all of the white text blocks transparent.

Step 11: Lingo and Loops

You've already animated your score. But if you play it back, it stops when it reaches frame 30. Let's use some simple Lingo scripting to create a loop that causes your project to go back to frame 1 and repeat when it reaches frame 30.

To loop back from frame 30 to frame 1, open a Score Script window in the script channel at frame 30. After the script window is open, type the following inside its frame:

```
on exitFrame
   go to frame 1
end
```

After this text has been entered, close the Score Script window. The next time you play the project, when you reach frame 30 in your score this script instructs the playback head to return to frame 1, and the sequence begins anew.

Test your animation by playing the project from the Control Panel. You should see your name split into four copies of itself and fly off the window in four directions, only to reappear at the center of the stage and repeat. When you tire of watching your name in lights, press the Stop button in the Control Panel.

Congratulations! You've just created a working Director project. After you've patted yourself on the back, we'll continue with additional steps to complete Project One. But before you tackle these more advanced steps and include some user interaction in the project, we'll help make you a better-educated Director user. To that end, we cover Director's menu commands next.

A Look at Director's Menu Commands

Macromedia Director offers more than 90 menu commands, so a complete survey of them falls well beyond the scope of this book. We only cover the handful of menu commands necessary to complete our projects. These items are structured to be understood easily. For simplicity, we work our way from left to right across the menu bar in Director, briefly discussing the menu and those items you use in your projects.

The File Menu

The File menu contains the commands that you see in most applications. Most of these menu items are self-explanatory or may be found in the manuals for Director. But some of them require more explanation about the functions they perform and how we use them in your projects. The File menu is depicted in Figure 3-12.

You need to understand four menu items in the File menu to complete our projects: Import, Create Projector, Movie Info, and Preferences. Each of these items opens its own window when selected.

The Import Menu Item

You use the Import menu item to include files in your project. Director can import many types of image files, sound files, and movies. Figure 3-13 shows the Import window and its options.

Figure 3-12: The File menu contains both common and some Director-specific selections.

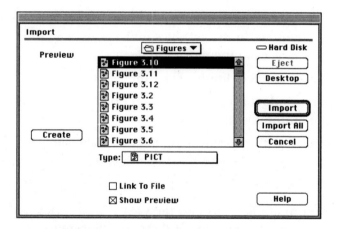

Figure 3-13: The Import window is used to import graphics, sound, and movie files into your projects.

Steps to Import Media into Macromedia Director. The following steps allow you to import a single item into Macromedia Director:

1. Open the Import window by selecting Import from the File menu. This opens the window depicted in Figure 3-13.

2. Select the file type you want to import from the Type pop-up menu near the bottom center of the Import window.

3. Make sure Link to File is unchecked. Linked media are incompatible with the current version of Shockwave.

4. In the scrollable window within the Import window, select the file you want to import. After you select a file, choose the button labeled Import on the right-hand side of the Import window.

Importing Multiple Items into Macromedia Director. You can import more than one item at a time if you organize your items by type in a folder or directory. Then, you can open the folder in the dialog box and click the Import All button at the right-hand side of the Import window. You can use this technique to organize the items in your Cast window by following these steps:

1. Make three folders or directories named *graphics, sounds,* and *movies.*

2. Place all of your graphics in the graphics folder, sounds in the sound folder, and movies in the movies folder.

3. From within Director, select Import from the File menu.

4. After the Import window is open, select and open the graphics folder. Click the button marked Import All.

5. Repeat this process with the remaining folders. Make sure that the correct Type is selected; otherwise, your files may not appear in the scrollable window.

Director will import multiple items into the Cast window. However, it's important to realize that the amount of RAM you allocate to Director (for Macintosh users) or have available (for Windows users) can affect importation of multiple items into the Cast window.

If you encounter memory problems, try one of these steps:

• Increase the memory allocated to Director (Macintosh only).

• Add memory to your system.

• Manually import items one at a time.

You'll find other organizational tips and tricks in Chapter 6. You can use the organizational structure and techniques found there to guide your project's general organization.

The Create Projector Menu Item

The Create Projector menu item converts your Director project into a self-running application, called a projector. Note that you can't convert a projector into a Shockwave .DCR file. Rather, you must access the original copy of the Director project, or film strip, to create a Shockwave document. This means that you won't need to use the Create Projector menu item when creating a project for conversion into a Shockwave document. We will, however, discuss using this option to test your project later in this chapter. Create Projector's window is depicted in Figure 3-14.

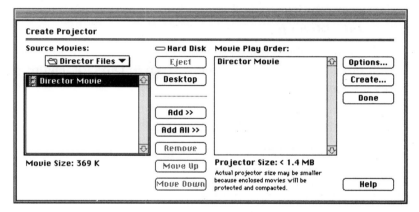

Figure 3-14: The Create Projector window converts your Director projects into self-running applications.

Note: Be sure not to save your projector in the same directory with the same filename as your film strip file. Otherwise, you won't be able to edit the projector. So be sure to keep the film strip file in case you later need to edit it.

To create a projector, follow these steps:

1. Open the Create Projector window by selecting Create Projector from the File menu.

2. Select a source movie on the left-hand side of the window. Notice that the filesize of the source movie is displayed in the bottom left-hand corner of the Create Projector window.

3. After the movie file you want is selected, choose the Add >> button in the middle of the window.

4. Choose the Options button in the top right-hand corner of the Create Projector window. Look at the section labeled When Opening File and make sure that Re-size Stage and Center Stage on Screen are checked, then click OK.

5. Now choose the button labeled Create. You'll be prompted to save the file. After you name the file and click Save in the dialog window, the conversion of the file to a projector is made.

The Movie Info Menu Item

The Movie Info menu item opens the Movie Info window and contains information on the movie that's currently open in Director. Figure 3-15 shows this information.

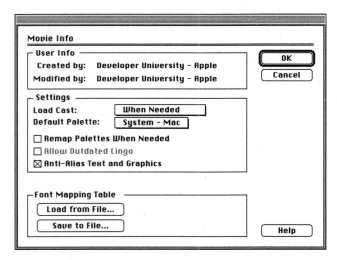

Figure 3-15: The Movie Info window provides details about the current movie in Director.

The Preferences Menu Item

Preferences is the final File menu item that we cover. Choosing this item opens one of the most important windows for our project. This Preferences window is where you control details such as stage size, movie positioning (when opening), and stage location—all of which are vital to your control of the project. Figure 3-16 shows the Preferences window and its options.

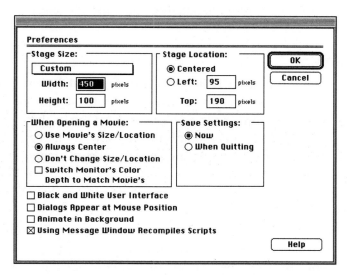

Figure 3-16: The Preferences window provides control for critical project details.

Stage size is the most important aspect in your Shockwave project because, as we stated earlier, Director's default stage size (640 pixels wide by 480 pixels high) is too large to fit into most Web browsers' default window. You need to resize the stage to ensure that your project fits on your users' desktops.

The Edit Menu

The Edit menu contains the standard content editing controls in Director. This menu supplies common options such as cut and paste, along with some Director-specific options such as Disable Lingo.

The Window Menu

The Window menu is where you can open and close all windows in Director, including the stage. Director automatically hides any open windows if you choose the Stage window from this menu, so you need to use this menu frequently to bring closed windows back to your desktop.

The Cast Menu

The Cast menu allows you to get information on a cast member, to paste images into the Cast window, and to sort or find cast members in your project. This window is useful in organizing and controlling your project's cast.

The Score Menu

The Score menu offers options such as Setting Sprite Blend, Tempo, Palette, Transition, and Sound. You can control most of these options from the Control Panel window or the Score window. One of the commands that you'll use from this menu is the In-Between Linear command, which allows you to incorporate simple sprite animation into your project.

The Text Menu

The Text menu controls text fonts, sizes, styles, alignment in text, paint, markers, and more. This menu is useful for control over all of the textual aspects of your project. The Text menu also contains choices that allow you to recompile one script in your project, or multiple scripts at the same time.

Tip: When you format or delete text in Director, then type new text, the new text appears in the default format. Deleting all of the text in a text field on the stage or in the text window deletes the formatting. So it's a good idea to save one character from something you delete if you plan to replace it with text that should take the same style. You can enter the new text and maintain style and formatting information from the one remaining character, then delete the character after you enter the replacement copy.

Other Menus in Director

Macromedia Director includes various other menus, including Paint, Effects, Lingo, and Palettes. We address two of them within the presentation of our following examples—Paint and Effects. Because our goal in this chapter is limited to giving you an introduction to the Director authoring environment, we won't cover other aspects for these two menus. If you need more information about any of Director's windows, please consult the product manuals.

Finishing with an Interaction

Now that you've seen more Director menus than you probably ever wanted, it's time to jump back into Project One. At this point, we add some interactive controls to keep the project from looping back from frame 30 to frame 1 until the end of time.

We mentioned earlier that you would make the circle that appears as cast member 5, channel 6, a clickable object. We'll also show you how to make a set of screen credits appear when the user clicks on that circle. First, you need to make some credits, then script your circle and your score so the credits appear when the circle is selected.

Step 12: Credits Where Credit Is Due

Begin by creating a credits cast member. To do this, follow the same steps you used in step 3 to create text. Open the Text window by choosing it from the Windows menu. If an existing cast member appears in the Text box, click the + (plus) button in the Text window to jump to the next blank cast slot (cast member 7). Otherwise, you may edit an existing cast member that should be left alone. After the correct text window opens, type your name. Make the text look like this:

```
Project Created By:
Joe Doe
```

Next, create another cast member (8) with text that reads:

```
Click here to continue
```

Place these two new cast members on the score. Put cast member 7 at channel 2, frame 35. (Notice that you now have two different cast members in the same channel.) Next, place cast member 8 at channel 3, frame 35. Move each of these items to its proper position. (We suggest placing the credits just above center, and the *click here ...* text just below that.)

Step 13: The Pause That Refreshes

Now, add another score script to the script channel at frame 35 by double-clicking the script channel cell. After the Score Script window opens, enter the following text:

```
on exitFrame
  pause
end
```

This pauses the playback head whenever it reaches frame 35. (You may be asking yourself how, with the loop scripted at frame 30, your project ever reaches frame 35. Proceed, and be illuminated!)

Step 14: Click Here to Continue . . .

Adding a script to an object makes it a clickable object. (A clickable object is an object that, when clicked, executes an attached script.) To make your credits work as they're supposed to, make the circle, otherwise known as cast member 5, a clickable object with an appropriate Lingo script. Here's how: Select cast member 5 in the Cast window and choose Open Script from the Cast menu. This opens a Script editing window, into which you must enter the following Lingo script:

```
on mouseDown
  go to frame 35
end
```

Because we made this object clickable, the default stub script starts with the *on mouseUp* command. To make the script work, we must change this to *on mouseDown*. The preceding Lingo script causes the playback head to move to frame 35 from any other frame between 1 and 30 when the circle is clicked.

To test your script, reset the playback head to frame 1 in the Control Panel, then click Play. At any point during the loop from frame 1 to frame 30, click on the circle object. The playback head will jump immediately to frame 35, and your credits should be visible. If this doesn't work, retrace the last step or two to make sure you did everything correctly.

When a click on the circle invokes your credits, there's no way to return from frame 35 to the main sequence. The solution is to add a script to cast member 8, the associated text that reads *Click here to continue*. Highlight cast member 8 at channel 3, frame 35, by clicking on it in the Cast window, then select Open Script from the Cast menu. Enter the following text into the Script window that appears:

```
on mouseDown
  go to frame 1
end
```

This causes the playback head to return to frame 1 when you click on the text defined in cast member 8. Voila—you've established a way to get back from the credits frame to your main sequence!

Step 15: Testing 1, 2, 3 . . .

Play the project from within Director. Click on all scripted objects and check the results. If you have a problem with any of your scripts or the actions of any of your cast members, back up and try again. If you click on the circle and see the credits, then click on the text element to restart the animation, you've successfully completed the project!

Step 16: Save Your Work!

Because you will use this project again and may also use it as the basis for more advanced projects of your own, save your work in its current state as a file of its own. To do this, select the Save As entry from the File menu and enter a nice, descriptive name for the project in the filename text entry box. (May we suggest project1.dir?)

Note: Remember once again that you will not be able to save your work with the version of Director included on the CD with this book. Luckily, we've included a saved version of Project One, so you can continue with Project Two.

Project One Summary

With Project One complete, let's review what you've learned. We've covered quite a bit of territory for one short lesson, including how to:

- Create simple text cast members
- Create basic graphic cast members
- Use sprite animation in the Director score
- Use Lingo to control loops and frame position, and to make cast members interactive

These are simple aspects of Macromedia Director, but they represent the fundamentals necessary to claim a working knowledge of the application. We now move to our second project to learn some intermediate Director techniques.

Project Two

This second example is much shorter than the first, yet covers a few new topics. You'll import a background, change some Lingo, and create special Lingo effects. By following the steps we describe, you learn the techniques required to achieve these effects using the same score as in Project One.

Step 1: Once More, with Feeling!

Open the score from Project One, if it isn't already open. You'll modify items within this score so that you don't have to start from scratch.

Step 2: Grab a Graphic by the Toe . . .

Import any picture into the Cast window. The graphic should be in PICT format for the Macintosh or in .pcx format for Windows.

To import the image, simply click once to highlight an available cast member slot in the Cast window. If you followed the first example instructions precisely, the next available member is number 10.

Next, choose Import from the File menu. Make sure that the Type pop-up selection is set to your file's format in the Import window. After you've picked the file you want to import, click the Import button on the right-hand side of the window.

Step 3: Make Your Own Background

After the file has been imported into your cast, make it the background for your project by dragging and dropping the cast member from the Cast window into the Score window at channel 1, frame 1.

Note: If you recall, we left channel 1 open when we created this project. Now you know why: Director places cast members on the stage sequentially, with each subsequent element layered atop previous ones. Placing your background image in channel 1 puts it behind the rest of the cast members on your stage, thus achieving the desired effect.

After you've positioned the background, you must also place the same image into channel 1, frames 30 and 35. Instead of dragging from the Cast window, this time click on the cell at frame 1, channel 1, then

choose Copy from the Edit menu. Now, click frame 30 and choose
Paste from the Edit menu; repeat with frame 35.

Note: Notice that you not only can drag cast members from their windows, but you can also copy them from one score cell to another. What's more, copying an element from a cell also copies its position and other characteristics. This means that you won't have to duplicate modifications to cast members in the score or manually maintain consistency between a cast member's characteristics from one part of the score to another.

Next, select the background cast member at channel 1, frame 1, and
at channel 1, frame 30. After you have the two cast members selected,
use the In-Between Linear command from the Score menu to fill in the
rest of the channel between frames 1 and 30.

Step 4: Do the Lingo Limbo

Now that your background is in place, you must modify your Lingo
scripts so that instead of clicking on cast member 5, the circle, and
going to frame 35, you click and hold on cast member 5 to see the
credits. When you release the mouse button, the credits disappear and
cast member 5 reappears on the stage. Change the script for cast
member 5 from:

```
on mouseDown
    go to frame 35
end
```

to:

```
on mouseDown
    set the castnum of sprite 6 to 7
    updatestage
    repeat while the stilldown
        updatestage
        end repeat
on mouseUp
set the castnum of sprite 6 to 5
updatestage
end
end
```

Edit the script by highlighting the circle in the Cast window and choosing Open Script from the Cast menu. Select the line that reads *go to frame 35* and replace it with the new lines. When you're done, close the Editing window.

This script changes the behavior of your project so that, when you click on the circle, cast member 7 (the credits) appears in place of the circle as long as the mouse button is held down. Try playing the project from within Director and click on the circle. If you have difficulties seeing the credits, experiment with its placement. You may have positioned it within the stage so that the credits appear off the screen.

Step 5: Stop the Presses!

Next, you add a way to stop your project during playback. You use cast member 4 to do this. If you have followed the lessons, cast member 4 moves slowly across the stage. You want to make cast member 4 a clickable object so it will pause playback. But you also want your script to allow playback to resume when the mouse is released. Therefore, you need to create the following script for cast member 4 to meet both of these objectives. You must select cast member 4 from the Cast window, then select Open Script from the Cast menu. Here's the script you should enter:

```
on mouseDown
  pause
  updatestage
  repeat while the stilldown
    updatestage
    end repeat
on mouseUp
go to the frame
updatestage
end
end
```

Step 6: Save Your Work!

Because you may want to review this project again or use it as the basis for more advanced projects of your own, it's probably a good idea to save the project in its current state as a file of its own. To do this, select the Save As entry from the File menu, and enter a nice, descriptive name for the project in the filename text entry box. (May we suggest project2.dir?)

Project Two Summary

You've just learned how to do several things in Macromedia Director. In this example, you learned to:

- Import graphics into your project
- Use Lingo to switch cast members on the stage
- Use Lingo to pause playback while the mouse is down

These are just a few of the things that you can add to your projects using importing and Lingo. Importing allows you to add many different types of sounds, graphics, and movies to your projects. Lingo provides precise control over your project through script commands. Try using the *Lingo Dictionary* that accompanies Macromedia Director to learn more about Lingo and what it can do for your projects. (You'll also learn more about Lingo commands and syntax in the next chapter.)

Summary

You have worked exclusively within Director with these lessons. You created a Director project and gained familiarity with the way the application works. Yet as you can no doubt tell, we've barely scratched the surface.

We invite you to continue fiddling with what you've created, importing other media or adjusting sprite animation, colors, and scripts. But be sure to save one copy the way you created it in these two lessons, because in the next section of this book you'll convert it to Shockwave format and ready it for access over the Internet!

Part II

Applying Shockwave Technology

*t*he second tutorial includes Chapters 4 through 6 and covers the ins and outs of using Shockwave technology to package Director movies for Internet delivery. It also covers the basics of Director content, including file formats, save commands, and built-in scripting language.

Chapter 4, "Principles of Shockwave Conversion and Lingo Usage," takes you through Director's many options to create output files and explains what kinds of input files are necessary for Shockwave input. It also covers installation of the Afterburner compression tool and provide a high-level overview of Director's built-in Lingo scripting language, including a discussion of the commands that can and can't be used in projects destined for Shockwave treatment.

Chapter 5, "Converting Your Project for Shockwave," covers the details of performing a project conversion. It begins by explaining the minimum system requirements to run Afterburner, then explores

Afterburner's architecture and capabilities in some detail. The chapter concludes with step-by-step instructions to help you convert one of the projects you built in Chapter 3 into Shockwave format.

Chapter 6, Shockwave Tips & Tricks, gives you a brain dump of useful tips and tricks for authoring Director movies to get the best performance from Shockwave. We gleaned these tips, both basic and advanced, from our own experience in the school of hard knocks and from all of the experts and on-line resources on Shockwave that we uncovered while researching this book. We think you'll find a good deal of useful information in this chapter and hope it will keep you from making some of the mistakes that we did while learning this material!

At the end of this tutorial, you will understand what's involved in installing and using Shockwave and how to extract its best performance and capability.

CHAPTER 4

Principles of Shockwave Conversion and Lingo Usage

*t*his chapter takes a closer look at the principles that underlie Shockwave. After reading this chapter, you'll have a better understanding of the file formats Director can create, and the different features and abilities each format possesses. You'll also understand the basics of Afterburner and why powerful compression technology is critical to serving multimedia on the World Wide Web.

This chapter also provides background on Lingo, the powerful scripting language built into Director. In our discussion of Lingo, we provide a list of commands that are legal and illegal within a Shockwave project.

Differences between Film Strips and Projectors

You have two significantly different ways to save the content you create in Director projects. Your choices are *film strip* and a stand-alone Director *projector*. These methods serve different purposes and carry different amounts of overhead.

The Director film strip method of saving should be used when creating Shockwave content for the Internet. Regardless, a knowledge of both methods in Director provides a better overall understanding of the application and its capabilities, and how different ways of saving Director content can be used within your projects.

What Is a Director Film Strip?

A Director film strip is the standard file that's created when a document is saved in Director. Film strips can be reopened and edited with Director, just like a standard text file can be opened and edited with a text editor. If you have several computers with Director installed, film strips can be transported between machines and edited.

A film strip carries a recognizable icon that resembles a small piece of movie film. The film strip is the format of choice for playing Director content through Shockwave-savvy Web browsers. When used on the Internet, Director film strips must use a .dir or .dcr suffix to be served properly from an Internet server. Examples of properly named Director film strips intended for use on the Internet are myfile.dir and myfile2.dcr. A film strip requires Director for any type of modification or editing. Likewise, the Director application or a Shockwave-savvy Web browser is required to view a Director film strip.

What if a Film Strip Won't Open in Director?

If you can't open a Director film strip with the Director application, the file could have been corrupted. This could be due to a damaged media source or interrupted network transfer; unfortunately, this problem can occur with almost any type of file.

With basic troubleshooting skills, you may be able to determine what is wrong with the file. It's important to keep backup copies of your Director projects in filmstrip format as this is the only format in which you can edit your project's content!

The Save and Compact Command

The Save and Compact command lets you save a movie under its original name so that it's optimized for playback. Because this operation reorders the cast and compacts the file, it takes longer than the Save command, especially for a very large file. However, this produces smaller, more efficient movies.

Use the Save and Compact instead of the Save command to:

- *Reduce a movie to its minimum size.* Save and Compact rewrites the file's entire contents so that any wasted space in the original

(continued)

file is eliminated. This command differs from the Save command because the Save command only saves the cast members or other elements that have changed since you last saved the movie.

- *Gain optimum performance for playback from a CD-ROM drive or a slow hard disk.* For large files, you want to use Save and Compact when you're finished authoring.

You can save room on your hard drive by compacting Director movies and still be able to let other people open these files or process them with Shockwave. Save and Compact is most often used by CD-ROM producers who want to place a film strip on media where the file will be accessible to the end user in a compact format. With the current version of Afterburner, there are no problems with "burning," or compressing, a film strip that has been saved with Save and Compact.

What Is a Projector?

A projector is a film strip that has been transformed into a stand-alone application. After Director content is saved as a projector document, the file can be viewed on any supported computer or platform. The only constraint is that Director running on a Macintosh can't build projectors for Windows, or vice versa.

A projector doesn't need Director on the machine on which it runs, because all components and elements are saved within the projector. Many CD-ROM based titles contain content saved as a Director projector. This lets viewers of the CD-ROM experience the content without purchasing and installing the Director application.

After content is saved as a projector, it can't be edited or modified by the author or any viewer. This is a nice way to protect the content, but be sure to keep film strip versions of that content for future changes. Projector filesizes can be much larger than film strips owing to the overhead of the code that gives the film strips the ability to run as stand-alone applications.

How Can Film Strips and Projectors Be Used with Shockwave?

Director film strips can be served and viewed over the Web, as long as the filenames end with the file extension of .dir and the Web server has been properly configured. Film strips can also be processed by the Shockwave Afterburner compressor, which reduces filesizes without affecting content.

Projectors cannot be served over the Internet or used with Shockwave. The code that enables projectors to act as stand-alone applications isn't necessary for Shockwave files, and the Shockwave Afterburner compressor won't process them. The Shockwave plug-in makes enabled Web browsers the Director viewing agent, so only film strips or Shockwave documents are required and supported.

Another way to look at the Shockwave plug-in is as the runtime environment that's usually embedded in a projector. The plug-in lets Director projects run as they would inside the application itself.

Basic Afterburner Concepts

Because Afterburner is necessary to convert Director movies into Shockwave files that can run on the Internet, it's important to understand what Afterburner is and how it works.

What Is Afterburner?

Afterburner is a software tool that is separate from Director and used to compress film strip data into smaller files that can be sent across the Internet in a reasonable amount of time. Afterburner uses powerful, proprietary compression algorithms that significantly reduce filesizes without reducing image quality.

Often, advanced Shockwave files are smaller after Afterburner compression than the original .gif images used in the project! This is accomplished through a variety of compression schemes that are applied to the various media elements in a project according to each element's specific media type.

After Afterburner has finished processing a file, the result is a Shockwave file. The proper suffix for such a file is .dcr.

Figure 4-1 shows the filesize of a .gif file, while Figure 4-2 shows the size of a Directory movie that incorporates the same image after the file has been processed using Afterburner.

Figure 4-1: This is the filesize of a .gif file.

Figure 4-2: This is the filesize of a .dcr file containing the same .gif file.

How Does Afterburner Work?

It's important to remember that the proprietary compression scheme used in Afterburner resides in both the Afterburner compression tool and in the Shockwave plug-in for Web browsers. In today's world of open standards and open systems, you might ask why Macromedia chose to make their compression scheme proprietary. From the company's perspective, the answer is simple: With Afterburner on the publishing end and Shockwave on the viewing end, a closed system is created. So, it makes no difference to the viewer or the creator if the transport format between the two is proprietary or open, because no one sees the raw files.

Afterburner is required for the publishing side and the plug-in is required for the viewing side, so interim transport needs can be met by any compression schemes understood by both parties. From an objective standpoint, the only limitation in this closed circuit between publisher and audience is that projects must be developed using Macromedia's authoring tool, Director, and none other. This may eventually change based on the historical precedents for proprietary file formats licensed to third-party developers to increase the size of the overall market. But because Director is currently the *de facto* standard for multimedia authoring, this is not a concern today.

In any case, Macromedia has future plans for Afterburner and Shockwave that include creating a more open system. The Xtras folder familiar to users of Director is also present in Afterburner's root folder. This is Macromedia's version of a plug-in architecture. In the future, Macromedia will use it to allow users to drop in a variety of codec, or COmpressor/DECompressor, extensions to post-processing applications.

As a part of their Open Architecture initiative, Macromedia plans to publish the Afterburner Xtras specification. Thus, third-party developers will be able to create their own codec extensions.

Why Is Afterburner So Important?

Afterburner's purpose in life is to compress Director movies into as small of a size as possible for travel across the Internet. This type of compression can convert a file that starts around 3.5-4MB to a transport format of about 100K. Filesize reduction of this magnitude has never before been enjoyed by Director movies, but is essential for the success on the Internet. The Web shows little tolerance for large filesizes, which result in slow retrieval and display of documents.

The majority of Internet viewers connect to the Internet via modem at relatively slow speeds—9.6 and 14.4 Kbps. At these rates, viewers only get about 1 Kps of effective throughput. This translates into painfully slow transfers when attempting to access graphically-intense Web sites. If a viewer's Internet service provider or the Web server being accessed is overloaded, this rate can drop even lower!

Internet viewers have a wealth of resources at their finger tips. If graphics and files are too large to download in a reasonable amount of time, viewers will go elsewhere. On the other hand, it's important for publishers to provide high-quality content that adequately represents their products and services. High quality often means large filesizes, so it's up to compression technology to establish a happy medium that mixes high-quality content with reasonable download time.

Comparing File Sizes

After burning, or compressing, your first Director movie, the first noticeable difference will be in filesize. A file processed through Afterburner will usually be less than half the size of the original. Figures 4-3 and 4-4 illustrate this difference.

Figure 4-3: This is the size of a typical movie before burning.

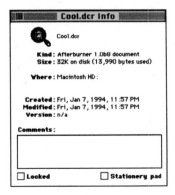

Figure 4-4: This is the size of the same movie as used for Figure 4-3, but after burning.

The next element you notice is that a burned file cannot be used as a regular Director film strip. This burned file is ready for transport across the Internet and requires a Web browser equipped with the Shockwave plug-in to be viewed.

Installing Afterburner on the Macintosh Platform

The general instructions for installing Afterburner on a Macintosh appear in the following list. As new versions of Afterburner are released, the filenames and specific instructions may change. The instructions that follow explain the installation process and show how easy Afterburner is to use on your system.

1. Download the latest version of Afterburner from http://www.macromedia.com.

2. Double-click the file named afterburner.sea. If prompted for a destination, choose an appropriate location in the dialog box and click *OK*. The file will be uncompressed onto your hard disk.

3. The resulting folder contains:

    a) The Afterburner drag-and-drop compressor

    b) An Xtras folder

4. Completed Director film strips are dragged and dropped onto the Afterburner icon to initiate compression.

Installing Afterburner on the Windows Platform

The general instructions for installing Afterburner on a PC running Microsoft Windows appear in the following list. As new versions of Afterburner are released, the filenames and specific instructions may change. The instructions that follow explain the installation process and show how easy Afterburner is to use on your system.

1. Download the latest version of the Afterburner software from http://www.macromedia.com.

2. From File Manager, move aftburn.exe into an empty directory on your hard drive.

3. Double-click aftburn.exe. It will unzip and deposit several files, including setup.exe.

4. Double-click setup.exe to install Afterburner.

5. After Afterburner is installed, open it and select .dir files for compression.

Using Lingo with Shockwave

When one or more of your projects is destined to become a Shockwave file, you have a number of choices to consider during the authoring process. One of the main concerns is your use of Lingo scripting, because that may prevent a project from being converted to Shockwave. Conversely, several new Lingo commands have been developed especially for Shockwave. We'll review these new commands and provide a list of those commands that can't be accommodated within your Shockwave projects.

The lessons you completed in the first section of the book included some basic Lingo scripting, but the language is complex enough that it deserves a more formal overview. A powerful language, Lingo enables publishers to add extensive interactivity to multimedia productions. Its object-oriented commands provide reusable code and simplify the development process.

Lingo allows external movies to be played within a Director movie with almost any amount of additional interactivity. Lingo also lets you test and set a variety of cast member properties, including type, registration points, and color depth. You also can control the action, size, location, and appearance of windows. In addition, Lingo provides a list feature for simple arrays, as well as mathematical functions including sine, cosine, and tangent.

Lingo and Shockwave

The Lingo command environment has been slightly modified to work with Shockwave. To make Shockwave fully operational, new commands were added to Lingo and several original commands were restricted. These restrictions are designed to prevent Shockwave movies from intentionally or accidentally performing operations that could cause problems on a viewer's computer. This includes protecting viewers who download Shockwave movies from viruses or system damage resulting from commands within a Shockwave movie.

If you use Lingo, some commands may need to be removed from your projects to convert them to Shockwave. In addition, commands that were recently added to support Shockwave must be understood to fully exploit the Internet as a delivery platform.

New Lingo Commands in Shockwave

Several new Lingo commands provide a Shockwave movie with access to the Internet. A network is essentially an asynchronous environment; this means that it takes time to get things from the Internet, just as it would from any other network.

During downloading, a user can continue to interact with a Shockwave movie. Most of the network commands involve starting an operation, then checking to see if it's complete, and finally obtaining the results. Lingo network extensions thus differ from most Lingo commands, which return their results immediately.

Table 4-1 introduces these new commands with a brief description of each. Following the table will be a more detailed discussion of these new commands.

Table 4-1: New Lingo commands that will enhance Shockwave projects

Category	New command	Command description
Beginning asynch I/O	GetNetText	Initiates retrieval of an HTTP item to be read by Lingo as text
	PreloadNetThing	Initiates preloading of an HTTP item into the local file cache
Checking asynch I/O	NetDone()	Checks the state of an asynchronous operation
	NetError()	Monitors the success or failure of an asynchronous operation
Retrieving results	NetTextResult()	Returns the text result of a network operation
	NetMIME()	Returns the MIME type of an HTTP item
	NetLastModDate()	Returns the date-last-modified string from the HTTP header
Canceling operation	NetAbort	Cancels a network operation

(continued)

Category	New command	Command description
Managing operation	GetLatestNetID()	Retrieves an operation's network identifier
Synch commands	GotoNetMovie	Retrieves and goes to a new Director movie or "burned" file from the network
	GotoNetPage	Opens a *uri* that may specify either a Director movie or some other MIME type

Let's now look a little deeper at each of these commands and their syntax. It's important to remember that Lingo commands may change, or that new commands could be added to increase functionality or to enhance present features. We suggest that you continue to check the Macromedia home page for the latest information on Lingo available for use with Shockwave.

`GetNetText uri`

This command starts the retrieval of an item via the HyperText Transport Protocol (HTTP) to be read by Lingo as text. The *uri* parameter is a *universal resource identifier*, which specifies an HTTP item to be retrieved. At present, only HTTP URLs (Universal Resource Locators) are supported as valid *uri* parameters.

`PreloadNetThing uri`

This command starts preloading an HTTP item into the local file cache. The *uri* parameter specifies the HTTP item to be referenced. An HTTP item can be anything, including a Director movie, an HTML page, or a graphic. This command also supports only HTTP URLs as valid *uri* parameters. In general, an item that has been preloaded can be viewed immediately, because it's read from the local disk cache rather than from the network. However, it's impossible to determine when an item may be removed from the local disk cache.

`NetDone()`

This function returns true when the asynchronous network operation is finished. Until then, it returns false.

`NetError()`

This function returns an empty string until the asynchronous network operation is finished. At that point, it returns OK if the operation was completed successfully or if a string describing the error if the operation failed.

`NetTextResult()`

This function returns the text result of an operation. For a GetNetText operation, this is the text of the HTTP item.

`NetMIME()`

This function returns the MIME type of an HTTP item. MIME stands for Multipurpose Internet Mail Extensions, a scheme to identify a data element's media type. Although MIME was originally developed for use in Internet e-mail, it has been adopted into the HTTP standard as a way for Web servers and browsers to identify data types.

`NetLastModDate()`

This function returns the date-last-modified string from the HTTP header for an item. This string reflects the date the movie file or other object was last edited.

NetTextResult, NetMIME, and NetLastModDate functions can be called only from the time that NetDone or NetError reports that an operation is complete until the next operation is started. After the next operation begins, Director discards the results of the previous operation to conserve memory.

`NetAbort`

This command cancels a network operation without waiting for a result.

Each of these functions—NetDone, NetError, NetTextResult, NetMIME, NetLastModDate, and NetAbort—allows an optional parameter to specify the unique identifier for an operation, as we explain below.

It is possible to have more than one operation active at a time. When two operations start simultaneously, the Lingo script needs a way to keep them straight during downloading. After one operation starts and until the next operation begins, the following function retrieves its unique identifier.

`GetLatestNetID()`

The unique identifier returned by this function can be optionally supplied to any of the functions listed earlier.

```
GotoNetMovie uri
```

This command retrieves and goes to a new Director movie from the network. The new movie occupies the same display area as the calling movie. The *uri* parameter specifies an HTTP item containing the movie. At present, only HTTP URLs are supported as valid *uri* parameters. The URL can specify either a filename or an anchor within a file. For example, both of the following URLs are valid:

```
http://www.yourserver.com/movies/movie1.dcr
http://www.yourserver.com/movies/buttons.dcr#Contents
```

After retrieval, the movie is played in the browser's window.

```
GotoNetPage uri
```

This command opens a *uri* that may specify either a Director movie or some other MIME type. Using GotoNetPage opens a new page within the browser.

The Lingo commands we've just covered were created specifically for cross-platform Shockwave usage, but please remember that not all Lingo commands work in a cross-platform environment. If you're unsure about a Lingo script's cross-platform applicability, test it on as many different machines as possible. If you can't test the script this way, try consulting the *Lingo Dictionary* or the *Using Lingo* guide that accompany Macromedia Director.

Illegal Lingo Commands in Shockwave

A set of restrictions has been designed to prevent Director movies from performing operations that could cause serious problems on end users' machines. These restrictions protect users who download Shockwave movies from malicious or unintentional damage to their system resulting directly from the movie. To provide that level of safety, several features have been disabled in the Internet version of the Shockwave plug-in, including XObjects, XCMDs, and XFCNs in a movie that interacts with external software and hardware.

Table 4-2 represents the features and commands that have been disabled in Shockwave. Following the table will be a more detailed discussion of these illegal commands.

Table 4-2: Lingo Commands that cannot be used with Shockwave

Category	Illegal command	Command description
XObjects	FileIO	Reads and writes text files to the local file system
	SerialPort	Creates multiple instances of an object in memory
	OrthoPlay	Controls devices that play video and audio source
Director-related commands	OpenXLib	Opens external function library
	OpenResFile	Opens resource file
	CloseXLib	Closes external function library
	CloseResFile	Closes resource file
	open	Opens local resource
	close	Opens local resource
	importFileInto	Replaces a file member with a specified external file
	saveMovie	Saves a Director movie to a designated file
	printFrom	Prints the stage display
System-related commands	open	Launches and closes specified applications
	quit	Exits Director
	restart	Restarts your computer
	shutdown	Shuts down your computer
	filename	Returns fully qualified filename from file system
	file path properties and functions	Returns file path and attribute information from file system
	fileName of cast	Returns associated file for imported cast member
	fileName of window	Returns associated file for imported Window contents
	getNthFileNameIn Folder	Searches local file system directories/folders
	moviePath	Returns fully qualified file path for external movie
	pathName	Returns fully qualified path name for file
	searchCurrentFolder	Searches local folder/directory in file system
	searchPaths	Establishes a search hierarchy for files and resources
	mci	Passes specified strings to the Windows media control

Please note that these commands could be enabled in future versions of Shockwave, but there are no announced changes as of this writing. Each command is further discussed below, followed by an explanation of what the command does from within a Director movie.

```
FileIO XObject
```

Reads and writes text files to the local file system that contain information such as user responses, names and addresses, and interactive game information.

```
SerialPort XObject
```

Creates multiple instances of an object in memory, such as controlling Director movies on two computers from a Director movie on a central computer.

```
OrthoPlay XObject
```

Controls devices that play video and audio source material such as videodisk, videotape, and audio CD players.

The following commands, which are meant to control the Director environment, are also disabled in Shockwave.

```
OpenXLib
OpenResFile
CloseXLib
CloseResFile
```

These resource and Xlib commands control resource files located outside a Director movie that are related to the prohibition on linked media.

```
open window
close window
```

These commands, respectively, open and close a window that can play a Director movie.

```
importFileInto
```

This command replaces a file member with a specified external file.

```
saveMovie
```

This command saves a movie to a designated file.

```
printFrom
```

This command prints whatever is displayed on the stage for a frame or a range of frames.

System-Related Commands

There are 14 other Lingo commands that interact directly with the local machine and have been deemed illegal for Shockwave projects.

```
open
```

This command launches and closes specified applications.

```
quit
restart
shutdown
```

These commands exit (or quit) Director, restart, and shut down the computer, respectively.

```
filename
file path properties and functions
fileName of cast
fileName of window
getNthFileNameInFolder
moviePath
pathName
searchCurrentFolder
searchPaths
```

These commands link to external files, windows, paths, and so on. They are useful in Director projects based around a CD-ROM, but aren't listed as legal Lingo for use with Shockwave at this time.

```
mci command
```

This command passes specified strings to the Windows media control.

Because all of these commands interact with the local machine's data and operating system, they represent potential areas for mischief. This may seem like a potential limitation to Shockwave projects, but because most of these commands were designed for use in CD-ROM based projects, none of them is absolutely necessary for on-line Shockwave use.

In fact, the availability of resources over the Internet through the new Lingo functions provided for Shockwave, in conjunction with an imaginative use of CGIs, Javascript, and Java itself, more than adequately compensate for these banned features.

The Future of Shockwave

Now that we've presented an overview of today's Shockwave technology, you may wonder what changes are in store for the immediate future. Macromedia has already announced Shockwave version 1.1; and by the looks of it, they will take care of some of the biggest existing problems and provide substantial advances to the technology.

Planned Shockwave Version 1.1 Enhancements

Specifically, Shockwave version 1.1 will include enhanced audio support as well as support for streaming data across the Internet while a project plays. Let's look at each of these coming attractions in turn.

Audio and Afterburner

Currently, Afterburner can't compress audio information. This means that if you process a Director project with an audio file as a cast member, the portion of the project comprising the audio data will stay at its original size. For example, assume a 250K project file contains a 150K audio file. Instead of enjoying the usual compression from Afterburner, which would result in a filesize of 95–130K, the compressed file's size would be 190–210K.

Historically, audio data has been more troublesome to compress than other media types. While highly efficient algorithms have been devised for text, graphics, and video, the same cannot be said for sound. The problem lies in the fact that our ears are sensitive to any degradation in sound quality, so lossy compression schemes often result in unacceptably "noisy" or inaccurate data.

Nevertheless, Macromedia plans to address this problem soon. The audio compression method for version 1.1 has yet to be announced, but they're evaluating the best technologies available. Integrating any one of these audio compression methods would greatly improve Shockwave technology.

Streaming and Shockwave

Streaming is the process of sending data in the background while a user interacts with data that has already been sent. As an example, a Web page with Shockwave content might download a 15K Shockwave movie to the client. After it is downloaded, that document could request more data from the server while the initial chunk of data is playing. The server could in turn send that data to the client so that the movie can continue seamlessly.

Streaming is a big step toward delivering cutting-edge multimedia content via the Internet. Through streaming, a developer can split a 300K module into three 100K modules, then chain the pieces together to recreate the original content. This enables the adaptation of much larger Director projects for the Internet than in the past. Developers will be able to increase the interactivity, performance, and effectiveness of projects through the proper use of this planned Shockwave enhancement.

Possible Future Enhancements to Shockwave

Many improvements to Shockwave are likely, but a few of them seem like a natural progression to us. These can be viewed as kind of a wish list for Shockwave improvements. Let's look at just a few of the "wishes" that we would like to see in version 1.x (or 2.x).

Afterburner Built into Director?

The first thing we'd like to see is a menu option in the next version of Director that would allow users to save a project directly to a compressed Shockwave file format. It would be a big improvement to see some sort of Save and Burn option in the File menu, much like the Save and Compact option that exists today. This would eliminate several intermediate steps in the production of Shockwave Web sites. Figure 4-5 illustrates our take on how this feature might work in a future release of Director.

An Afterburner with More Options?

Afterburner itself has room for improvement, either as a stand-alone application or integrated into Director. Many options could add substantial value to Afterburner, including multiple compression options, compression estimates, and batch processing.

What all these features need is a useful, graphical interface. This would allow users to specify options as well as display useful information before files are burnt. The mock-up interface shown in Figure 4-6 supports the features we discussed here as well as provides a framework for whatever other features eventually make it into Afterburner.

Chapter 4: Shockwave Conversion and Lingo Usage

Figure 4-5: This Director File menu illustrates our proposed Afterburner save option.

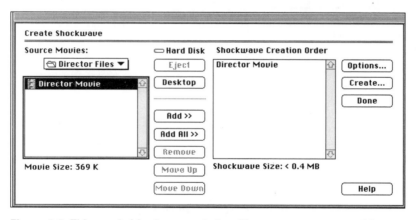

Figure 4-6: This mock Afterburner window illustrates our proposed features.

With batch processing included in a stand-alone Afterburner application, the developer could pick and choose files to burn, then arrange the order in which they are processed. This would make Afterburner more of a production tool. This might look like Figure 4-7, which shows our "wish" for this kind of feature.

When you create a projector within Director, the first thing that happens when you select a file is that an estimate of the projector's filesize is displayed. This seems like a natural feature to migrate to our proposed Afterburner-of-the-future. Figure 4-8 shows what we think it could look like.

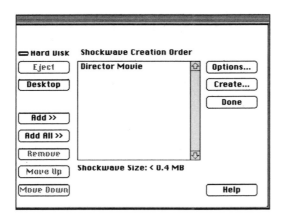

Figure 4-7: This illustrates our mock Afterburner Batch Process window.

Figure 4-8: This is Afterburner with our proposed filesize estimate feature.

The possibilities for Shockwave's conversion and compression stages alone are exciting, and we've just scratched the surface. The plug-in side offers the potential for another host of potential enhancements. It's clear that, while Shockwave 1.0 is a giant leap forward in some ways, it needs time to mature into a full-featured, broad-based technology.

Summary

In this chapter, we sought to deliver an in-depth look at those aspects of Shockwave technology that you as a developer will use the most. Specifically, this includes the Afterburner conversion utility used to create

Shockwave versions of Director film strips. We examined installing and using Afterburner, discussed what it does and why, detailed which Lingo commands can and cannot be used in Shockwave projects, and briefly dabbled in some crystal ball gazing.

With this foundation, you are now ready to try Afterburner yourself. In the next chapter, we step you through converting your tutorial file into Shockwave format and look a little deeper into some of Afterburner's inner workings.

CHAPTER 5

Converting Your Project for Shockwave

*t*he process of converting Director movie files, known as Film Strips, into the Shockwave file format using Afterburner is fairly simple. This chapter helps you to understand the conversion process, and the underlying technology and system requirements that enable Afterburner to function. We present technical information on these topics to improve your understanding of the issues related to Afterburner use.

Using Afterburner

In practice, Afterburner is extremely easy to use. After a file is created in Director, the file icon is either dragged onto Afterburner's icon or opened from within Afterburner, depending on your operating system. Afterburner automatically analyzes the file and dramatically reduces its size through intelligent compression technologies.

The end result for the original Director movie is a file in Shockwave format. The suffix of the file changes from .dir to .dcr, and the project is now optimized for Internet delivery. Figures 5-1 and 5-2 show Afterburner in action on a Macintosh. Figure 5-1 shows how to start the conversion process, while Figure 5-2 shows the window that appears as conversion is underway. This displays a progress chart that estimates how much of the file has been converted.

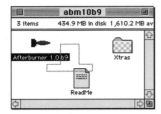

Figure 5-1: A file is dropped on Afterburner to start the process.

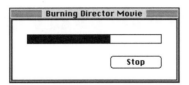

Figure 5-2: The Afterburner window shows progress toward completion.

System Requirements for Afterburner

The system requirements for Afterburner are also quite simple. Afterburner can function on a wide variety of systems. As with most multimedia applications, the more powerful your computer is, the quicker Afterburner and Director process your data. The current minimum system requirements for Macintosh and Microsoft Windows systems are listed in the two accompanying sidebars.

In most cases, if you can run Director on a Macintosh or Windows PC, you'll have little trouble meeting Afterburner's system requirements. Free RAM, hard disk space, and processor speed are key elements for Afterburner's or any other multimedia application's successful operation. Here's a quick rundown on why each of these elements is important to performance.

Minimum System Requirements for Macintosh

- Macintosh computer with 68030, 68040, or Power PC processor
- 640x480 display with 256 colors
- 2MB of available hard disk space
- 8MB of RAM
- MacOS System 7.5 or later

Minimum System Requirements for Windows

- IBM-compatible PC
- Intel 80386 processor running at a speed of 25 MHz or faster
- VGA or better graphics resolution
- 5MB of available hard disk space
- 8MB of RAM
- DOS 6.0 or later
- Microsoft Windows 3.1 or later (including Windows 95 and Windows NT)

RAM

Eight megabytes of RAM is the practical minimum for both Macintosh and Windows-based computers. Although 8MB is enough to run the operating system and Afterburner, chances are high that you won't have enough memory to simultaneously run additional applications. This adds extra steps to your project's post-processing as you quit Director after saving the project, compress, and launch Director again. Sixteen megabytes would be more convenient, and 24–32MB are even better. In multimedia, possibly more than any other area of microcomputer applications, you can never have too much RAM!

Hard Disk Space

The minimum requirement for free hard disk space is 2MB for Macintosh and 5MB for Windows-based machines. But these requirements only cover room for the Afterburner application itself and for a few small projects. Depending upon the size and number of your projects, you'll probably want much more.

Processor Speed

The processor and its co-processors are responsible for calculating the mathematical equations and other operations necessary for software applications to function. Many types of processors are available on the market today, but the most prevalent CPUs include the following:

- the 680x0 series from Motorola
- the Power PC processor, developed with the combined efforts of Apple Computer, IBM, and Motorola
- the Pentium processors from Intel

The two most powerful entries in this short list are the Pentium and Power PC processors. Currently, the Pentium is found mainly on computers running Windows, while the Power PC primarily drives computers running the MacOS from Apple Computer. The x86 and 680x0 processors are predecessors to the Pentium and Power PC, respectively, and usually process data at slower speeds.

Afterburner requires a 386 processor or higher on the Windows side, and a 68030 or higher on the Macintosh side. However, any serious development efforts should be driven by the most powerful machines within your means. In addition, because clock speed plays a role in any processor's overall performance, you want the fastest-rated chip in whichever family you purchase.

It may seem like overkill to explore basic characteristics of a desktop computer in such depth, but for newcomers to multimedia or Web development, the preceding information holds a simple but vital message: In development environments, time corresponds directly to money. Production houses that complete projects quickly command premium rates from their clients. Therefore, whatever the scale of your undertaking, allocate as much of your financial resources as possible toward hardware. It is ultimately an investment in your own marketability.

In Depth: Compression and Afterburner

Afterburner is the cornerstone of Shockwave technology. Without Afterburner's powerful, advanced compression features, it would be much more difficult, if not impossible, to transport Director-based projects over the Internet. Without Afterburner, filesizes would simply be too large for average users to download.

We've already touched on Afterburner's technique of applying different compression techniques to the various parts of a project according to the media type. Here, we delve deeper into Afterburner's specifics and present a general overview of how compression works and what it does to a file.

What Is Compression?

Understanding compression is simple: It describes a process by which data is reduced to its essence. When something is compressed, some portion of the data is usually replaced with a smaller representation of the larger.

Most compression tools are actually algorithms designed to find multiple instances of the same information and mark the places where that information occurs. Then, they replace that information with special code that represents not only the information but the multiple places where it appears in the original file too.

Depending on the compression scheme, compressed files may be restored to their original form or, for some kinds of images, a form with lower image quality or resolution. A method that faithfully restores the original is called lossless compression, while one that only restores a semblance of the original is called lossy compression.

There are many compression techniques, but in general it's important to use a method that achieves a good compression ratio without degrading quality to unacceptable levels. It's essential to understand that Afterburner cannot revert a file that has been burned: Always keep a copy of your original Film Strip for future editing.

The two parts of Shockwave, Afterburner and the plug-in, contain several codecs. Afterburner contains the compressors and the plug-in contains the decompressors.

Compression can be generic or type specific. Type-specific compression can achieve much higher compression ratios because it knows something about the type of data being compressed. As discussed in Chapter 4, compression schemes can be proprietary or based on open or public standards. In version 1.0 of Shockwave, the system is essentially closed, but a framework exists for opening this technology to third-party codecs.

Table 5-1 shows the compression algorithms that are used in Shockwave.

Table 5-1: Codecs used in Shockwave technology are media specific

Media type	Compression name	When used
Generic	LZ77	No type-specific compression available
Graphic	Macromedia Image	For graphics data (e.g., PICT or .pcx cast members)
Audio	To be determined	For audio data in version 1.1 only

Afterburner transparently chooses the correct compression algorithm. An author need only run a complete Director movie through Afterburner to ensure its proper compression. It isn't necessary or even possible to make decisions or tweak compression options; Afterburner understands the formats contained in a Film Strip and applies the appropriate compression algorithms.

Compression Technology: The Lempel-Ziv Algorithm

Though it isn't necessary for developers to understand compression to use Afterburner, it's helpful to understand the underlying technologies. While the Macromedia Image codec is proprietary and available details about it are sketchy, the Lempel-Ziv compression algorithm used by Afterburner to compress generic data is well known.

Two Israeli software developers named Lempel and Ziv developed a lossless compression algorithm named LZ77 in 1977 that has become one of the most popular and powerful lossless compression schemes available. Their algorithm uses repetition as the key to compression. If a repetition is found, it is represented by a reference back to an earlier occurrence in the input string. Repeated data is replaced by <offset,length>, which means "move back *offset* bytes in the input string, and copy *length* bytes from there."

An example before Lempel-Ziv compression is as follows:

```
Peter_Piper_picked_a_peck_of_pickled_peppers.%%
A_peck_of_pickled_peppers_Peter_Piper_picked.%%
If_Peter_Piper_picked_a_peck_of_pickled_peppers,%%
where's_the_peck_of_pickled_peppers_Peter_Piper_picked?%%
^Z
```

%% is a two-byte representation for end of line and carriage return and ^Z is a one-byte representation for end of file.

This data requires 202 bytes to represent the original form. The same data looks like this using Lempel-Ziv compression:

```
Peter_Pip<6,3>picked_a_peck_of<17,5>l<18,3>peppers.%%
A<28,24>_<73,18>.%% If_<97,44>,%%
where's_the<38,24><83,19>?%%^Z
```

The data is now 78 bytes in size. If you look closely at both data samples, you see what has changed. This shows what happens to a file when it is compressed with the Lempel-Ziv algorithm. By replacing repeated strings with pointers to previous occurrences, the data has been compressed for a savings of 124 bytes (59.6 percent).

As a general principle, the more assumptions a compression algorithm makes about its target data, the more efficient it is. This is why Macromedia has chosen a multi-codec approach to Shockwave—to achieve maximum compression efficiency for all types of data in a project.

Compression Maximization Techniques

While the compression provided by Afterburner is quite efficient, it would be a mistake to rely on compression alone to produce files of manageable size. Remember that compression efficiency is measured in percentage and not absolute savings, so it is common sense to note that the smaller your original file is, the smaller the end results will be.

Therefore, when creating projects in Director for Shockwave, keeping the sum of the parts as small as possible should be a high priority. We'll discuss some advanced techniques in the next chapter, but one area is appropriate here because it involves a simple type of compression that you can implement yourself before you turn to Afterburner to finish the job.

Simply put, you should do what you can to reduce the size of the images in your project by minimizing the data included in your graphic file. Although the standard palettes used by graphic files come in 1-, 2-, 4-, 8-, 16-, and 24-bit increments, most images use an odd number of colors that falls somewhere between these defaults. Luckily, many utilities and applications can trim your palette to optimal size.

Adobe Photoshop

The best example of an application that trims palettes is probably Adobe Photoshop, because it is a popular graphic tool for both Macintosh and Windows users. With Photoshop, reducing the data in a file is simple. When you complete your image manipulation, change its image type to Indexed by choosing that option from the Mode menu. The resulting dialog box allows you to choose exactly how large the image's palette will be, to a maximum of 8 bits or 256 colors. If the image has less than 256 colors, you will also be given a Custom option with the exact number of colors indicated. If this option is available, choose it. It produces the smallest possible file for the image's data.

If the image contains more than 256 colors, additional colors will be dithered, or approximated, using colors from the 8-bit palette.

Note: For MS-Windows, if the current image is already in Indexed mode you must first switch to RGB mode, then back to Indexed mode, to further reduce color depth. For example, an 8-bit (256-color) image can be reduced to a 7-bit (128-color) image only if you switch to RGB mode, then to Indexed, 7-bit mode.

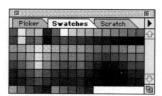

Figure 5-3: Photoshop's palette for choosing the blend of colors for your project.

After a palette is specified, you may save the file in PICT or .pcx format, then import it into your project's cast. It's a good idea when "downsampling" your image in this way to save it to a different filename that indicates the kind of change that's been applied. This not only identifies the smaller image at a glance, it also preserves your original in case you ever need to edit it further with its entire palette intact.

Other Suitable Applications

Photoshop is by no means the only program that allows palette minimization. Debabelizer, Graphic Converter, and a host of other utilities are available for the Macintosh. When running Windows, you have a similarly wide array of choices, including Paint Shop Pro and Lview.

Whichever program you use, the general principle remains the same: Reduce the file's palette to the bare minimum required by the image before saving and importing.

Other Techniques

The total size of your cast members in any Director project is the single factor that rules the final size and corresponding effectiveness of your

Shockwave project. As a rule of thumb, unless a cast member is essential to your project, discard it. Regardless, make sure that only used cast members are present when you burn and that you have removed any obsolete media.

Sound data currently has no specific codec assigned to it in Director; therefore, it can be particularly troublesome. This is especially true because anything that reduces the original's size will also typically reduce its sound quality. Such reduction techniques can include lowering the sample rate, the bit depth, or the number of channels.

Eleven kilohertz is a suitable sample rate, carrying a healthy savings over 22 kHz sounds but still offering decent quality. Similarly, 8-bit sounds are half the size of their 16-bit counterparts, yet the noise level remains acceptable, especially for data delivered via modem. Finally, stereo sounds are nice, but are probably overkill in this context. Switching to monaural won't affect the noise level, but cuts filesizes in half.

All of these sound modifications appear in any sound-manipulation application with a decent feature set. SoundEdit 16 is a Macromedia application that easily allows you to make these changes. There are also simpler, less expensive applications, many of them shareware or freeware, that are available on the Internet.

If you put a little effort into precompressing your data in the ways we outline, you will be rewarded with smaller Shockwave files. Afterburner will receive a file that is already as small as you can make it, and the percentage its compression saves will have a greater impact on the final size of the file.

Afterburner Issues

While Afterburner is simple to use, the application comes with a few potential gotchas. To prepare you to use Afterburner, we review these issues.

First, remember that Afterburner won't compress Director movies saved as Projectors, and that only Film Strip format is suitable for Afterburner processing. This should emphasize the importance of guarding the original saved version of your project. If you overwrite a Film Strip with a Projector version of the project with the same name, you will not only be unable to burn the project, you will also lose the ability to go back and edit the project. The bottom line is: Don't lose the Film Strip version of your project!

Afterburner can't compress Director movies that contain linked media. Linked media, can cause problems in an Internet environment because network traffic or other considerations can prevent retrieval of the linked media, even after successfully downloading a movie. Therefore, this often-used Director feature is absent from the Shockwave specification. According to Macromedia and Netscape, a solution is being investigated, but no release date has been set as of this writing. Existing projects with linked media will have to be modified or rebuilt before they can be converted to Shockwave.

Shockwave doesn't support QuickTime movies. Despite Netscape's planned support of QuickTime via the QuickTime Plug-In (which other Web browsers should also shortly support), Shockwave can't support QuickTime because it represents a form of linked media. Thus, the Afterburner compressor refuses to process a file containing a QuickTime movie. Here again, Macromedia hopes to resolve this in future releases of Shockwave.

Finally, with the beta version of Afterburner for the Macintosh we used while writing this book we noticed an issue that may disappear by the time the application is formally released. If you attempt to compress a project and see an error message that says that "Afterburner can't find the Xtras folder," this means you've moved the application from its installed directory. Our version refused to process files until we either put it back in its own folder or created a folder called Xtras in its new location.

Compressing the Tutorial Project

Now that we've taken you through Afterburner, inside and out, you're probably anxious to use it to ready your own project for the Internet. The Afterburner application is included on the CD-ROM accompanying this book. We have also included a sample project of the kind we walked through in the tutorial, lesson.dir. If you want to process it, copy Afterburner to your hard disk and follow the platform-appropriate installation directions that we outlined earlier. After you finish, compare the before and after filesizes. You should be pleasantly surprised!

If you own a licensed copy of Director, by all means experiment with your own projects using these same steps. We find it particularly interesting to compare the percentage of saved space among files of different types and numbers of cast members.

Viewing Shockwave Files Locally

When you produce a new, compressed file, you probably want to preview what it will look like when it is posted on the Internet. Normally, previewing Web documents is as easy as opening the file within your browser. The Netscape browser can be used in this way to preview not only HTML documents, but also nearly any graphic file it accepts in Web documents.

This is not the case with Shockwave files, however. This is because Netscape defines its MIME types and the corresponding suffixes for the types of media it supports internally. So when you open a file named image.gif, Netscape maps it to *image/gif* and handles it accordingly. However, Shockwave Director movies are handled externally by the plug-in; therefore, the MIME type is also defined externally.

There are two workarounds for this. The first is to upload the file to a Web server configured to serve Shockwave files. We cover exactly how to set up this configuration in Chapter 7, but in essence what this does for our current purpose is to educate the server about Shockwave's MIME type and its file suffixes. Therefore, if you request a file from the server that ends in .dcr, the server responds with the correct MIME type and Netscape loads the Shockwave plug-in.

The other workaround avoids the Internet entirely. To view a Shockwave file locally, simply create a small file that contains the following HTML source code:

```
<HTML><HEAD><TITLE>Shockwave Test</TITLE></HEAD><BODY>
<EMBED HEIGHT="100" WIDTH="448" SRC="lesson.dcr">
</BODY></HTML>
```

Here, HEIGHT and WIDTH are the actual dimensions of your file, and SRC specifies the path to, and name of, the file. We created the <EMBED> tag here so that it contains the correct dimensions for the tutorial project and loads a file called lesson.dcr that resides in the same folder as the HTML file. Make sure to save the file with an .html extension, or .htm for a Windows 3.x machine. Then, from inside Netscape, open the HTML file.

The EMBED tag instructs Netscape that the source file requires a plug-in. When you launch Netscape, it registers all of its available plug-ins and maps them to file suffixes. Therefore, the combination of the EMBED tag and the .dcr suffix causes the plug-in for Shockwave to load and the file to display correctly inside the browser. This suffices for previewing the file locally and ensures that your conversion to Shockwave format worked properly.

Summary

At this point, you not only have a burnt project of your own, but also understand Afterburner and Shockwave on many levels. We have discussed installing and using Afterburner, as well as the minimum and optimal system requirements for running Afterburner.

We also have explored the theory behind compression technology. We had our reasons for exposing you to the theoretical side of things. With an understanding of compression principles—namely, reducing data to its barest essentials—we outlined ways in which you could prepare data so that Afterburner will operate even more efficiently. Finally, we touched on possible issues that you may encounter when compressing projects and instructed you in trying Afterburner for yourself. In the next chapter, we rip the covers off Shockwave technology and share tips and tricks to help you get the best from its use.

CHAPTER 6

Shockwave Tips & Tricks

in this chapter, we look at basic and advanced techniques you can use to improve the performance of your Shockwave projects. Many things in this chapter may seem more like workarounds than tips or tricks. In some cases, this is valid because Shockwave only adds multimedia to the Internet—it doesn't solve all of the various Internet issues that challenge developers.

Alone or in combination, many factors affect the download of a Web page. Pages with short download times often leave users with a page starved for graphical content. Conversely, pages rich in graphical content can take much longer to download. Additionally, most people who visit your Shockwave site travel the Internet using a 14.4 Kbps connection, so it's important to keep filesizes for your Shockwave projects as small as possible.

Most of the tips and tricks in this chapter are common-sense steps to reduce filesizes. Others are more advanced techniques that use Lingo to control various aspects of a project. We want to stress that Shockwave is moving forward at an incredible pace: Tricks that help you solve problems today may soon no longer be necessary.

Most of the techniques we cover are intended to help with bandwidth problems that are purely Internet related. We recommend keeping movie sizes as small as possible—even before using Afterburner. You can do some imaginative and creative things with small movies. Most users aren't willing to, and won't, wait for what appears to be an excessive amount of time for Web pages to load.

Obviously, time is relative. Many people are willing to wait longer for a game to download than for an animated banner, a cool introduction to a site, or a sound clip. Be sure to consider the value of what's being downloaded when trying to decide what's too big or too small.

You may already use some of these techniques in your Web site designs, but some of them may be new to you. In writing this chapter, we sought to provide the best available techniques; whether you've used them before or they're brand-spanking new, we hope your Shockwave documents benefit from the material we provide.

Basic Tips & Tricks

We consider the following techniques basic because they are mostly techniques you should consider using before creating a Shockwave movie. Rescaling images and using flat colors to create your artwork are commonly used techniques to reduce the filesizes of graphics that are incorporated into Web sites.

To give you an idea of the effects you can create with small filesizes, we suggest that you examine some of your favorite Web sites and pay attention to filesizes and their content. Chances are good that you'll witness the results of some of the methods we cover here. Seeing them in action may help to inspire you to create better looking Web pages using simple graphics with smaller files.

Creating Images for Shockwave Movies

When creating images for Shockwave movies, keep one word in mind: small. Make each bitmap image and sound file as small as possible. You can use the Cast Member Info button to check cast members' filesizes in Director and to keep a running tab on the total size of your project.

While you develop your project, remember that, at this point in Shockwave's history, the only real problem you'll run into is your users' expectations. The technology's capabilities are awe inspiring, but users can be disappointed by how long it takes to download the content.

Rescaling Images

You can save substantial file space by rescaling images after they've been imported into Director. Try rescaling images on the stage to make them appear larger or smaller rather than creating them full size in your graphics application.

When using scaled bitmaps, test their performance before you complete your project. Whenever possible, test scaled bitmaps on a Windows system. These images often have problems in the Windows environment because performance is typically slower than on a Macintosh.

Many people forget about the Sprite Info dialog box and continue to resize bitmap images on the stage. As mentioned earlier, this can cause a performance hit. Here are the steps for rescaling images most effectively:

1. Import or create your image in Director's Cast window.

2. Drag the cast member from the Cast window to the stage. The cast member now appears in your project's score.

3. Select the cast member in the Score window, then choose Sprite Info from the Score menu. The window depicted in Figure 6-1 opens and contains several settings that pertain to the way your sprite appears on stage, as well as where it appears.

4. Resize the sprite in one of two ways—by changing the scale percentage or by adjusting the sprite's width and height.

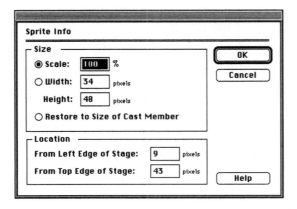

Figure 6-1: Director's Sprite Info window is used to rescale images.

Adjusting the size of the sprite through the Sprite Info dialog box doesn't change the size of the cast member. This means that if you use the cast member in another frame by dragging it from the Cast window into the Score window, the sprite won't be the same size as the one that you adjusted in the previous frame. To ensure that you don't get confused, when populating another frame in the score, don't drag the cast member that you adjusted in the Sprite Info dialog box into the Score window at the desired frame. Instead, use Copy Cells from the Edit menu to copy the sprite that you've already adjusted. Then, select the frame you want to populate and use Paste Cells from the Edit menu to place a copy of the adjusted sprite into that frame.

When resizing, remember that integer scaling requires less calculation than custom scaling. In simple terms, this means that if you drag a bitmap onto the stage and scale it via the Sprite Info dialog box, it plays more smoothly than if you scale the bitmap by dragging the sprite's bounding handles on the stage.

Tip: Bounding handles are commonly used to increase the size of a bitmap image on the stage, but this is not the best technique. Whenever possible, use the Sprite Info dialog box to change the size of bitmap images.

We've included an example Director film strip and a "shocked" version of the same material, which shows the use of a resized image, on the CD-ROM that accompanies this book. You'll find it in the \examples subdirectory in a file named ch06ex01.dir (the film strip) and ch06ex01.dcr (the Shockwave version). You also find the original graphic in a file named ch06gr01.jpg in the same location.

Note: Throughout the remainder of this chapter, you'll find numerous examples listed. In each case, you also can view the Shockwave versions of these examples at the *60 Minute Guide to Shockwave* Web site, located at:

```
http://www.idgbooks.com/idgbooksonline/shockwave/shock60.html
```

Applications Suitable for Palette Minimization

- Adobe Photoshop
- DeBabelizer
- GraphicConverter
- Picture Compressor

Applications that reduce the bit depth of your graphics save you a good deal of file space. In some cases, people won't be able to detect any difference between the original and a color-reduced version. Many people who visit your site will have a monitor that displays only 256 colors.

Using Flat Colors in Your Graphics

Use flat colors whenever possible in the artwork you create for Shockwave. In other words, avoid shading because each gradation is treated as a separate color in the palette. If you create your designs to take advantage of flat areas of color, they will not only perform more smoothly, but they will also require less memory.

One of the best ways to exploit this technique is when importing images. When you import images into Director, choose to remap the image instead of dithering. If your cast member contains only a few colors, use one of the image processing applications listed in the sidebar to transform the image to 1-, 2-, or 4-bit depth before importing it into Director.

You can use Director's Transform Bitmap command to convert imported images back to 8 bits. If you're using a 1-bit image, you can keep it as a 1-bit image in Director and not worry about conversion. The compressor in Shockwave performs best using lower bit-depth images. One-bit and 8-bit bitmap images are recommended.

Numerous applications for both Mac and Windows platforms can reduce filesize. Many of the same effects are also available from Director.

Reducing Bit Depth in Director

Follow these steps to reduce bit depth while working in Director:

1. Select a cast member in the Cast window whose bit depth you want to change.

2. After the cast member is selected, choose Transform Bitmap from the Cast menu to open the Transform Bitmap window, as shown in Figure 6-2.

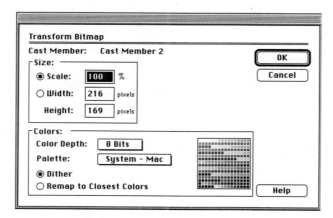

Figure 6-2: Director's Transform Bitmap window reduces a cast member's bit depth.

3. Select the bit depth for the cast member by choosing a bit depth from the pull-down menu for Color Depth. Supported bit depths include 1, 2, 4, 8, 16, and 32. The lower the bit depth, the better.

Tip: When transforming an image's bit depth, choosing Re-map to Closest Colors, located underneath the Color Depth pull-down menu, works much better than dithering the image.

Figure 6-2 also depicts a choice to scale the cast member. Use the technique we described previously instead of making adjustments in the Transform Bitmap window. Using the choices for scaling an image in the Transform Bitmap window doesn't confer the same advantages or performance as using the Sprite Info dialog box.

Reducing Image Size in Other Applications

Cast member images are often created or manipulated in applications such as Adobe Photoshop before being imported into Director. Taking care to reduce image size in the editing phase in these other applications can be a real boon to the final product.

In Chapter 5, "Converting Your Project for Shockwave," we described how to reduce color palettes in Photoshop and mentioned that most other graphics applications have similar capabilities. But limiting your use of colors in other ways is also helpful.

For example, you may want to use a simple gradient made of three basic gradations instead of one with many more. A good gradient tool confers the ability to control the number of transitions. Remember that each variation in shading represents another color in the file's palette.

It is difficult to think of graphics without thinking color today, but seriously consider whether all your images need to be in color. Maybe simple grayscale images can look just as good on your Web site. For example, consider the name of a company cut out of a black square. Add a simple drop shadow and you may have a nice looking graphic with a small palette. Eight to 10 shades of gray blend better than the same number of colors, and image quality is higher.

You can also use grayscale images saved in Photoshop for color effects in Director. Import grayscale images into Director and place them on your stage. Use the Tools Palette to add single colors to your grayscale images. Try using different Ink Effects when applying different colors to your grayscale images. This process helps save some of the memory that a full-color image would use and makes Afterburner processing more efficient. In addition, doing something in unusual ways can produce unique and interesting effects.

To view an example of Ink Effects, check out the example 2 materials on the CD-ROM. (Remember, you can view the finished materials at our Web site too.) You'll find the example materials on the CD-ROM in the \examples subdirectory in the files named ch06ex02.dir, ch06ex02.dcr, and ch06gr02.jpg for the original image.

Using Tiling to Create Backgrounds

Tiling a cast member in Director is an efficient way to build backgrounds into Shockwave movies. Tiles can be square or rectangular, and are one of Director's greatest hidden features. With tiles, you can use custom textures as backgrounds with extremely small costs in memory and performance.

In a way, tiles are similar to patterns in Director. However, unlike patterns, tiles are displayed using screen coordinates. What this means is that a tiled graphic that moves across the stage seems to reveal an underlying texture on the stage rather than the texture being carried with the graphic as a default pattern.

You can use multiple custom patterns defined from a single bitmap image simply by overlaying multiple shapes. Each shape can be related, yet have a different custom pattern. You can produce intriguing designs with little impact on memory or performance. In the hoary words of the old commercial: Try it, you'll like it!

1. Select a blank cast member, then choose Paint from the Windows menu. This opens the Paint window and creates the Paint menu choice at the top of your screen.

2. Choose Tiles from the Paint menu. This opens the Tiles dialog window.

3. In the Tiles window, depicted in Figure 6-3, you can view the eight built-in tiles or create a tile from an existing cast member. To create a new tile, select a tile to replace and click on the *Cast Member: #* radio button. Use the arrows below this radio button to select the cast member. (If you need to create a cast member to make into a tile, exit this area, draw the cast member, then return here.)

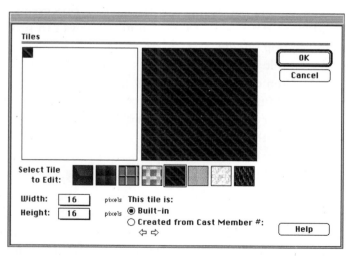

Figure 6-3: The Tiles window from Macromedia Director is used to create tiles.

4. If you create your own tile, you can alter the Selection box. It can be moved in the left-hand side window, and its size can be

changed using the pull-down Width and Height menus. The effects of your actions display in the right-hand side of the Tiles window.

5. After you create your tile, close the Tiles window and return to the Paint window. If you click and hold the rectangle directly below the choices for foreground and background colors, your tile appears in the bottom row of the displayed patterns.

6. Select the Tile you created earlier, then select a paint color. Now, choose one of the Tools on the left-hand side of the Paint window to create some art. When you start painting in the window, the tile shows instead of a solid color.

To use a tiled pattern to cover the stage, you must draw an object that has the tiled pattern big enough to cover the stage area. Otherwise, you can draw the tiled object and, after placing it on the stage, you can resize it to cover the entire stage. Both of these techniques help you get more from your Shockwave creations with little impact on filesize.

Tiles represent a good way to create patterns using more than two colors. When you choose a portion of a cast member (as described above) to make into a tile, that cast member becomes a building block for a pattern created within a field of tiles.

For an example of effective tiling on a background, check out the example 3 files on the CD-ROM (in subdirectory \example, files ch06ex03.dir, ch06ex03.dcr, and ch06gr03.jpg).

Creating Two-Dimensional Animation for Shockwave

Animation can add value to any Shockwave movie. You can use two-dimensional animation in a movie without creating a large, slow file. In our animation example that follows, we focus on ways you can create lots of movement with little increase in project size.

Using the Tools Window to Create Objects

Use the Tools window in Director, shown in Figure 6-4, to create objects for your Shockwave movies. The Tools window can be used to create a multitude of objects, including geometric shapes, text, buttons, and even tiles. These objects use little RAM and disk space.

Figure 6-4: This is Macromedia Director's Tools window.

By using the color palette to change the color of individual images within film loops, you can make the best use of this window without creating new cast members. The following steps create 1-bit film loops:

1. Create a series of 1-bit PICTs (.pic or .pct on the PC) in a graphics application such as Photoshop. Make sure these PICTs use indexed color. In Photoshop, make these menu selections to do so: Mode, Indexed Color, Other, and finally 2 Colors.

2. Import these images into Director using the Import or Import All command covered in Chapter 3, "Assembling and Authoring your Project in Director."

3. Place each of the new imported cast members in the score on a single channel in the order in which you want the animation to occur.

4. Select each cast member in the Score window and use the color palette in the Tools window to alter the foreground color (forecolor) and background color (backcolor) properties of your shapes and 1-bit images.

5. Create an animation in the Score window by using the In-Between Linear command discussed in Chapter 3.

6. From within the Score window, select those cells that contain the sequence of cast members that you want to use to create the film loop.

7. Drag the selection into the Cast window. As you do so, a blinking bar indicates where the selection will be inserted.

8. Release the mouse button to insert the selection to the right of the insertion bar. Director will prompt you for a name for the film loop.

9. Enter a name for the film loop and click the OK button. The film loop will be inserted into the cast to the right of the insertion bar. Any cast members to the right of the insertion bar automatically shift to make room for the film loop.

About Film Loops

Film loops are useful when adding animation to Shockwave movies. After you have created a film loop, you can add it into the score anywhere you choose. Just drag the film loop from the Cast window to a channel and frame in the Score window. Next, highlight the cast member you just dropped and highlight the frames for the length of animation, then select In-Between Linear. When your Director project is played, the film loop repeats as many times as needed to fill the play length you designated. You can find more information and instructions on creating film loops in the materials that accompany Director.

For a nice example of an animated film loop, check out the example 4 files on the CD-ROM (ch06ex04.dcr and ch06ex04.dir).

Creating Three-Dimensional Animation for Shockwave

Three-dimensional animation can add interest and excitement to your Shockwave projects, more so than two-dimensional animation. Let's go over some techniques on how you can use three-dimensional animation while maintaining manageable filesize.

Changing the Frame Rate Using Director's Control Panel

Director plays animated sequences one frame at a time; using a VCR-inspired metaphor, the control over frame display is called the playback head, and the speed at which frames are displayed is called the frame rate. To change the frame rate of the playback head, follow these steps:

1. Choose Control Panel from Director's Windows menu.

2. Now, increase or decrease the frame rate by clicking the up or down arrows located in the center of the Control Panel window. The number that you see displayed directly above the clock symbol in the Control Panel window represents your current frame rate.

Using the 2-bit Rendering Technique for Shockwave

One of the key elements in keeping graphic filesize small is the image's bit depth: The lower the bit depth is, the smaller the filesize of your image will be. Although a 2-bit image lacks the richness and detail of higher bit depth images, it allows you to create 3-D animation for the Web within small files. The following are the steps necessary for using the 2-bit rendering technique:

1. Create a model in a 3-D modeling application, such as Macromedia's Extreme 3D program (for both Mac and Windows).

2. Animate and render the model in an animation application; for the Mac and Windows, you could use something such as Ray Dream Designer.

3. Export or save the animation as a series of PICT or .pcx files.

4. Import these images into a graphic utility that allows control over bit depth, such as Adobe Photoshop.

5. Reduce the images to 2 bits. Then, reduce the image size to approximately 180x120 pixels. This size works well for Shockwave.

6. Export or save the images as a PICT or .pcx sequence.

7. Import the sequence into Director and proceed as you would for a regular Director movie. Set up each image as a frame in a movie in the Score window. Then, experiment with different frame rates and see how speeding up and slowing down playback of the image sequence affect the appearance on stage.

   Remember: End users probably won't have machines as powerful as the one you use to build this material. Therefore, be sure to view your work on a "typical end-user machine" as well! This will help to keep your frame rates and image sequences more realistic.

Overall, you can create an assortment of graphical sequences that imitate two-dimensional and three-dimensional animation sequences. Many people question whether you can have decent animation using the types of techniques we just covered. In fact, with a little experimentation, creativity, and effort, even the simplest ingredients can conspire to deliver eye-catching animation!

You find a catchy three-dimensional example file on the CD-ROM in the files named ch06ex05.dir and ch06ex05.dcr in the \examples subdirectory. (Be sure to view this one from the Web site too to get an idea of the impact of filesize and complexity.)

Additional Tips and Tricks for Animation

Another trick to try is to combine two- and three-dimensional graphics and animation in your Shockwave movies. Each of the following items should help you get more use from your animation files.

- Try using Director's sprite animation abilities to move things up and down, left and right on the stage.

- Change layers of various elements in your project during the animation so that one element emerges from behind another, then passes in front of it, by switching a cast member from a higher-numbered to a lower-numbered track.

- Use Director's native animation abilities in combination with the three-dimensional perspective, shape, and shape changes of your animation tool.

- Use Director to composite different layers of an animation (or several animations) in real time on the stage.

- Yet another trick is the proper use of flat shading in your three-dimensional rendering application. Consider using flat shading instead of Phong or other methods. You should especially avoid using ray tracing and any graphic files made using ray tracing. Flat shading, or Lambert shading, applies the same color to an entire polygonal face in your model and saves considerable memory, thereby reducing filesize.

- If you use a high-end rendering application that supports rendering spline-based modeling, or rendering at very low adaptive sampling rates, use those effects. Also, use shape changes with flat shading to make crystalline shapes with a much more impressive effect. These shapes can be tightly compressed yet give a real three-dimensional impression of an object. Many other three-dimensional rendering techniques are worth exploring; consult the manual or tutorial for your rendering application for other ways to get smaller, great looking files.

141

Using Ink Effects in Director

Ink effects within Director are too often underutilized. These effects provide an opportunity to create single cast members with multiple colors. Ink effects are also easy on the size constraints of successful Shockwave Web sites.

In Director, applying ink effects to different sprites for the same cast member can provide many different looks without having to duplicate a cast member. If used properly, this saves a large amount of memory in the cast and provides a more complex look to your project. Using 1-bit images is a particularly good way to create areas of complex, or irregular, detail. These are areas you usually can't create using shapes in the Tools window.

You can use a combination of freeform shapes and other patterned shapes in conjunction with complex ink styles to obtain some rather amazing effects with very little memory. You can also use these along with animated foreground colors to generate many other effects in your Shockwave movies.

When following the steps below, try to think of 1-bit graphics in terms of their overall shape and curvature rather than relying on them for photo-realistic detail. The purpose of these images and effects is not to create mind-blowing detail; rather, it creates clean, simple effects that don't consume much memory. You can get a great deal of efficiency by using bitmaps for shape and the Tools window shapes for texture. Try the following steps in one of your Shockwave movies.

1. Create a new file in Director and keep the stage white.

2. Draw a large, free form shape such as a square or circle in the Paint window, as shown in Figure 6-5.

3. Reduce the object's color depth to 1 bit.

4. Drag the object from the Cast window into channel 1 of the score.

5. Create a rectangular shape in channel 2 of the score using the Tools window.

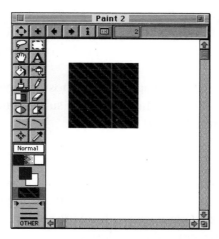

Figure 6-5: This Paint window contains a free form figure.

6. Scale the rectangular object to cover the stage by using the Sprite Info dialog box.

7. Assign a pattern to this shape in the Tools window.

8. Try to apply the Ghost ink effect to the rectangular object. If you're not sure where the ink effects are, examine Figure 6-6.

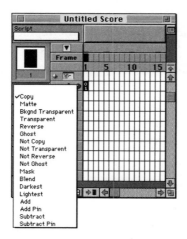

Figure 6-6: The Score window shows Director's ink effects.

The pattern displays only in areas of the free form shape you created in step 2. This is a good example of how you can use ink effects in

Director. Try repeating the steps, but instead of the Ghost ink effect use Reverse, Add, Subtract, or any of the other effects. Try using different colored backgrounds, and animate the foreground color of the bitmap sprite to fade it in and out.

To better understand the interesting properties of Ghost ink, please check out example 7 on the CD-ROM in the \examples subdirectory in the files named ch06ex07.dir and ch06ex07.dcr.

Using Text in Director

Using text made in Director instead of text rendered or saved as bitmapped text from other applications provides a great advantage in managing Shockwave movie size. Compared to bitmapped text, text created with the Text tool in Director takes up less disk space and, in turn, less memory in your Shockwave movie. This is because Director saves only the information that defines the text, not each pixel that represents the text image.

Choosing Fonts

Choosing your fonts is an important decision. Remember that a computer can display only those fonts it has installed; someone who views your Shockwave movie may not have the same fonts that you have. If the font you choose isn't available on another system, that system substitutes another font. When this happens, the results usually don't produce the effects you want. The safest approach is to use standard system fonts for Macintosh and Windows systems.

Macintosh system fonts are:

- Chicago
- Courier
- Geneva
- Helvetica
- Monaco
- New York
- Palatino
- Symbol
- Times

Windows system fonts are:

- Arial
- Courier New
- Symbol
- Times New Roman
- Wingdings

If you choose a standard Macintosh system font and someone runs the movie on a Windows computer, Director automatically substitutes a standard Windows system font, and vice versa. Therefore, check your movie on both platforms to see how it looks.

The memory savings that creating your text within Director can achieve is illustrated in the following example.

Savings from Creating Text in Director

To illustrate the memory savings from creating text within Director, we created two files. First, we created text in Adobe Photoshop using its Text tool. We made no fancy patterns and didn't use any filters; we typed the text using a flat color. The filesize of the Photoshop text was approximately 41K. Figure 6-7 shows the Get Info box for the Photoshop file.

Figure 6-7: This Get Info box shows details of a simple text file created in Adobe Photoshop.

After we imported the Photoshop file into Director and placed it on the stage at frame 1, we added a score script at frame 1 to pause the playback at that frame. This means that our project has only one cast member at frame 1. This is the smallest Director project we can possibly create.

We created another file with the same design, except this time we didn't import the graphic. Instead, we created the text within Director. Table 6-2 outlines the filesizes of these two movies after we saved them.

As you can see, the movie for which we created text instead of importing a graphic of the text is much smaller. Next, let's examine Afterburner's effect on these two files. As you can see by comparing

Figures 6-8 and 6-9, the files maintain their size difference even after processed with Afterburner.

Table 6-2: The saving in filesize between imported and native text is striking

Application used to create text	Filesize
Adobe Photoshop	43,672 bytes
Macromedia Director	8936 bytes

Figure 6-8: This Get Info box shows details for a file containing text imported into Director, following Afterburner processing.

Figure 6-9: This Get Info box shows details for a file containing text created in Director, following Afterburner processing.

By creating text in Director, we produced a file that is roughly one-third the size of the file into which we imported the text. This is just an example; actual filesizes will vary based on such factors as color, cast size, and bit depth.

Sound and Shockwave

Today, there's no way to compress audio data with Afterburner, so when creating Shockwave movies you must be a little more creative with your sounds to keep files small and effective. This also means that when you import a sound file of 30K into a Shockwave project, you will increase the size of your Shockwave movie by about the same amount.

Even with this big price to pay for sound, we don't recommend that you forsake audio to keep your movies small. Think of the difference between watching your favorite movie without sound compared to watching it in THX Dolby stereo. Allocating a certain percentage of the total size of a movie for sound can greatly enhance its impact; a good rule of thumb is reserving 20–30 percent of your project's total size for sound.

Despite the lack of a codec specifically designed to compress sounds, here are several strategies you can use to keep the data small.

- One of the simplest techniques to reduce the size of sound files is to lower the sampling rate. The lowest usable sampling rate is 11.025 kHz. Anything less may sound distorted on Windows machines because of the limitations of many PC sound cards. For the best sound, use a sampling rate of 22.050 kHz whenever possible.

- Avoid creating sound for sound's sake. It's better to have a slightly longer download time and a great sound than to suffer through listening to a bad sample at 11.025 kHz. Review your work on a typical end-user platform to make sure your audio files sound okay. If necessary, stick to 22.050 kHz to make your sounds clear, along with your intentions. It's better to use shorter but clear sound clips than longer but muddy or choppy clip.

- Loop sounds for longer background tracks. Try looping the sound in a sound-editing application such as Macromedia's SoundEdit Pro. After you hear how it sounds, adjust the loop setting to make it play smoothly. Avoid skips and choppiness, and make the loop seamless. Make sure to set the edit point for the loop carefully. A loop on every four beats for 4/4 music provides an easy edit point. The source track greatly affects how easy it is to edit the loop.

- Check the size of the loop in the Sound Cast Member Info dialog box. Figure 6-10 shows the options you see in this box for a sample loop.

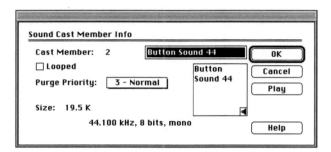

Figure 6-10: The Sound Cast Member Info dialog box in Director shows the size of sound loops.

- Get the most from your sound channels by using lots of small sound clips overlaid upon one or two large clips (15–30K) that play in the background behind the small ones. Spread the small clips around to add variety, and try using Lingo to call those sounds randomly. If you're using a sound loop as a background, fade it out or stop it after it plays a few times. Sounds that repeat endlessly become annoying.

We eagerly await the arrival of a sound codec for Shockwave; in the meantime, including sound is worth the extra effort required to keep filesizes manageable. Shockwave makes it appear that sound is seamlessly built into a Web page—a totally new and unexpected effect. Keep this in mind, and use these tips to make your pages sing!

Using Video with Shockwave

Although Netscape 2.0 has a QuickTime plug-in, because Shockwave doesn't support linked media, you can't include a QuickTime movie inside a Director project as of this writing. An alternative to using QuickTime is to use a 2-bit screen PICT sequence, similar to the 2-bit animation we demonstrated earlier in this chapter. The following steps are necessary for converting a QuickTime movie to a PICT sequence:

1. Import a QuickTime movie into a graphics utility program such as DeBabelizer for the Macintosh, or LView Pro for the PC.

2. Convert the QuickTime movie, reducing the color depth to 2 bits and the image size to approximately 180 x 120 pixels. This is the optimum size for Shockwave.

3. Save the images in PICT or .pcx format, then import these images in sequence into the cast in Director.

4. Place the sequence of cast members in the Score window. Make sure that they are positioned in the score in the correct order. Many times, filenames can be sorted out of order if simple mistakes are made. For example, suppose you are working on a sequence that has 17 image files. If you name the files IMG1, IMG2, IMG3, and so on, they would be imported into Director incorrectly if you used the Import All command. The reason is that, if you save these files into a folder from which to import them, they would be imported in the following order:

    ```
    IMG1
    IMG11
    IMG12
    ```

    This continues until image 17, when the order would look like this:

    ```
    IMG17
    IMG2
    IMG3
    IMG4
    ```

    This happens because of the way most systems organize filenames in folders or directories. (It's based on the collating sequence for ASCII characters.) To get around this, add a 0 (zero) to filenames with only one digit in their sequence numbers, like this:

    ```
    IMG01
    IMG02
    IMG03
    ```

    This helps organize items that must maintain a specific order when importing them into Director.

If your QuickTime movie has sound, use a sound-editing application such as SoundEdit Pro to strip out the audio track from the QuickTime movie and save it at 22.05 kHz. If the audio track isn't synched, import it directly into Director and place it in one of the sound channels.

If the sound needs to be synched to the QuickTime movie, the process is a bit more complicated and involves the use of Lingo commands. However, it's essentially the same process you would use in a regular Director movie using Lingo.

For an example of programming synched sound in a Director movie, download the source code for Terry's Head from the Macromedia Shockwave Developers Guide Web site and look at the movie score. Other information on synching sound to frame rate is contained in Macromedia's *Tips & Tricks* guide for Director. This guide also includes many other useful pieces of information.

To find the source for Terry's Head, jump to the Macromedia movie listing at the following URL and search on the string, *Terry Schussler*:

```
http://www.macromedia.com/Tools/Shockwave/sdc/Dev/Moviedocs/
   corpsite.htm
```

Insane Tips & Tricks

In this section, we cover some of the more challenging tips and tricks. All of these techniques require the use of Lingo. Because we only covered the basics of Lingo in previous chapters, we recommend the following: Use the Lingo commands in this section; if you need more information about basic Lingo or find yourself lost, use the handy *Lingo Dictionary* that accompanies Macromedia Director.

Using the *goToNetMovie* in Lingo

Proper use of Lingo's *goToNetMovie* command can go a long way toward helping manage your Shockwave projects. This command allows you to open another Shockwave movie from the currently playing movie. This can be useful in breaking one large movie into several chained, smaller movies. Here is an example of what this command looks like in a script:

```
on exitFrame
goToNetMovie "http://www2.outer.net/shockwave/William.dcr"
end
```

Using this script, you could link the current movie to the movie named William.dcr when you exit the last frame of your current movie. Here's another example:

```
on mouseDown
goToNetMovie "http://www2.outer.net/shockwave/William.dcr"
end
```

This Lingo script takes you to the William.dcr movie when you click on the object associated with the script, such as a button or a switch. This Lingo command retrieves and skips to a new Director movie across the network. The new movie occupies the same display area as its predecessor.

Using Lingo Instead of *Wait For* Settings

The current Shockwave release doesn't support the *Wait For* settings in Director's Tempo dialog box, so you must use Lingo commands to build a pause into a movie.

To create a pause, follow the approach that follows. *Pause* is a basic Lingo command that can be assigned to a number of different types of scripts.

Choose the way you'd like to initiate the pause—does a button pause the playback, or does the playback pause when a certain frame is reached? After you know where or how the pause will commence in your movie, insert the following Lingo script into the appropriate place in your score. We give three examples of this script.

```
on mouseDown
  Pause
end
```

Use the above script to cause a button or area of an image to pause when it's selected. Place this script into the cast member's script that you want to associate with the pause.

```
on exitFrame
  Pause
end
```

This second script pauses playback at a designated frame. Place this script into a score script at the frame in the score channel where you want the pause to occur.

This pause statement lasts indefinitely. If you have no other scripts that interrupt the pause state, the movie will remain in the pause state forever. There's no automatic function in Director that will time out a pause state.

For example, let's assume we've built a Director movie that includes the preceding script in the last frame of its score. Let's call this frame 30 to keep things simple. In this movie, we also have a button at frame 30. In the script info for the button cast member, we place this script:

```
on mouseDown
    go to frame 50
end
```

When playback of the score stops at frame 30, it remains paused until some other action breaks the pause. In this case, though the playback of the score is paused, you can still click on items on the stage. Thus, if you click the button, *go to frame 50* is selected, causing the playback head to resume at frame 50. This is just one example of how the pause state can be interrupted in Director. Try other Lingo commands that control timing in your Director movies too.

You can also use the following Lingo command to pause playback only while the mouse is down on a certain object. To do this, first select the object that will act as your pause button, then enter the following script in its cast member script:

```
on mouseDown
    Pause
on mouseUp
    go to the frame
end
end
```

This can be modified so that playback pauses when the button is first clicked, then continues when the button is clicked a second time. This acts like a toggle between pausing and resuming playback.

Creating Loops with Lingo

Loops can be useful in Shockwave movies, so it's important to understand associated Lingo commands. The following steps help you build loops for your Shockwave movies:

1. Create the sequence of frames you want to loop in your Director movie.

2. Drag a frame marker to the first frame of the sequence. Give the marker a name.

3. In the script channel of the final frame of the sequence, type this script:

```
on exitFrame
   go [loop]
end
```

For *[loop]*, substitute the name you gave the marker in the first frame of the sequence. A sequence can be a single frame, but remember that film loops require that the playback head is moving. If you use film or sound loops, you must use a sequence that is at least two frames long.

More Lingo Substitutes for Tempo Commands

Here are some additional Lingo substitutes for commands that are customarily used in Director's Tempo dialog box. Try them in your next Shockwave movie.

Wait for Sound to Finish

In the script channel of the final frame of the sequence, type this script:

```
on exitFrame
   if soundBusy(1) then go to the frame
end
```

This Lingo command checks to determine if the sound that was playing in Sound Channel 1 of your score is still playing. If so, the playback remains at the current frame until the sound finishes playing. In this case, when the sound is finished, the playback head moves to the next frame.

For example, if the playback head reaches frame 30 and encounters the preceding script, it checks to determine if a sound is currently playing in Sound Channel 1 of the score. If a sound is indeed playing, the playback head loops back to the beginning of frame 30. Upon reaching the end of frame 30, the playback head checks again. This behavior continues until the script checks at frame 30 and finds no sound playing in Sound Channel 1 of the score. If no sound is playing at frame 30 when the script checks the Sound Channel 1, the playback head advances to frame 31.

Wait for Mouse Click

In the script channel for the final frame of a sequence, type this script:

```
on exitFrame
  go the frame
end


on mouseUp
  go the frame + 1
end
```

This script uses Lingo to wait for a mouse click on the stage. If this script is stored in a score script at frame 30, the playback head loops on frame 30 upon reaching this script. This means that upon reaching the end of frame 30, the playback head returns to the beginning of frame 30. But if you click the mouse at any point during this loop, the playback head breaks the loop and continues playback at whatever point was designated in the mouseUp or mouseDown script. Here, the script reads:

```
on mouseUp
  go to the frame + 1
end
```

Thus, if you click the mouse, the playback head resumes at *the frame + 1*; in our example, this is frame 31 of the score.

Wait for N Seconds

In the script channel of the final frame of a sequence, type the following script. For *[seconds]* in the second line of the script, substitute the number of seconds you want playback to pause.

```
on exitFrame
  set seconds to [seconds]
    if the timer > (seconds * 60) then startTimer
    if the timer < (seconds * 60) then go the frame
end
```

Branching with Lingo

It can be useful to spice a series of short, related animated sequences by jumping randomly among them. This command can be a powerful tool in creating your next Shockwave movie.

Sometimes a random element can be important to your project's interactivity. To randomly jump among a series of labeled frames (such as *frame 1*, *frame 2*, and *frame 3*), use the following script:

```
on exitFrame
   set targets to ["frame 1", "frame 2", "frame 3" . . . ]
   set theTarget to getAt (targets, random(count(targets)))
   go theTarget
end exitFrame
```

This script is tricky, so let's briefly explain what each part does.

```
on exitFrame
```

This Lingo command sets the script to start when the playback head exits the current frame.

```
set targets to ["frame 1", "frame 2", "frame 3" . . . ]
```

The preceding line sets the targets for the random jumps. In your script, you would replace the ellipsis (" . . . ") with any remaining label names you want to invoke. Each of the items in quotes matches some marker of the same name in this movie's score.

```
set theTarget to getAt (targets, random(count(targets)))
```

This part of the script randomly chooses a target (named *theTarget*) defined in the preceding line and passes that target to the next portion of the script.

```
go theTarget
```

At this point, the playback head jumps to the target passed from the preceding line of the script.

```
end exitFrame
```

This ends the sequence of actions associated with the *on exitFrame* command.

Each time this script as a whole is initiated, one of the targets (or markers) is randomly selected. Then, the playback head advances to the frame where the target (or marker) resides. This selects a random choice each time the script is called.

Using the *StartGetNetText* Lingo Command

Check out the movie, Shockhead, on the Macromedia Web site to see a cool example of a new Lingo command, *StartGetNetText*. This command lets you chain multiple Web pages or Shockwave files within the context of a single Lingo script. (This is the equivalent of letting one program call another program or one subroutine in a program call another, except that it doesn't return control to the calling program or subroutine). Here is the movie's URL:

```
http://www.macromedia.com/Tools/Shockwave/sdc/Dev/Moviedocs/
    shckhead.htm
```

When you click the blackboard above the Shockhead character in this movie, he turns around and the blackboard descends. Then, he writes a quote on the blackboard. This is an example of using the *StartGetNetText* Lingo command in a Shockwave movie. The Lingo script to initiate this sequence is:

```
on exitFrame
  StartGetNetText "[url]"
  go the frame + 1
end
```

Then, Director tests the state of the asynchronous operation and posts its results using the following Lingo script:

```
on exitFrame
  put NetError() & NetTextResult() into field "star"
  updatestage
end
```

Summary

If you're new to Director or to the Web, you'll find that you're able to create sophisticated content without too much difficulty. For best results on the Internet, you want to go beyond simple authoring. We've provided the collection of techniques in this chapter to help you make your movies smaller, faster, and more effective.

Despite the many tips and tricks we covered, we still just scratched the surface. You have an almost infinite number of techniques to improve your movies. Ultimately, you must find your own way and your own techniques to make killer content and to develop a style all your own. The wealth of tools at your disposal and the richness of Lingo supply a blank and bountiful canvas for creativity!

In the next chapter, we show you how to put what you've been learning to use as we explore how to integrate Shockwave content into your Web documents.

Part III

Internet Shockwave Delivery

*t*he third tutorial, which includes Chapters 7 through 9, takes an in-depth look at integrating Shockwave content into Web pages and at what's involved in making this work on the server side. This part of the book covers how to deliver Shockwave materials to users over the Internet.

Chapter 7, Integrating Shockwave with HTML, begins with step-by-step instructions on how to incorporate Shockwave content in a Web document. It then moves to a discussion of the design issues that can crop up when you integrate multimedia content into your Web pages. This chapter also describes how to accommodate visitors to your pages who may not be using Shockwave-enabled browsers without running them off. Then, we examine two Web sites that incorporate useful Shockwave content to see how this works in real applications.

Chapter 8, Shockwave on the Internet, examines the issues involved in serving up Shockwave content on the Internet. It begins with a detailed discussion on selecting and situating your Web server. Then, it provides detailed information on how to configure and tune your server to deliver Shockwave content.

The first half of Chapter 9, Testing Shockwave Sites, concludes the tutorial portion with a comprehensive overview of content testing and maintenance techniques. Here, we place a heavy emphasis on keeping your site current, fresh, and fully operational.

After a look at these delivery-focused issues, in the second half of Chapter 9, The Future of Shockwave, we turn speculative and discuss Shockwave's potential, along with recommended applications, Shockwave's shortcomings, and future research and implementation directions. Throughout, we try to use concrete examples and to point to accessible Web sites wherever possible.

By the time you conclude this tutorial, you will not only be ready to tackle a real Shockwave project of your own, but you also will thoroughly understand the implications and responsibilities inherent in making your content available through the Internet!

CHAPTER 7

Integrating Shockwave with HTML

n ow that you have a completed Director project in hand and have taken care of your Shockwave compression, you're just two steps away from viewing your site "live on the World Wide Web!" First, you must wrap your Shockwave files inside valid HTML code, then you must upload your materials to your Web server.

In this chapter, we cover how to use Shockwave in Web pages. We explore many of the issues you'll encounter, including the tags for embedding Shockwave files, strategies for proper display, and style considerations. We assume you already have a working knowledge of HTML and will only cover those aspects of Web documents specific to Shockwave. Finally, we take an in-depth look at four examples of Web pages containing Shockwave Director content to show you how it's done. After this chapter, you will have the information you need to produce professional HTML pages with Shockwave Director content.

Custom Tags

To support plug-in content such as QuickTime movies, VRML worlds, and Director movies, Netscape has introduced yet another proprietary HTML tag, EMBED. Its presence signals Netscape (or any other plug-in aware browser) that the material referenced in the tag will be handled by a plug-in. The exact plug-in loaded is determined by the file's extension and the MIME type to which it corresponds.

The syntax of the EMBED tag varies slightly with each type of plug-in content because the options supported by each plug-in also vary. An EMBED tag for Shockwave Director movies is constructed like this:

```
<EMBED SRC="path/filename.ext" WIDTH="n" HEIGHT="n"
    TEXTFOCUS=focus>
```

The SRC parameter specifies a URL for the file. This URL can be relative or absolute, local or remote. The extension of the file in most cases should be .dcr, though .dir and .dxr also trigger the Shockwave plug-in. The WIDTH and HEIGHT parameters specify the dimensions in pixels for the window in which your project will display. Make sure the width and height agree with the stage size for the Director movie. Netscape crops the image to the size you specify, and positions movies inside too-small windows in surprising ways.

The final parameter, TEXTFOCUS, is optional and specific to Shockwave Director content. It dictates how the Shockwave plug-in responds to keyboard input from the user. The possible values for TEXTFOCUS are *onMouse* (default), *onStart*, and *never*. The corresponding behaviors of these values are outlined in Table 7-1.

Table 7-1: TEXTFOCUS values control keyboard behavior

Value	Behavior
onMouse (default)	Keyboard input is accepted after the user clicks anywhere in the movie
onStart	The plug-in accepts keyboard input as soon as the movie begins playing
never	All keyboard input is ignored

The TEXTFOCUS tag can be important in determining the overall behavior of your page. If you have elements in your Shockwave project that require user input, you may want users to be able to provide that input immediately. If you mix HTML form elements with Shockwave movies, you must consider your total user interface to decide what's appropriate.

SRC Option Details

The SRC parameter points the browser to the location and filename of the movie to load into the EMBED area. The possible values for the SRC option are as varied as your content, but they tend to fall within a few categories.

Earlier, we mentioned two of the main categories that apply to all URLs—relative and absolute links. Relative links are those that rely on the existing path to the active HTML file for resolution. That is, the file may be located by appending the Web page's position on the server to the link's path. Consider the following tag fragment:

```
SRC="movies/no1.dcr"
```

To find this file, the Web browser appends the path part of the page's URL to the relative path. Assume the preceding HTML fragment resides in a file with this URL:

```
http://www.outer.net/singe/shockwave.html
```

When the browser requests this URL and receives a file in return, it separates the filename, shockwave.html, from the path to the file, http://www.outer.net/singe/. Then, when the browser parses the EMBED tag and attempts to load the movie, it constructs this URL:

```
http://www.outer.net/singe/movies/no1.dcr
```

It's a simple concept, but understanding how relative links work helps to troubleshoot problems. The most common issue you'll encounter is when links break because an HTML file is relocated. Relocation changes the URL's path to the file, so the relative link may no longer properly resolve.

To test this possibility, enter the new folder or directory where the HTML file is placed, then attempt to follow the path specified in the link. Or, if you can't directly access the file system where your files reside, construct the media file's URL by hand and try opening it with your browser.

Relative paths are popular among developers while Web sites are under development because they allow developers to preview links, inline graphics, and movies locally. However, we suggest that just before or after posting content on the Internet, you convert relative links to their absolute form. That makes site files and their related media much more portable. Then, if a file is relocated, the graphics and movies it references still link properly because absolute links work from anywhere. Because the URLs are fully qualified, they can pinpoint the location of content anywhere on the Internet. In fact, by using absolute paths throughout your site, you can more easily distribute your Web site across multiple machines.

Distributing content can be important if you're lucky enough to have a popular site. Spreading files over multiple machines also distributes the processing load and ensures a more pleasant user experience through faster load times. Absolute URLs point to the actual server on which the content is located, so splitting the site across two or three locations is easy to accomplish. For example, you may want to serve HTML pages and static images from one server, and Shockwave Director movies from another.

Link management is often one of the biggest tasks involved in maintaining a Web site. You may find yourself tracking broken links, converting large numbers of relative links to absolute links, or changing URLs in a collection of files that have moved from one machine to another.

Fortunately, an increasing number of utilities are designed to aid the harried Webmaster. If you're interested in such applications, this area is changing so rapidly that we suggest you start looking on-line to see what's available. On the noncommercial front, a multitude of free UNIX utilities are available to handle such changes. Also, numerous programs will traverse entire Web sites or servers at preset intervals to verify all links. The same kind of functionality is now also available in Mac and Microsoft Windows applications.

EMBED and Web Page Layout

In general, the EMBED tag behaves much like the IMG tag does when placing static graphics on a Web page. This is especially true if you're using the Netscape IMG tag extensions—specifically, HEIGHT and WIDTH options. When these are defined, the browser draws a frame for the image when it parses the HTML page, then loads the content into that frame.

The EMBED tag causes the browser to do the same, reserving space for your movie as it renders the page. The browser then requests the data referenced in the SRC option, loads the plug-in, and passes that data to the plug-in to be played.

It is desirable to establish in advance how wide and tall your movie is, both from an HTML developer's and the user's point of view. For the developer, it means more conscious awareness of the physical size of the movie on the page and how it compares to other elements that may be present. Sensitivity to context and placement are essential for production of a good, clean, tight Web page; it's still too rare to see work that displays good design.

From the user's perspective, enabling the browser to properly reserve space for an image or a movie is also desirable. Because the full text of the HTML file is retrieved before the inline content is requested, reserving the right spaces means that the page won't have to be redrawn after the content is downloaded. This speeds page delivery and access to its content.

Like the IMG tag, the EMBED tag can also be placed inside other HTML tags, including layout directives or a table. This can be useful to control exactly where an element is displayed on a page. For example, you can use the CENTER tag to ensure that a movie is centered on the page.

But if you need more precise control over a movie's placement, consider wrapping it inside a table. Data inside a cell can be very precisely laid out by cell tag options or by constructing the table exactly as you desire.

One example is to wrap text and static graphic elements around a movie in an area of fixed width. If you have an image, a Shockwave movie, and a chunk of text that you want to combine, you could create a single table with an HTML source similar to this one:

```
<TABLE BORDER="0" CELLSPACING="1" CELLPADDING="0">
<TR>
<TD COLSPAN="2"><IMG WIDTH="292" HEIGHT="58"
   SRC="http://www.outer.net/singe/banner.gif"></TD>
</TR>
<TR>
<TD WIDTH="210" VALIGN="BOTTOM">
<FONT SIZE="5">T</FONT><FONT SIZE="4">This text
exists in a cell on the same row as the <I>Director movie</I>.
It should have the appearance of <I>wrapping</I> along the side of
the movie. The second half of the text data will be in a
```

```
double-width cell below this row. If you are successful, the two
halves should meet up to form one</FONT><BR></TD>
<TD ALIGN="RIGHT"><EMBED HEIGHT="126" WIDTH="80"
SRC="http://www.outer.net/singe/flyingON.dcr"></TD>
</TR>
<TR>
<TD WIDTH=292 COLSPAN=2><FONT SIZE=4>body of text. You may have to
experiment with font sizes, line breaks and with moving bits of
text back and forth, but we think that the end effect is worth the
effort.</FONT></TD>
</TABLE>
```

When viewed with Netscape Navigator 2.0 on a Macintosh, this page displays as shown in Figure 7-1.

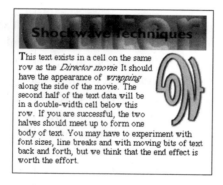

Figure 7-1: Table formatting allows for complex, precise layout of Web pages.

If you have Internet access, you can view this table with the Shockwave movie-in-action at this URL:

```
http://www.outer.net/singe/shockwave.html
```

Remember that different platforms and different browsers render this page differently. On a Windows machine running Netscape 2.0, the absence of the Palatino font referenced in FONT SIZE="4" on a Mac causes the text to consume more vertical space. This interferes with the layout somewhat, but it still looks okay. Other browsers that support Netscape tables may render it differently. This is a factor you must consider when building pages that incorporate Shockwave content.

The example shown in Figure 7-1 is fairly simple. Still, it demonstrates that you can get tables to bring most of the control found in desktop publishing programs to your Web offerings with a little twiddling. For example, you could wrap text around all four sides of a movie for an on-line magazine effect. More important, you can mix static and moving graphics to create the illusion of movies that look larger than their frame sizes would ordinarily indicate. In the size-conscious world of the Web, this trick is valuable!

Note: For more information on tables and their associated options, consult the Netscape documentation at this URL:

```
http://home.netscape.com/assist/net_sites/tables.html
```

Design Considerations

Positioning your content is critical to the success or failure of your Shockwave pages, because moving images and interactivity demand more careful interface design. Because movies may start playing as soon as the data finishes loading, make sure that the contents of the EMBED tag are visible within the typical browser window.

We've already seen Shockwave-enabled Web pages that are frustrating to use because of this problem. Test your page with different sized windows or on different sized monitors to make sure that it displays its Shockwave content effectively.

Tip: If you include a Shockwave Director movie that requires user interaction before play can begin, inform your users. Use a notice that appears in the first frame of the movie, or in a text or graphic element that is positioned nearby. If users don't intuitively sense that they must click on the movie to start play, they may never notice that it's not a static image and all your hard work will be in vain!

The same advice applies to any interaction you expect from users with your Director movies. Remember that most Web pages don't require two-way communication with their users. As an exotic, unfamiliar type of medium on a page, users may not automatically respond appropriately when they view your Shockwave project.

Your ability to effectively communicate with your users is what will make your Shockwave content work, just as it governs other aspects of their experiences at your Web site. If you put yourself in your users' shoes, you'll know what they want (or need) to see and hear to fully understand what's happening. Even if you can't make that leap, you can ask test users to help you get it right!

A Grasp of the Obvious Can Be Amazing!

Something that's obvious to users when they view a movie on a CD-ROM, for instance, may completely escape them when the same content appears on a Web page. This will change as the general public acquires the interactive vocabulary for Web-based interaction; in the meantime, this is an important consideration for your page designs.

Aesthetically, integrating inline movies on a Web page is more challenging than laying out simple text and graphics. Because of the media's richness, Shockwave movies often dominate the pages on which they appear. Moving pictures (and possibly sound) can overwhelm the rest of a page's content or make it seem out of place. If you work hard to avoid this, you won't inadvertently create an impression that the movies only appear to show off new technology rather than to complement the entire site.

If the Movie Doesn't Fit, Don't Use It!

Here is a good measure to apply to all of the movies on your pages: Does a given movie add or subtract from the overall value of a page? Ultimately, the World Wide Web is a communication medium, so you must consider whether each movie aids or hinders your site's message.

In these early days of Shockwave, we've already seen too many pages on which movies were obviously inserted into a page as if to say, "Look! We do Shockwave! Isn't it cool?" If that's all you want to convey, consider grouping your movies on a page or pages as a kind of portfolio, and identify your efforts as such. That way, both people looking specifically for cool Director-on-the-Web content and people who want to get value from the rest of your site will be happy.

In fact, you may want to use a jump page—a movie-free page from which users can choose which of your movies to view, where each movie is lovingly described, where its size is stated, and where a link can be followed to view it. This helps viewers combat the tendency for

Director projects to become quite large, and lets them select the movies they really want to see.

Tip: A top-level "welcome" to your site might include only text and graphics, and thus be quick to load and display. It can inform users about what kind of content you offer, along with the filesize for each linked page. This is a throwback to the early days of the Web, when high-speed modems were still luxury items and the rule of the day was to inform the user of the size of each linked graphic image. Given that Shockwave content ups the ante in terms of filesizes, this rule of thumb is probably due for a revival!

We've repeatedly harped on filesizes and download times, but it is truly one of our most important messages. Not only should you do everything you can to keep individual movies small, but you also need to consider the total size of a page inclusive of all of its linked media. Even if your average movie is less than 50K, 10 of them on a single Web page will frustrate and drive away users in droves.

Non-Shockwave Browsers

Speaking of frustration, another thing to consider is how your pages look to non-Shockwave browsers. You don't want your site to look bad simply because users who lack Shockwave-enabled browsers can't properly view your inline movies. Because Shockwave technology is so new, you must anticipate that the Web audience will adopt it slowly over the coming years.

Even after Shockwave has penetrated the marketplace, a significant portion of the user community will remain unable to view your content the way you've designed it. Many users fail to keep up with the latest and greatest browser enhancements, as you can discover for yourself by looking at statistics that describe the distribution of browsers on the Net today.

We encourage you to keep an eye on the browsers in use by visiting sites that track such things. One excellent source for information like this is found at:

```
http://emporium.turnpike.net/J/jc/public_html/stats.html
```

Moreover, because plug-ins are optional, even users with plug-in capable Web browsers may not yet have installed Shockwave Director capabilities. Happily, you can work around these difficulties when you design your pages.

To address that portion of the audience that can use the Shockwave plug-in but doesn't yet have it installed, consider a strategy similar to that used by sites designed to be viewed with Netscape. Place a prominent notice on your page to explain that you use movies that require the plug-in and include a link to Macromedia's site to download the plug-in. This message also warns those users whose browsers can't use plug-ins that they'll encounter content they can't see.

Netscape's plug-in architecture includes features designed to handle this problem: Users running Netscape 2.0 who load a page that demands a specific plug-in that they lack see a link in the EMBED frame that leads to a Web page with information about the plug-in. This feature isn't yet entirely functional; clicking the link usually returns an error. However, this should be fixed by the time you read this book. In any event, a notice on your Web page should alert users to the need for a plug-in.

A simple notice works best when you have a welcome page on your site that lacks Shockwave content. That way, the page loads normally and presents users with links to your pages that require the plug-in. But if you think your site's impact will be substantially diminished by an intermediary step between your users and your content, and you want to include movies on your site's entry page, you should take further action to universalize your content.

Hiding Movies Using NOEMBED

Along with the introduction of the EMBED tag to support inline Director movies in HTML, Netscape added another tag to its bag of proprietary tricks. This tag, NOEMBED, is meant to complement the EMBED tag and supplies content to load if a browser doesn't support plug-ins. A proprietary tag that helps Web browsers deal with another proprietary tag at first may seem like sheer folly, but NOEMBED works contrary to what you might expect.

By capitalizing on the HTML parsers built into Web browsers that ignore tags they don't understand, the browser reveals whatever the tag was wrapped around by ignoring its start and end tags. Typically, this is an image or text meant to replace the plug-in content. Thus, a typical use of the NOEMBED tag resembles the following:

```
<EMBED HEIGHT="100" WIDTH="348" SRC="movies/mymovie.dcr">
<NOEMBED><IMG SRC="images/noplugins.GIF"></NOEMBED>
```

Any tag or tags can be used within the NOEMBED tag. When a plug-in aware browser parses the page, it recognizes the NOEMBED tag. Because it supports EMBED, the content between the NOEMBED tags isn't rendered. Thus, NOEMBED works in reverse: It shows alternate content to browsers that don't understand it, and hides that content from browsers that do!

Note: The only potential downsides to the NOEMBED tag occur if the browser fails to parse HTML as the specifications dictate. The EMBED tag may display as a "broken image" icon on some browsers, for example. Alternatively, the browser may ignore the tags between the NOEMBED tags as well as the NOEMBED tags themselves.

If you want to add another level of bullet-proofing to your pages, you may want to dip into a little scripting, as we indicate in the section that follows.

Hiding Movies Using JavaScript

Version 2.0 of Netscape's Navigator Web browser includes support for a scripting language that was originally called LiveScript, but now is known as JavaScript. This language is distinct from Java, but supports some of the same functionality in a simpler, more approachable format. JavaScript is straightforward; using some of its commands makes the inclusion or exclusion of Director movies even more seamless.

As with the NOEMBED tag, it isn't immediately apparent how you can use features not present in incompatible browsers to mask still more incompatible features. JavaScript, however, follows different parsing rules than HTML. For example, a JavaScript in the middle of an HTML comment parses and runs perfectly. The HTML parser, on the other hand, ignores all content inside comments.

Using this difference, you can write a simple script that causes Shockwave content to be included in the page, then insert the script into an HTML comment. Only browsers with both plug-in support and JavaScript will see the Shockwave movies. At the moment, this means the only browser that works in this way is Netscape Navigator 2.0. But as this technology is further licensed and adopted, both capabilities will spread to other browsers in parallel.

The HTML and JavaScript source for this technique looks like this excerpt:

```
<SCRIPT LANGUAGE="livescript">
<!- begin HTML comment. JavaScript below
Document.write ( '<EMBED SRC="/movies/test.dcr" WIDTH="100"
    HEIGHT="250">' )
<!- finish comment ->
</SCRIPT>
```

Let's look at each of these lines of code separately.

```
<SCRIPT LANGUAGE="livescript">
```

This tag is ignored by browsers that don't support JavaScript and LiveScript.

```
<!- begin HTML comment. JavaScript below
```

Begin the HTML comment, but don't close it. This causes the browser to ignore everything until you close the comment.

```
Document.write ( '<EMBED SRC="/movies/test.dcr" WIDTH="100"
    HEIGHT="250">' )
```

This JavaScript command spits out the HTML tag and its contents to the browser, and the Shockwave movie appears on the page.

```
<!- finish comment ->
```

Having completed the script commands, you can close your comment. Note that the line again begins with a begin-comment tag; this is required so that Java- and Shockwave-capable browsers parse the line correctly.

```
</SCRIPT>
```

Outside the comment, you can end your SCRIPT tag. This will also be ignored by incompatible browsers.

To review, what you've constructed here acts like a conditional statement that controls the inclusion or exclusion of your Shockwave content. Normally, you would now add a NOEMBED portion to explain what users who can't see the movie are missing.

Shockwave Today

We turn now to real-world examples of what we've been discussing. While writing this book, we kept a close eye on ongoing Shockwave development efforts. The following sites represent some of the best examples of how it's being done. For each site, we look at the source behind the rendered page and explore how the principles we've been discussing have been put into action.

The Apple Interactive Training Site

The Apple Austin Training Group was among the earliest adopters of Shockwave technology. Fueled in part by one of this book's authors and armed with every beta Macromedia product in existence, this group launched a Shockwave-enhanced site the day the technology was announced.

This site distinguishes itself from many of the other Shockwave sites by attempting to put the content to practical use. To the group, the marriage of Director interactivity to Internet distribution is perfect for presenting their materials to a vast audience.

The group plans to move much of their training to Shockwave Web sites, which promises two major benefits. First, it will reduce the time to deliver new training materials when products are announced. Second, it will reduce the costs associated with CD-ROM and paper production and distribution.

Austin Training's site also exhibits all of the signs of careful design. Its movies are consistently small—the average falls between 50K and 100K. The layout carefully balances HTML and static graphics with Director movies to achieve an elegant overall feel.

The page depicted in Figure 7-2 is an interactive tour of the Apple QuickTime Conferencing Camera. The page is clean and well balanced; and although it contains four separate Shockwave Director movies, it requires a total download of only slightly over 200K. Each interactive element adds to the page, although the design team's enthusiasm for Shockwave technology may be a bit overdone.

Interactivity is difficult to describe with only text, but some of the interactive elements used here are clever enough to warrant a description.

The roll-over buttons in the navigation bar's top and bottom are a nice touch. Although Web users are accustomed to seeing navigation bars on Web pages, they will be totally surprised when they move the cursor over a button and see it light in blue. This is a good example of exploiting the new context for Director movies. Had these buttons been on a CD-ROM, they would be commonplace. On the Web, they are exotic—a small but pleasant change from the usual, static medium.

Figure 7-2: This Apple Interactive Training site demonstrates careful planning.

The centerpiece of the site is the QuickTime Conferencing Camera training, and it does not disappoint. Its first frame includes prominent instructions to click areas on the camera to see an explanation of a particular part. This prompts users to interact when they might not have otherwise been inclined to do so.

Each click evokes a short explanation of that part's function and causes close-up images to appear or, in the case of Figure 7-2, provides a link to a tech support article regarding the product. This is an excellent example of integrating Internet elements into traditional multimedia and calling attention to the synergy thereby created. The link is highlighted with a different text color and a large chain link icon. Without these interface elements, a user might pass right by that part of the project without knowing what to click.

A quick look at the Interactive Training Site's code reveals the same clean design as the rendered page. Each element is carefully designed to take maximum advantage of white space. One element sits on top of the other without any complex HTML layout, and it works as a whole because the concept of the page was followed throughout. The code begins with:

```
<HTML><HEAD>
<TITLE>QuickTime Conferencing Kit</TITLE>
<BODY BGCOLOR=#FFFFFF></HEAD>
```

After a standard HTML HEAD in which the title and background color are set, the file starts right with the first Shockwave movie.

```
<CENTER>
<SCRIPT language="LiveScript">
document.write ('<embed height="120" width="480"
   src="hqtccam.dcr">')
</SCRIPT>
```

Notice the use of the LiveScript tag. This page was created before the name change to JavaScript. The two are mostly interchangeable, so the presence of the old name doesn't affect the page. This first movie is the top navigation bar with the Apple logo and the "computer" text message.

```
<P>
<SCRIPT language="LiveScript">
document.write ('<embed height="300" width="592"
   src="camtest.dcr">')
</SCRIPT>
```

The code for the second Director movie is much like the first. All of the movies are wrapped in browser script fragments to prevent broken icons in browsers that aren't Shockwave capable.

The entire site runs NetCloak, a Macintosh Web server add-on that serves different pages to different browsers. Essentially, what happens when the user's request arrives is that NetCloak looks at the type of browser and instructs the Web server to return an appropriate type of page.

This lets the Interactive Training Web site serve Shockwave pages only to those browsers that are capable of viewing them. As an aside, NetCloak can do a lot of other cool stuff based on other information extracted from user requests. To learn more about it, check out the following URL:

```
http://www.maxum.com/netcloak/
```

This second Shockwave movie is the actual Camera training content. The HTML source continues with the third and fourth scripts, and EMBED combinations.

```
<P><SCRIPT language="LiveScript">
document.write ('<embed height="60" width="480"
   src="fqtccam.dcr">')
</SCRIPT><P>
<SCRIPT language="LiveScript">
document.write ('<embed height="110" width="288" src="exit.dcr">')
</SCRIPT><P>
```

These code fragments place the bottom navigation bar and the movie that acts as a button to return to the Interactive Training home page. With the multimedia content out of the way, the page finishes with a traditional HTML link to an Apple copyright notice document.

```
<A HREF="http://www.apple.com/notices/copyright.html"> &#169;
 1995  Apple Computer, Inc. All rights reserved.</A><P>
Last modified by <B>DAP</B> on 12/06/95
</CENTER>
</BODY>
</HTML>
```

Because the site is really a proof-of-concept for the training group's idea of Web-borne training materials, we look forward to watching their pages mature and their number of offerings increase. To see these pages for yourself, follow this URL:

```
http://selfpaced.info.apple.com/
```

DreamLight Multimedia's Web Site

Naturally, a large number of the sites that feature Shockwave Director movies in these early days were created by multimedia and Web developers to tout their abilities with this new technology. Sadly, many of these sites look like nothing more than an HTML page with a movie stuck in the middle as an afterthought. This is pardonable, because the normal rules for gratuitous content don't really apply when showcasing a new media type. However, some developers' pages rise above the rest by displaying more thought and care in their design.

One such developer's page belongs to DreamLight Multimedia. The average user, with no other knowledge of the quality of work done by DreamLight, is sure to come away from this site with a generally favorable impression. We had this impression ourselves, so pleased were we to see a change from the current slapdash offerings. View this page at:

```
http://www.dreamlight.com/dreamlt/gallery/pumpkin.htm
```

We were especially impressed to see examples of nearly all of the principles outlined in this chapter illustrated on DreamLight's pages. The placement of the central movie in Figure 7-3 is nicely balanced, with the text and HTML elements on three sides. The text to the right of the pumpkin movie not only has an indicator of the movie's size and a time-to-download estimate, but it also provides a brief explanation of what's happening on the page. The nature of the movie is explained, as is the kind of interaction that the movie expects from the user.

The movie at this site loads in two parts. A tiny movie loads initially, displaying information about DreamLight and a message stating that the movie is loading. The second, larger part of the project is then retrieved over the Internet using the Lingo command, *PreloadNetThing uri*. When the smaller movie is finished displaying, it is replaced by the larger one, which is depicted in Figure 7-3.

Figure 7-3: This portion of DreamLight Multimedia's Shockwave page demonstrates many of this chapter's principles.

The HTML code for this page reveals careful coding and even more precautions taken for the portion of the audience that's not running Netscape 2.0. The code begins with document setup and a standard sampling of HTML code to build the button bars at the top of the page.

```
<HTML>
<HEAD>
<TITLE>DreamLight&reg; Gallery: Pumpkin</TITLE>
<!-Copyright 1995 DreamLight Incorporated, Stoneham MA. All
  Rights Reserved.->
</HEAD>
<BODY BACKGROUND="../images/dli_noise.gif">
<A NAME="top" HREF="../studio/index.html"><IMG
    SRC="../images/dreamlight_up.gif" WIDTH="138" HEIGHT="44"
    ALT="[DreamLight]" BORDER=0></A>
<A HREF="../news/index.html"><IMG SRC="../images/news_up.gif"
    WIDTH="44" HEIGHT="44" ALT="[News]" BORDER=0></A>
<A HREF="index.html"><IMG SRC="../images/gallery_dn.gif"
    WIDTH="44" HEIGHT="44" ALT="[Gallery]" BORDER=0></A>
<A HREF="../insights/index.html">
<IMG SRC="../images/insight_up.gif" WIDTH="44" HEIGHT="44"
    ALT="[Insights]" BORDER="0"></A>
<A HREF="../shareware/index.html">
```

```
<IMG SRC="../images/shareware_up.gif" WIDTH="44" HEIGHT="44"
    ALT="[Shareware]" BORDER="0"></A>
<A HREF="../surf/index.html"><IMG SRC="../images/surf_up.gif"
    WIDTH="44" HEIGHT="44" ALT="[SurfSite]" BORDER="0"></A>
<A HREF="../welcome.html#webtop">
<IMG WIDTH="44" HEIGHT="44" SRC="../images/top_up.gif" ALT="[TOP]"
    BORDER="0"></A>
<BR>
```

Note the use of relative paths to all image files. As we mentioned earlier, such paths are useful during development but can turn into an Achilles heel after your site is up and running. If files move or directory paths are rearranged, every relative link may be affected. To make this page more robust and portable, these links could be changed to absolute URLs.

After some more buttons, navigation aids, and links (which we skip here) you encounter the code that handles the Shockwave content.

```
<HR>
<H2><A NAME="halloween" HREF="#halloween">3BD's Shockwave
    Halloween Pumpkin!</A> </H2>
<SCRIPT LANGUAGE="LiveScript">
<!- Hide this script from non-Navigator 2.0 browsers.
document.write( '<EMBED HSPACE="8" VSPACE= "8" ALIGN="left"
    WIDTH=320 HEIGHT=240 SRC="movies/DLILoading.dcr">');
```

The movie loaded by the EMBED tag in the first portion of the JavaScript is the small, introductory movie, DLILoading.dcr. This movie internally handles the loading of the larger movie, which is displayed in the frame created by the first movie's EMBED options.

It is interesting to note that DreamLight uses standard IMG tag options such as HSPACE, VSPACE, and ALIGN in the EMBED tag. We could find no documentation that states that these options are supported. In fact, Netscape's own documentation explicitly states that the EMBED tag supports only the three default options we discussed at the beginning of the chapter. It seems likely that the DreamLight HTML coders simply experimented and found that the options work. This is indeed good news for developers, because it affords more control over the appearance of your movies on a page.

```
document.write('<H3>Simply Shocking!!</H3>');
document.write('<P>This Shockwave movie is 150k and will
    take about one minute to load, at 28.8kbps, before it will begin
    to play. ');
document.write('Please be patient. Once the pumpkin with
    3BD in it appears, you may interact with 3BD. Have fun, and try
    not to be too scared! Here is a hint: Do not click the mouse too
    soon!</P>');
document.write('<P>This is only a simple example of what
    DreamLight can do with Shockwave. ');
document.write('There are many ways
        <A HREF="../studio/services/multimedia.html">DreamLight
        Multimedia</A> can work for you.</P>');
document.write('<P>If you see a broken picture icon, your
    browser may not be <A HREF="#note">configured properly</A> to
    view this movie.</P><BR CLEAR="left">');
<!- Done hiding from non-Navigator 2.0 browsers. ->
</SCRIPT>
```

Note that, like the Apple Interactive Training site, DreamLight has been careful to send plug-in code only to browsers also equipped with LiveScript or JavaScript. DreamLight has gone further than simply hiding the embedded movie, however. Also wrapped in the script commands are the text and links that go along with the movies. It makes sense to do this, because people who cannot view the movie have little interest in the information meant for those who can.

```
<NOEMBED>
<IMG WIDTH="320" HEIGHT="240" SRC="images/3BDpmk3.gif"
    ALIGN="left">
<H3>
<IMG WIDTH="34" HEIGHT="34" SRC="../images/caution.gif"
    ALT="[*!*]" BORDER="0">I'm sorry.</H3>
<P>
This page <STRONG>requires</STRONG> the following software which
    you may download here.</P>
<UL>
<LI><A HREF="http://home.netscape.com/comprod/mirror/index.html">
    Netscape 2.0</A>
```

```
<LI><A HREF="http://www.macromedia.com/Tools/Shockwave/">
    Shockwave</A>
</UL>
```

Not content with the precautions they already took for nonplug-in browsers, DreamLight also makes use of the NOEMBED tag to display information about how to get the software to view Shockwave movies. Links to Netscape and Macromedia give users a chance to equip themselves and return. This is an excellent strategy for a little evangelism for your site, because many people appreciate the help in finding the necessary pieces and will return to see your Shockwave content.

```
<P>
You may also, download a <A
HREF="../shareware/screenbits.html#halloween">self contained
    version </A> of this movie to run independently of your browser.
<BR CLEAR="left">
<BR CLEAR="left">
</NOEMBED>
```

We think that providing the option to download a stand-alone version of the movie will be appreciated by users. Even those who decide to get the browser and plug-in (or not to bother with Web multimedia at all) will notice the effort DreamLight put into making its offering as flexible as possible. The attempt to provide a rich set of options to users is rewarded with gratitude and a loyal user base.

Other nice touches to the site contribute to a pleasant user experience. The link to the larger, more complex Director project gives those with fast connections or burning curiosity a chance to see more involved content. The further explanation of the software needed and links at the bottom of the page also ensure that everyone gets the message.

Overall, the DreamLight site is excellent. Our only complaint is that the pumpkin movie seems somewhat large for the amount of content it represents. At 150K, it can take a decent amount of time to retrieve; for the relatively small number of cast members and frames it contains, it could have been smaller. Perhaps with the application of the techniques presented in this book, their later efforts will match the quality present on the rest of the page!

Summary

Including inline Shockwave movies in HTML content is rather easy—at least at first glance. Its tags and options strongly resemble those of the IMG tag, and are certainly no more difficult to master. But the nature of multimedia and its novelty on the Internet make for some unique design constraints. Take care to place a movie on the page so that it is neither lost off screen, nor overwhelms the rest of the page. Bandwidth, too, is always a potential problem.

Available provisions can deal with all of these issues. Thoughtful consideration of the way the page looks to users, what you want to offer them, and how they will experience your site all lead to informed design decisions.

Shockwave represents a revolution in the way Web pages look, feel, and behave. The multimedia revolution also presents challenges for Web and multimedia developers, and will force them to find new ways to put the technology to best use.

Now that you know how to integrate Shockwave content into Web documents, the next chapter tackles the issues involved in delivering that content over the Internet. Along the way, we help you understand not just the technology, but some of the business issues that must be considered.

CHAPTER 8

Shockwave
on the Internet

S o far, we've covered the authoring environment and the compression phase of Shockwave technology. You've also learned how to integrate burned Shockwave files into HTML documents. At this point, you're ready to investigate the very *raison d'être* of Shockwave—serving multimedia content from an Internet-accessible server.

In a perfect world, bringing Shockwave content to the Web would be as simple as taking a completed Shockwave project, placing it on a Web server, and telling the world where to find it. However, the Internet and its various applications are always in a state of flux and don't provide the ease of use you might expect from more mature, stable technologies.

Along the way, you face several steps in serving Shockwave from a Web server, and many potential issues. In this chapter, you gain a conceptual understanding of these steps along with concrete illustrations. Likewise, where potential issues arise, we arm you with the kind of information that can be applied generally instead of die-cut solutions for specific problems. We believe this is the best approach because of the fragmented, multifaceted nature of the World Wide Web.

In fact, every one of this book's readers will face a different mix of server hardware, client and server software, and connection types as they attempt to serve their projects to the public. It's our hope that all of you will be able to find the specific solutions needed for your own unique situations armed with the general principles we present here.

Understanding Servers

The first step to placing content on the Internet is to identify and understand the Web server you'll use. This process should begin with a careful assessment of your needs and research into the potential solutions the market offers.

The scale of your project and the amount of money you have to spend on the server are the strongest factors in your ultimate decision. If you operate on a limited budget or this is an exploratory venture onto the Web, you probably want to merely rent space from an Internet service provider, or ISP. Conversely, if your company is deeply committed to a lasting Internet presence and has deep pockets, you probably want to purchase at least one Web server, and possibly more. Each of these scenarios is discussed in more depth later in this chapter.

Connectivity

Merely identifying and paying for a Web server is not the only hurdle you must leap, no matter what kind of server you choose. Any server that isn't connected to the Web does you little good. In addition to researching your hardware and software requirements, you must also carefully research what kind of connection to the Internet you need. Here again, you must weigh several factors when choosing an Internet connection for your Web site.

The first factor to consider is the size of your audience. If this is a pilot project or a demo for a few select individuals, a fairly low-bandwidth, inexpensive connection should suffice. A fast modem can provide a proof-of-concept connection but little else, as the maximum speed of 28.8 Kbps and the slow response time of analog devices are unsuitable for any real traffic volume. An ISDN connection provides a 64 Kbps or 128 Kbps connection, and is suitable for modest audiences. If you expect more than 10 to 15 people to access your pages simultaneously, however, an ISDN link will bog down and cause frustration for your users.

The next step up is some kind of T1 connection, which usually consists of a connection at 256 Kbps or 512 Kbps, called a fractional T1, or at 1.544 Mbps, called a full T1. Any of these connections provides substantial bandwidth, especially at the 1.544 Mbps maximum speed, and is able to sustain traffic from 100 to 300 simultaneous users.

It's important to consider outgoing as well as incoming traffic when determining traffic volume. In many cases, your connection must also serve local users as their primary route to the Internet as well as providing outside access to your Shockwave server. If this is true in your company, you must anticipate the traffic your users will generate and factor that into the aggregate traffic your connection must handle, along with incoming visitors to your Shockwave and other Web materials.

If even a T1 is not enough, the next step up is to aggregate multiple T1 lines, or to obtain a T3 connection, depending on the services available in your market. Multiple T1s provide 3, 4.5, 6, or more megabits per second. A T3 can carry incremental traffic up to 45 Mbps. Both types of connections carry high price tags, so be prepared for sticker shock!

For ISPs, Internet connectivity typically costs between $200 and $20,000 per month, depending on the speed of the connection and your ISP's other charges. Remember that installation and hardware costs also factor into this equation. Typical costs for a T1 connection appear in Table 8-1.

Table 8-1: These are estimated costs for a T1 Internet connection. Actual charges depend on current market prices.

Item	Estimated Cost
Equipment (router, CSU/DSU)	$4000
Installation (telco)	$2500
Line charges (telco)	$750/month
Setup (Internet service provider)	$1500
Connectivity charges (ISP)	$2000/month

Ultimately, your financial resources will be the primary deciding factor. Given unlimited capital, everyone interested in the Internet would purchase the maximum bandwidth available. If you can't afford the connection your audience will demand, there are several ways to maximize available funds, as you'll see in the sections that follow.

Outsourcing

While your Shockwave site requires a dedicated connection to the Internet, that connection does not necessarily have to be your own. A multitude of Internet service providers offer Web site hosting services. By tapping into their facilities, you can utilize a high-bandwidth connection to the Internet without paying for the whole thing. This type of arrangement can also buy you the services of experienced system administrators and a well-equipped network operations center at a fraction of their actual costs.

A good place to start looking for such services is the Leasing a Server list at:

```
http://union.ncsa.uiuc.edu/HyperNews/get/www/leasing.html
```

We've come full circle to our starting point. That is, the decision to run your own Web server versus paying someone else to do the job is often decided by the need for bandwidth. If you want higher rates of connectivity than you can afford to buy, you must turn to a service provider and pay as you go. This is unfortunate because many other factors might indicate that a different solution is appropriate. Nevertheless, you may be locked into this particular option because of the overriding importance of bandwidth.

Locating your Web pages on an ISP's servers means losing direct control over your site. You'll have less flexibility and control over numerous aspects of the Web, such as statistics, CGIs, and ancillary services such as gopher and ftp. In addition, service providers typically serve a large collection of clients' sites from their servers, so access to your pages may be adversely affected by neighbor sites on the same machine.

If your site shares a server with another site that becomes immensely popular, the load on the machine will affect service to your users. This sometimes results in slow transfer rates and refused connections, both of which negatively impact your audience's impressions about your site.

We should also mention that a select few ISPs buck the general industry trend by offering Web server *homing* instead of Web site *hosting*. The difference is semantically slight, but in practice can be quite dramatic. Web site hosting requires that users place their Web site onto a machine owned and operated by a service provider, and situated at the provider's place of business. In Web server homing, the client provides a Web server while the service provider connects that server to the ISP's Internet backbone.

On a homed site, the service provider handles day-to-day care and administration duties, as with Web site hosting, but the machine remains the property of the client. Thus, if you have the budget for a server but not for the requisite Internet connection or the technical staff to maintain it, you can still have exclusive access to a high-powered machine dedicated to serving your customers. You also obtain lower-cost, high-bandwidth connectivity from the service provider as a part of this approach.

Internet service providers that offer this type of service are fewer in number and harder to find. Our exhaustive search on Yahoo! (http://www.yahoo.com) and Lycos (http://www.lycos.com) found only three providers that offer to locate your servers on their backbones:

```
http://www.outer.net/prodserv.html
http://www.internex.net/
http://www.forest.net/
```

Nevertheless, we think homing is a good compromise for those who are stuck in the middle between hosting a site at your ISP and establishing your own site.

Choosing a Server

If you decide to house your pages on your own dedicated server, you'll have to select some combination of hardware, operating system, and HTTP server software that is appropriate for your project. Again, the size of your intended audience and your budget requirements are the primary factors in making this choice.

But there's another important consideration in this case—familiarity with system administration. Running a Web server is never a trivial task. It can be quite difficult when you're faced with an unfamiliar server or operating environment, and you must climb a steep learning curve to master it.

Unless you have in-house UNIX expertise or the resources to hire outside talent, we can't recommend a UNIX server. Nevertheless, many advantages to hosting Web servers on UNIX machines may make the decision for you. If you expect your site to experience heavy traffic on an almost continuous basis, for instance, you may have little choice in this matter. UNIX was not only the first operating system on the Internet, it was also designed from its inception as a multiuser, asynchronous I/O, multitasking, kernel-based operating system. If you understand this gibberish, good for you! If you don't, take our word for it that UNIX is still unparalleled in its robustness and reliability. For "big kahuna" sites, you shouldn't dismiss these characteristics too lightly.

In addition, UNIX servers have almost unlimited flexibility in customizing a Web site. The operating system has user friendliness for power, speed, and broad capability. While graphical interfaces lend themselves well to simplifying complex tasks for users, they can also obscure much of what's going on behind the many layers of menus, buttons, and windows.

Each interface element limits the choices available to users and takes away some ability to customize the system. UNIX, on the other hand, leaves every part of itself exposed, so it is relatively simple and quick for a seasoned UNIX administrator or programmer to customize a system's behavior.

Log files are a perfect example of this: When Web servers run under graphical interface OSes, log file formats and the post-processing applied to them to produce server statistics are usually somewhat constrained. By contrast, in a UNIX environment virtually any action you want to perform and any format you can imagine can be achieved or created. Or rather, tools to massage the data into exactly the form you desire are easy to build and customize under UNIX.

If UNIX is on your horizon, you have a wide range of choices of hardware platforms and server software. Various flavors of UNIX run on a huge number of platforms, from lowly 386 and 68030 machines all the way to multiprocessor RISC systems from Sun, SGI, HP, and DEC. Make your choice according to the flavor of UNIX your system administrator knows and what your budget allows.

For example, if you hire a system administrator with Solaris experience, pick the Sun workstation that fits your budget and choose one of the many available server software packages. Don't think that just because a system administrator is smart enough to master Solaris he or she can turn around and instantly master Windows NT—or vice versa.

For most companies, however, UNIX expertise is harder to come by than familiarity with the MacOS, Windows NT, or even Novell's

NetWare. Luckily, a number of Web server products have become available for all of these operating systems in the last 18 months.

In fact, the WebSTAR server package from Quarterdeck Corporation accounts for approximately 10 percent of the Web servers on the Internet, primarily in its Macintosh implementation (although an NT version shipped at the end of 1995). Various other servers such as Alibaba, Netsite, HTTPS, and Website are popular on Windows NT servers. Recently, Novell announced a product that permits NetWare servers to provide HTTP services. This came as a great relief to the many businesses that exclusively run Novell on their networks.

All of the Web servers we just mentioned are fine products and offer much easier configuration and installation than their UNIX-based counterparts. However, their relative immaturity and their operating systems' limitations somewhat handicap them. The MacOS-based WebSTAR, for instance, can't keep up with a comparable UNIX server in number of simultaneous connections or raw file I/O speed. NT servers suffer from many of the same weaknesses. But for most sites, the kind of volume that a Mac- or Windows-based server can handle is more than adequate. That's why understanding your visitation rate is such a key ingredient in selecting your Web site's operating environment.

After you select the operating system and software for your server, you must evaluate how much you can spend for server hardware. We recommend that you buy the fastest machine with the most RAM you can muster. A 100 MHz or faster PowerMac with 24MB of RAM, or a 120 MHz Pentium with 32MB of RAM, is a good place to start for a medium-sized site.

When evaluating potential server solutions, you may want to consult one of the many comparison charts on the Web, such as:

```
http://www.proper.com/www/servers-chart.html
```

This chart has a good rundown of the various features and limitations of the available products, and may help you catch some things you might otherwise miss.

Learning Someone Else's Server

For many people—especially those creating their first Web site—running their own servers may seem too daunting to tackle right away. The majority of Web newcomers start out by renting space from a service provider. After your pages and content are developed and tested, and you have a better idea of how they fit into the Web, you can always migrate to a server of your own. There's certainly nothing wrong with starting this way; if it seems like the right approach for your Shockwave site, by all means follow it!

Placing your content on someone else's server doesn't obviate your need to understand its Web server software. Even if you've paid big bucks for someone to create and maintain your site and you're simply providing the Shockwave projects, you will still benefit from familiarity with the package in use, no matter how cursory.

This is common sense, if you stop to consider it for a moment. If something goes wrong with your pages or your content, a modicum of familiarity with the Web server and its operating system will better prepare you to troubleshoot the problem. Even if you can only glean information regarding the symptoms but can't come up with an explanation, this information makes explaining the problem to your service provider—and resolving it—much easier.

Here are a few key points to apply to leasing space on almost any type of Web server. First and foremost is the issue of permissions. You should have a folder or directory designated as your own on the ISP's machine to which you may post all of your files, and where you can create file hierarchies.

If a problem occurs with your write privileges, it's useful to be able to identify the problem by its symptoms. This is the most common problem for users on hosted Web sites. Because you won't have full privileges to the entire file system as you would with you own server, you must rely on your ISP to fix the problem. At odd hours and on weekends, this may be a serious problem.

The second consideration involves your privileges regarding CGIs and external applications. ISPs usually provide some collection of standard CGIs such as e-mail gateways, guestbooks, imagemaps, and the like for their customers. However, you should find out if you may either customize existing CGIs or upload and run your own.

Differentiation and eye-catching displays are the keys to effective Web site design. While Shockwave content can go a long way, if your interactive CGIs are totally generic it reflects badly on you. Also, if you want your audience to access an information source through your Web site, you may need to determine what external applications you can run. You may also need to find out if you can install a gateway between your database and the Web server.

Finally, it is vital that you understand how to handle server log files and statistics. Without logs, you can't collect information on the traffic to your site. If you run a commercial site or rely on outside help, usage statistics are crucial to demonstrate the success or failure of your site.

Every ISP should be able to report on the Web sites they host, but you should also look carefully at what kinds and frequencies of reports they offer. Make sure these reports provide the details and the data you need. If their standard offerings don't meet your needs, find out if they'll customize reports for you and how much that will cost.

At this point, you should have identified the kind of server that will house your Shockwave site. Next, you must make sure it's ready to serve your content to the world.

Server Configuration

The process of selecting a Web server has multiple variables, many of which often pull you in opposite directions. So working through the decision-making process can be painful. But after you have your own server—or space on somebody else's server—what's left to do is fairly straightforward.

Essentially, this consists of making the server understand what to do with Shockwave content and getting the content onto the server. After these two steps are accomplished, your project will be accessible to the entire world, and you can sit back and watch how well it's received!

MIME Types

Thankfully, the process of configuring a server to handle Shockwave— or any other type of new Web content—is relatively easy and consistent across most server software. This is because, long before HTTP became the basis for commercial applications, it was defined with the flexibility to incorporate new types of media.

This flexibility derives from the standard upon which all media identification and handling is based in HTTP. This standard is called Multipurpose Internet Mail Extensions. MIME defines a method to consistently identify data types so that the requesting software knows how to unambiguously handle incoming data streams. When you browse the Web, for example, all HTML documents and image files are identified by their MIME types and displayed appropriately.

When you request a document from a server, it responds not only with the content of that page, but also with a MIME header that identifies the data type for each element of the page. Before the server sends the content, it tells the browser that the content is HTML source so that the tags will be properly parsed and rendered by the recipient's browser.

Similarly, when your browser requests images, the server identifies them as .GIF or JPEG files so the browser can appropriately route the data for display. If there's a link on the page to a compressed binary file, the server identifies it as such to the browser. If the browser has a helper application identified for that particular MIME type, it passes the file to that application after the transfer is complete.

The MIME identification of the data arrives in an HTTP header called *Content-type*. The server provides this header every time it responds to a request for data, along with type and subtype names—and sometimes other information about the data. The Content-type header for an HTML file reads like this:

```
Content-type:    text/html
```

In this case, *text* is the data type and *html* is the primary subtype. The header value for a .GIF image is:

```
Content-type:    image/gif
```

We're sure you get the idea and probably know where we're going with this discussion. For Shockwave files to be properly transferred and viewed across the Internet, the server must identify them. Thus, Shockwave must have its own MIME type. This type and subtype are:

```
Content-type:    application/x-director
```

The *x-* before *director* indicates that this is an external data type, one that requires the intervention of a helper application for delivery. That's the Shockwave plug-in, in case you haven't already guessed!

With the MIME type for Shockwave files properly established, all that remains is to ensure that the server identifies Shockwave content and provides the proper MIME type to browsers that request it. By following the steps specific to your server for adding support for a new media type, you can add the necessary information. As a demonstration of what's involved, we cover several examples in the sections that follow.

NSCA httpd Configuration

We begin by describing how to configure the UNIX Web server from NCSA, called *httpd*. This is a good example because it's one of the two original HTTP servers, along with the former CERN server now supported by the World Wide Web Consortium, or W3C. NCSA *httpd* is the model for the look and feel of many other Web servers.

What's more, the NCSA server accounts for anywhere from 30 to 60 percent of the servers currently on the Web, depending on which survey you read. This is probably because NCSA *httpd* is free, robust, fast, mature, and easy to maintain. If you're setting up a UNIX-based Web server of your own, take a long, hard look at the NCSA server as a solution.

NCSA *httpd*'s method for identifying MIME file types is to establish a mapping between file extensions and MIME types. Thus, when requested by a browser, files with an .html extension will be properly identified as *text/html*, and the proper *Content-type* header value will be set. The file in which this mapping occurs is called *mime.types*, and resides in the *conf* directory under the server's root directory.

This file's format is simple: Each line starts with a type/subtype pair and, after a tab or some spaces, concludes with a comma-delimited list of extensions to which the MIME type applies. Our HTML example's entry looks like this:

```
text/html     html htm
```

Note that both *htm* and *html* are included as valid extensions. This ensures compatibility with the pre-Windows 95 DOS/Windows world, which doesn't allow file extensions longer than three characters.

To add support for Shockwave Director movies, the administrator simply adds the following line to the *mime.types* file:

```
application/x-director     dcr dir dxr
```

You may wonder why we map three different suffixes to this MIME type. The .dir and .DCR extensions should already be familiar to you; the former is the standard extension for Director Film Strip files and the latter for Shockwave-compressed Director files.

The last suffix, .dxr, isn't currently used but is specifically mentioned for this MIME type configuration in Macromedia's documentation. Our guess is that this extension will be used by some future twist on the Shockwave file format, perhaps for files that deliver content by streaming data across the Internet.

In any case, the .DCR suffix will probably be used more than any other, at least for now. Another thing to note about this configuration is that it is not case sensitive, so the MIME type statement properly recognizes and identifies files with the extension of .dcr, .DCR, or even .DcR.

Tenant Configuration

If you're a tenant on a server that runs NCSA *httpd* (paying for space on the server but having no control over the machine), you probably won't be allowed direct access to the *mime.types* file. There are two methods to add support for Shockwave to a hosting server without administrator access.

The first, most obvious tack is to contact your server's system administrator and request the changes we outlined earlier. We've given you enough general information to make yourself understood. So if you happen to be served by NCSA's *httpd,* you could probably walk the administrator through the process in a pinch.

The other method is to add support for the MIME type directly to the directory where your Shockwave files reside. To this end, you must create an *.htaccess* file to instruct the server that when it accesses this directory, it must add support for the MIME types needed by your content files. The default name for a directive file of this type is *.htaccess*—that is, a file extension without any explicit filename—though this will vary among server types. If you want to use this method to configure your server, check with your administrator or look at other directories to see if such a file exists and what it is named.

Whatever your server's naming convention is, you must create an .htaccess file in the directory that contains your Shockwave .dcr files, set its privileges to make it world-readable, and add directives to map from file suffixes to the appropriate MIME types. Assuming default naming, the easiest way to create such a file under UNIX is to type:

```
cat > .htaccess
```

Then, type the following directives for *httpd* to follow:

```
AddType application/x-director dcr
AddType application/x-director dir
AddType application/x-director dxr
```

To end input to the file, type ^*D* (hold down the Control key while you type the letter *D*). After you create this file, you must set its permissions. In UNIX, enter the following command:

```
chmod 644 .htaccess
```

This command permits the server software to open and peruse the *.htaccess* file when it enters the directory looking for one of your Shockwave files.

This method doesn't rely on the intervention of a system administrator, and the directives will be in effect for the directory in which you place the *.htaccess* file as well as its subdirectories. Unfortunately, as far as we know, this only works for the NCSA server and its derivatives, such as the Apache server. Any server that doesn't support *.htaccess* MIME directives may need to be configured by the system administrator.

Configuring Other HTTP Servers

To present a survey of all the currently available Web servers and the steps to add Shockwave support to each one would not only go beyond the scope of this book but would also be extremely tedious. Nevertheless, we'll touch on a few servers other than the NCSA server that form the largest part of the World Wide Web server population. Not only does this provide you with the steps for most servers you're likely to encounter, it also gives you the background to understand almost any other server's configuration.

W3C httpd. The second most commonly used server for UNIX is the product formerly known as *CERN httpd*. Now supported by the World Wide Web Consortium, all the server directives for this product are contained in one configuration file. This file takes the default path of /etc/httpd.conf. To add Shockwave support, include the following lines:

```
AddType .dcr    application/x-director 8bit
AddType .dxr    application/x-director 8bit
AddType .dir    application/x-director 8bit
```

Note that the *W3C httpd* handles only one extension per line and has a slightly different syntax from what we saw earlier. The order of extension and MIME type is reversed, and the encoding type (8-bit) is included as well. Since all server directives of any kind are included in this file, the

MIME directive needs to be identified by the keyword *AddType* at the beginning of the line.

Netscape Netsite. The single most popular commercial Web server is Netscape's Netsite. This is also a multiplatform server, with versions for UNIX and Windows NT currently available. While it has a file named *mime.types* that is similar to the NCSA server, its syntax differs somewhat. The entry to support Shockwave reads:

```
type=application/x-director      exts=dcr,dir,dxr
```

Strangely, though Netsite comes with an administration package that provides a Web interface for configuring the server, this interface does not allow you to add support for new MIME types. This is unusual for an otherwise cutting-edge Web server such as Netsite. The trend that nearly every other commercial Web server now follows includes a graphic interface for every detail of server configuration.

Quarterdeck's WebSTAR. Macintosh-based Web servers account for a startling 10 to 20 percent of the servers on the Internet. While it may seem strange that servers on the Net follow a distribution pattern that mirrors the rest of the computing world, it makes sense if you consider how the Macintosh has played into the hands of the Internet community.

Although UNIX machines were the first on the Internet and still comprise the vast majority of Internet servers, the Internet springs from government and higher education research facilities and campuses. These are long-time bastions for Macintosh users as well. TCP/IP client-server software has been available on the Mac longer than on Windows machines. Only when the commercial potential of the Internet was recognized and exploited did Windows machines become a viable market for TCP/IP software.

WebSTAR is an excellent example of the results of this history lesson. Begun as a shareware product by Chuck Shotten and distributed under the name MacHTTP, it was the first viable port of a Web server from UNIX. WebSTAR quickly developed a loyal user base that worked with its author to evolve the software into a commercially successful and technically impressive product. Purchased by StarNine and in turn by Quarterdeck, WebSTAR is not only the easiest Web server to install and configure, it's also extremely robust and reliable.

At the end of 1995, Quarterdeck introduced a Windows NT implementation of WebSTAR, and by all reports it too is being well received in the marketplace.

Here is what's required to add support for Shockwave media to the Macintosh version of WebSTAR. Like Netscape, WebSTAR includes an administration package that provides a graphical user interface for most common server tasks. WebSTAR Admin, as the program is called, uses a sophisticated Macintosh interface to control servers running on your own machine or on other machines accessible over AppleTalk.

Take the following steps to configure WebSTAR for Shockwave:

1. Launch the WebSTAR Admin application.

2. Choose your server in the dialog box that appears. (Your server must be running locally or be accessible via the Internet.)

3. Choose Suffix Mapping from the Configure menu. The Suffix Mapping dialog box appears.

4. Fill out the dialog box as it appears in Figure 8-1.

5. Click the Add button, then the Update button, to complete the configuration settings.

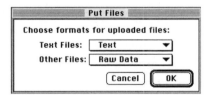

Figure 8-1: This WebSTAR Admin for the Macintosh's MIME configuration dialog box is filled in with Shockwave information.

Repeat steps 1 through 5 for .dir and .dxr suffixes.

As an alternative, WebSTAR provides a CGI-based remote administration package that performs some of the same functions as the Admin utility.

Configuration Principles

A common thread emerges from this peek at some of the most popular server packages: Though the particulars may differ—and interfaces do differ—the essential data remains the same across all HTTP servers. That information can be condensed under these three headings:

- Mime type: application
- Sub Type: x-director
- Extensions: .DCR, .DIR, and .DXR

If all else fails, you can give this information to your server's most experienced administrator, who should be able to take it from there!

Placing Files on the Server

After your server is properly configured to serve Shockwave files, the next phase is to upload your Web site's content. Typically, this involves a collection of HTML files, images, Shockwave movies, sounds, and other media from your development machines. The task that lies ahead is to get your local content onto the machine that will serve it to the Internet.

The simplest scenario is one in which your Web server is connected to your development machines over your LAN. Posting your content in this case is as easy as a regular network file copy. But in most instances, even when you own your server, chances are good that your development machines are separate from your server. A typical example is a UNIX server housed on an ISP's backbone with your development machines linked using PPP or an ISDN Internet connection.

In this scenario, your files must be collected and uploaded to the server via ftp. There are numerous free, shareware, and commercial ftp clients available for both Mac and Windows platforms; any of them should suffice. If the link to your server is slow, you might want to build an archive of all the content, compress it, and upload it overnight.

Better still, before or after you compress your archive, segment it into manageable parts and upload those parts one at a time. That way, if something goes wrong with any transfer, you only have to resend one segment instead of the entire package.

Archiving and Compression Issues

If you compress your files, be certain to use a format that you can decompress on the server. If your server and clients run on the same platform, this won't be a problem; but if you make cross-platform transfers, compression standards that exist on one platform may not exist on others.

Good bets for cross-platform archiving and compression include *tar* and *Z* compression. The former is an acronym for Tape ARchive; it can preserve folder or directory hierarchies as well as combine many files into one. UNIX compression affixes the letter *Z* to the files it processes; hence, it is commonly known as *Z* compression. It is a standard Lempel-Zev compression and, while not extremely efficient, it is adequate.

The advantage that both *tar* and *Z* formats enjoy is the existence of utilities that can create and extract them on UNIX, Macintosh, and Windows platforms. Therefore, if you're unsure what utilities are present on the server, or if you're unsure where your files will end up, these are your best choices.

File Formats

Compression formats are not the only potential pitfalls when moving files from one operating system to another. Depending on the specific mix of platforms, you may have to ensure that proper file translations occur. Because PCs, Macs, and UNIX machines handle data differently, you can't be sure about successful transfers, even when file formats are ostensibly the same. You won't encounter difficulties with the formats themselves, because you're dealing with a shared set of data types on the Web, such as .GIF, HTML, and JPEG. But that's not all that can go awry.

The two most common problems encountered when uploading files stem from differences in line breaks and from the Macintosh forked data format. Line breaks are handled quite differently on PC, Mac, and UNIX platforms. UNIX denotes the end of a line with a linefeed, Macs with a carriage return, and PCs with a carriage return followed by a linefeed.

If handled improperly, HTML and other text files may end up with data as a continuous line. This won't cause a problem for HTML files from the browser's perspective, because line breaks are ignored in favor of tags such as <BR> and <P>, which signify line breaks. But if a file that somehow acquires this characteristic is later downloaded to your development machine for editing, you may find yourself with a mess.

Most ftp clients handle line break translation automatically. In addition, a number of text and HTML editors automatically save files in a form that retains its integrity across platforms. The only times we tend to run into this problem are not when our data moves to one platform from another, but instead when it migrates among several platforms.

For example, data posted from a PC to a UNIX machine contains embedded carriage returns and linefeeds at the end of each line. It displays perfectly on a UNIX machine. However, if it's downloaded to a Macintosh, it will either be translated as stripped of the linefeeds or end up double spaced. If it's translated to display properly on the Mac and is then transferred back to the PC, the text will all be on one line. This issue can be tricky, but the good thing is that the integrity of the content itself is never compromised.

Some of the issues surrounding Macintosh files and their multifork structure are more complex and troublesome. Mac files can have three forks, or data partitions. One is the data fork, which contains the actual data, text, image, or other content. There can also be a resource fork and a file info fork. The resource fork of a typical data file may contain an icon or code fragments. For example, a self-extracting archive works because the code to decompress the file is contained in the resource fork. The file info fork contains information about a file, such as the date it was created or modified, and a version number.

In contrast, UNIX and DOS/Windows files are flat; that is, all their data is contained in one logically contiguous segment. If the Mac's various forks aren't handled properly, the file can become unreadable on other platforms. The customary solution is to use a utility that translates automatically to the target destination's preferred format. The Fetch ftp client for the Mac is available from Dartmouth University at:

```
ftp://ftp.dartmouth.edu/pub/software/mac/
```

Fetch is very good at this kind of translation. When you send a Mac file to a UNIX or DOS/Windows host, use Fetch's raw or binary transfer mode to ensure that superfluous file forks aren't preserved during the transfer. Fetch is illustrated in Figure 8-2.

For the files you'll be dealing with—HTML, .GIF, JPEG, and Shockwave files—all the content is in the data fork and thus will be transferred properly even when the other forks are removed.

Transfers in the other direction—from UNIX or PC to Mac—aren't problematic, because the Mac can handle flat data files as easily as it handles files with multiple forks.

Windows and Mac users who regularly ferry files between their platforms might consider two reasonably priced, industry-leading products from DataViz. Conversions Plus, a Windows product, not only faithfully translates a remarkable range of file formats between PC and Mac within an easy-to-use interface, it also reads from and writes to Mac disks while automatically handling Mac forks. MacLink provides comparable services for Macintosh users.

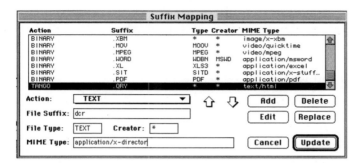

Figure 8-2: This is Fetch's filetype selection dialog box. Text translation is turned on, and only the data fork of binary files is sent.

Permissions

The files uploaded to a Web server must be assigned specific privileges for reading and writing. So your audience can see them, they must be accessible to every user on the system through read privileges. However, you don't want accidents, so write privileges must be assigned more precisely. A file's creator always has permission to edit or delete it; but in a typical scenario, this isn't adequate. Most sites, especially commercial ones, are created by teams of individuals, so the entire group needs the ability to create, edit, and delete files on their Web site.

Fortunately, any Web server platform is versatile enough to accommodate the permissions you need. If you're posting to a UNIX server, for example, you can directly modify your files to allow owner and write access for your group, and read access for everybody else. The UNIX *chmod* and *chgrp* commands make such changes. Let's assume your user name is *biffo*, your publishing group name is *publish*, and you uploaded a file named shock.dcr. Here's how you set appropriate permissions:

```
chgrp publish shock.dcr
chmod 664 shock.dcr
```

The resulting file's long listing should then look like this:

```
-rw-rw-r—   1 biffo      publish     17917 Jan  8 05:31 shock.dcr
```

Because *biffo* initially created the file, he or she already owns it. Therefore, all that was required (through the two commands that you just used) was to use *chgrp* to properly set the group permissions, then to use *chmod* with the argument *664* to set the permissions to:

- owner: read and write (6)
- group: read and write (6)
- all others: read only (4)

All other server platforms allow a similar set of permissions, though the method for setting them may differ. In some instances, you may have to ask the system administrator to set them for you. If possible, configure the site's home directory and your users so that each new file inherits the permissions and ownership that you desire.

If you have subdirectories in your main Web site directory, they must also have their permissions set properly. In the case of a directory or folder, all three categories of users, (that is, owner, group, and other), must be able to traverse the directory in addition to whatever other privileges they have. This means that they are able to travel into or through the directory while attempting to access files. For UNIX, this is referred to as *execute* permission, though of course it's only meant in its metaphorical sense when applied to such executable files as programs or scripts. On the Macintosh, the analogous permission level is See Folders and Files.

For our preceding example, the appropriate argument to pass to *chmod* on the UNIX platform is *775*, as in:

```
chmod 775 mydirectory
```

This adds the ability to traverse the directory to any privileges each type of user already enjoys.

With proper management, it is easy to ensure that your files and directories are accessible to the Web user community at large. Understanding your server and its operating system is the key. With it, the principles we have discussed can be applied.

Summary

In this chapter, we looked at the factors involved in placing your Shockwave project onto the World Wide Web. We examined the key ingredients—server hardware, server software, and a connection to the Internet—and discussed some of the factors that will decide your particular needs and solution.

This subject could easily fill a book by itself, so we attempted throughout to speak to the principles involved to help you understand the decisions you must make and the actions you must take. With a firm understanding of the underpinnings of what lies before you, you should be able to apply these principles to find specific solutions for your particular needs.

We also touched on the topic of posting your files to the server, and the issues and gotchas that sometimes lie in wait. Here again, we covered specific examples and discussed how to apply general principles to any of the multitude of different hardware-software combinations you will find on the Web.

With your content finally resident on your server, you now have a fully functional Shockwave Web site. Or do you? In the next chapter, we discuss some of the ways to make certain that your site works as expected, and how to keep it working.

CHAPTER 9

Testing Shockwave Sites; The Future of Shockwave

*t*his chapter comprises two topics. In the first part of the chapter, we discuss general concerns that should be considered when creating or posting a Shockwave movie. In addition, we cover steps you can pursue to test your own Shockwave site. We also review troubleshooting steps you should follow to pinpoint any problems that occur and provide tips on how to resolve them. Thereafter, in the second part of this chapter we examine the coming evolution of Director as we see it and as it's viewed by some multimedia industry luminaries.

Stop, Look, and Listen

Testing Shockwave sites may involve as much effort before you post a movie as after you've placed it on your server. For this reason, we cover some of the basic concerns that you should address before posting a Shockwave movie.

In general, your goal is to identify those items that could most seriously affect your content's performance, effectiveness, and cross-platform compatibility. This will be helpful as you build and test your Shockwave movies. We begin by examining a few of the issues that you should think about and test before you send your Shockwave projects into the cold, cruel world.

When Posting a Shockwave Movie . . .

Some general testing concerns that may arise when you post Shockwave content to the Internet are simple and stylistic. Other issues that can crop up, however, may be subtle and can come back to haunt you if you overlook them during the authoring stage. Some of the concerns we discuss here are related to Shockwave content's Director origins, while others are more specific to the Internet and its often-demanding bandwidth limitations.

After you peruse the following topics, all of which are related to delivering Shockwave content over the Internet, you should be able to formulate your own checklist of items to examine and test. Testing is a crucial component of any well-designed Web site, especially when you're dealing with a potential audience of hundreds, thousands, or millions of viewers. Try to make sure you address all of these concerns when creating your Shockwave movies, but don't overlook them during the testing process, either.

System Configuration Concerns

Your first concern should be the typical system configuration of your anticipated audience. While there is no way for you to accurately guess the configuration of every computer that may hit your site, making some assumptions can better your odds of success. If you plan your project for the lowest common denominator, you'll be far less likely to disappoint your visitors. Because average users use average computers, try asking the following questions to judge your project before you send it onto the perilous waters of the Internet.

1. *How much RAM has the average user that I'm trying to reach installed?*

    Sixteen megabytes is the greatest amount of RAM for which you should design; it's far more realistic to aim at 8MB, the typical RAM for which most off-the-shelf multimedia systems are configured today. *Never* assume anyone has more than 20MB. RAM is precious and expensive; after shelling out a few thousand dollars for a CPU, it's difficult for the average consumer to shell out half that amount (or more) for RAM. Always keep RAM at the top of your list of concerns, because it has the highest potential to disrupt users when they view your Shockwave movies.

RAM, or more specifically the way a particular system allocates RAM, should be a prime concern during the creation and testing of your Shockwave movies. Make sure that, when testing your movies, you try a variety of CPU and RAM configurations. This is especially important if a Web page contains multiple movies. Remember, each movie takes up a certain amount of the memory available to the browser. If testers or users report that they're unable to view all of the movies on your page, memory is the most likely culprit. If that happens to you, decrease the number of multimedia elements on your pages and, if possible, their sizes.

2. *What color depths will the computers used to view my site support?*

Be careful here! Those cool effects you put on your logo might actually look bad if you're thinking thousands or millions of colors and your user has only 256. Color mismatches have the second highest potential for making a visit to your Shockwave site less than satisfactory. All of us love those great digital images that can be created when you view them at thousands of colors, but what happens when you see the same image with only 256 colors?

Most of the time, an image at only 256 colors will only appear grainy, but backlit letters and other lighting effects can look rather rough. Figures 9-1 and 9-2 show a PICT of the same graphic as seen at the Macintosh "thousands" of colors setting (actually, it's 65,535 colors) and at 256 colors. This is a dramatic example, but gives a good feel for the kinds of effects color and color palettes can have on the users who are viewing your content.

Always try to view your art at 256 colors before you import it into Director and create your Shockwave project. This lets you experience what the majority of people who visit your site will probably see.

3. *How fast is the average user's computer?*

Your development machines are probably Pentiums or PowerPC 601s running at 75 MHz or faster. Unfortunately, developers are usually better equipped than those who cruise the Internet looking for cool new technologies such as Shockwave.

Figure 9-1: This is a welcome graphic at the Macintosh "thousands" of colors setting (that is, 65,535 colors).

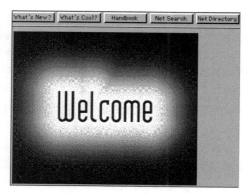

Figure 9-2: This is the same welcome graphic at 256 colors.

The average user may only be running at 60 MHz or slower. Keep this in mind when creating your Shockwave projects. Users may not fully utilize your offerings if they feel that operations in your Shockwave movie are taking too long. Try beta testing your projects on various CPUs with different speeds. This can save you a lot of trouble when your Shockwave project is shown to the masses.

We tested a Shockwave document to experience the differences between CPUs. We used two CPUs, the first a PowerPC 601 at 110 MHz, the second also a 601 but at 60 MHz. When we downloaded the same movie on to these two CPUs, we saw skips or lags in the movie on the slower CPU but not on the faster CPU. Because of processor-intensive activities that can occur while the movie is playing, a faster CPU is far less subject to such hesitations than a slower one.

Obviously, a faster CPU handles these operations at a higher rate of speed. This doesn't mean that a fast CPU with a fast connection to the Internet will have no problems. It's simply an example of how much more a slower CPU can magnify perceptual problems. While this isn't always a big issue, it can be.

4. *How fast is your average user's connection when viewing your Shockwave movies?*

   Count on your users having a slower connection to the Net than you do. Although you'd like to think that 28.8 Kbps or ISDN is in every home, all of us know in our hearts that most people we're trying to reach will probably be using a 14.4 Kbps modem—or slower. This is one of the most important things to consider when creating, reviewing, or posting a Shockwave movie. We touch on this issue later in the chapter, but remember that most people simply won't wait for larger movies to download. Always try to judge the size of your movie harshly, and the time it takes to arrive across a 14.4 Kbps connection.

Table 9-1 shows some benchmarks for download times for various filesizes. These are real-life examples, and though actual times can fluctuate in a real-world situation, they provide a good comparison guide. Three reference sizes are used: a 30K file, a 200K file, and finally a 1MB file. The range of times is meant to compensate for various levels of network activity. Remember, however, that network traffic is only one factor that affects download times.

The times in Table 9-1 were measured during several real-world trials. Notice the entry for downloading a 1MB movie file over a 14.4 Kbps connection. Twenty minutes is much too long to expect anyone to wait to see your page. Though this chart speaks of a single file of that size, if you link enough large media files to a page, your users can experience the same total download delay.

You should address some of the general concerns before, during, and after creating your Shockwave movies. Remember to imagine yourself at opposite ends of the scales of computing and connection power, speed, and memory. It's far too easy to create wonderful content for

Shockwave, post it on your server, view it from your CPU, and then gasp in horror at the time it takes to download via a friend's blazingly slow 14.4 Kbps connection.

Table 9-1: These relative download times are representative for various filesizes

Download times for a 30K file:

Connection speed	Download time
9.6 Kbps	23–45 seconds
14.4 Kbps	15–30 seconds
28.8 Kbps	5–15 seconds
56.0 Kbps	5–10 seconds

Download times for a 200K file:

Connection speed	Download time
9.6 Kbps	3–6 minutes
14.4 Kbps	2–4 minutes
28.8 Kbps	1–2 minutes
56.0 Kbps	30 seconds to 2 minutes

Download times for a 1MB (1024K) file:

Connection speed	Download time
9.6 Kbps	12–30 minutes
14.4 Kbps	8–20 minutes
28.8 Kbps	3–10 minutes
56.0 Kbps	2–5 minutes

Cross-Platform Concerns

Don't forget to check your Shockwave's cross-platform capabilities too. In the holy wars among computing platforms, it's quite common for developers to be unconcerned that their content doesn't work on the "other platform." This not only harms the developer, but also the computing industry as a whole.

Shockwave is a great technology that takes enormous advantage of the Internet and its ability to deliver content across many platforms. If you create content with limited compatibility and post it where millions can access it, you alienate a large portion of your potential market. With that in mind, it makes a lot of sense to consider a few of the potential compatibility issues during your design and testing phases.

Color Palettes

Color palettes can cause almost as much trouble for people viewing your site as insufficient bit depth. Color palettes are easy to overlook when creating movies in Director for multiple platforms. The problem can crop up when, for example, content is created on a Macintosh with a special color palette and someone on a Windows machine views it. The results are at best inconsistent, and at worst a total disaster.

Here is some easy advice to consider when approaching this problem: Use standard color palettes; if you must use a custom palette in a project, make sure it's imported into the cast before you save the project. This is usually automatically done when you import a graphic into Director that requires a custom color palette. In this situation, Director asks if you would like to install the custom palette into your cast. Installing that palette helps when creating the final version of your movie and the resulting Shockwave file that you post to the Internet.

When in doubt, however, early reports from Shockwave developers suggest that the Windows palette fares best in cross-platform use. This is because Macintoshes can adjust to a strange color palette more gracefully than Windows machines. Think of this phenomenon as an extension of the lowest common denominator effect, if you like.

Sound

Making sound work properly in cross-platform circumstances can be difficult if you don't watch closely. One of the most common mistakes occurs when Macintosh developers use System 7 sounds. Although the Macintosh can use multiple formats for sound playback, most Windows environments are more limited. Audio data should always be imported into Director as AIFF files. These files are cross-platform and can be imported into the cast of your Director movie, then controlled with Lingo. AIFF files provide good sound reproduction on most major platforms.

As we stated in Chapter 6, keep your sample rate at 22.050 KHz whenever possible. Lower rates result in signal degradation on Windows machines and, to a lesser degree, on Macs.

Lingo

Lingo is an excellent scripting language, but it can be a double-edged sword without proper cross-platform testing. Be aware that not all of Lingo is cross-platform. Many developers use undocumented Lingo, or

Lingo that has been developed for XObjects. These types of Lingo are often platform specific.

All of the Lingo mentioned in this book, however, can be used on either platform. If you use Lingo and want to know if it's usable across multiple platforms, consult the following sources of information:

- *Macromedia Lingo Dictionary*
- Macromedia's fax-on-demand system
- Macromedia's technical support line

In general, you shouldn't run into many problems with Lingo and cross-platform compatibility. However, test on both platforms before you show your work to the world.

You would be well advised not to try to incorporate platform-specific features into your Shockwave movies. This only frustrates users who view your site with another type of computer. If the user doesn't receive the full benefit of your movie, the parts they do see may not be enough to communicate your ideas.

Bandwidth Concerns

The most critical aspect to consider as a Shockwave developer is one that we repeatedly touch upon in this book—bandwidth. Bandwidth should head your list of considerations when creating a Shockwave movie. The speed of the Internet and network speeds in general are ever increasing, but unfortunately most people still connect at lower speeds.

Some estimates show the speed of networking and Internet access doubling every two years. At this rate, the average user will have an ISP-grade connection in just a few short years. To get an idea of the transfer rates you can expect from this kind of bandwidth in the future, consult Table 9-2, which shows sample filesizes and download times for a full T1 connection.

Table 9-2: These are typical download times for various filesizes with a 1.5 Mbps connection

File size	Download time
30K	less than 1 second
200K	1–2 seconds
1000K	4–7 seconds
2000K	9–14 seconds

As you can see from Table 9-2, a 1.5 Mbps connection to the Internet permits you to deliver much larger files. If you compare these figures to Table 9-1, you see that with this kind of connection you can download a file of 2MB in about the same time as a user with a 14.4 Kbps connection can download a 30K file. With faster speeds not too far off, it's a good idea to plan your long-term development path with bigger bandwidth in mind. For the immediate future, however, it's wise to plan your connections around 14.4 to 28.8 Kbps.

Keeping all of these considerations in mind while creating your content may somewhat slow overall production. However, this is time well spent because a happy user base is a loyal one, and loyalty is an essential ingredient to the success of your site.

Testing Your Content Online

We have already mentioned the kind of testing you should perform while developing your content. After you've finished the development cycle and have posted your content to the Internet, a whole new phase of testing begins. This phase must concentrate on verifying that the pages and media on your site load properly, link properly, and remain viable over the life of the site.

Page Rendering

Under the heading of loading properly, you want to concentrate on two main subcategories. The first and most obvious of these is to test whether the page and all of its linked inline data load completely into a browser's window.

You generally will run into only a few difficulties here. If your page isn't where you told the server it was, you'll get a *403 Not Found* error message or its equivalent. This may mean that you have a path or filename misspelled or improperly capitalized. Remember that UNIX servers are case sensitive, which can require an adjustment for Mac and Windows users. A *403* error may also be returned if the file's ownership or permissions aren't properly set.

If a browser finds the page, you can verify that all your HTML formatting works as expected. Because you have stared at these pages a thousand times during development, you probably won't find any errors. Errors in uploading or in text translation—remember the carriage return and linefeed issues from Chapter 7—have been known to introduce unexpected behavior.

The most likely problems you'll encounter when you first load your pages from the Web server will be related to your inline media. If you manage to load all your pages without a single broken or missing image icon appearing, our hats are off to you! Managing all of your content and creating files that tie them together error free can be a devilishly difficult achievement.

Incorrect paths, improper capitalization, and bad file formats can cause these dreaded image icons to appear. The best troubleshooting technique we know is to verify the URL to the piece of media on the server, then load it directly into the browser by opening its URL manually (that is, by typing it into the Open dialog box).

If the media loads, you have verified the path and the media's integrity. Then, you can assume that the path in the original HTML file is at fault. If you get a broken image icon again, make sure the file format is a correct one for the Internet. With the media's URL and format verified, you can return to the HTML source and verify that it has the right URL as well. It's simply a matter of applying the process of elimination to all the possibilities until the culprit is found!

The preceding discussion applies equally to Shockwave content as well as to inline .gifs and JPEGs. If a movie can't be found, the EMBED frame is drawn with a broken plug-in icon in its center. You may also get a dialog box stating that the plug-in for the content's MIME type cannot be found. (At least that was the behavior with the Macintosh Netscape 2.0b5.) By the time you read this, that behavior may have changed. In any case, you want to verify all inline Shockwave Director movies just as you would any static graphics.

To return to testing that a page loads properly, the second aspect to test is a page's overall appearance on multiple client platforms. You should have been looking at your page on as many machines as you could during the development cycle, but now that it's on the Internet, you can test with greater ease.

Because your site is accessible to the entire globe, finding a wide variety of machines with Internet access should be easy. You can look at how it loads across a variety of different link speeds, bit depths, resolutions, platforms, operating systems, and client browsers. While you cannot absolutely ensure that it properly renders on all of the possible client permutations and combinations, testing in this way can help you widen the base of users for whom the pages look okay, if not exactly as they should.

This phase of testing can include testing whatever masking of Shockwave content you did for nonplug-in browsers, as well as any layout and formatting. Expect Netscape's proprietary elements to look strange on browsers that do not adhere to Netscape's tag standards.

In general, expect your pages to look pretty strange on anything but the platform or two for which you developed. It's an unfortunate fact of life that Internet users suffer from a lack of standardization today, and this all too often makes all of the various parts of the Web uncooperative with each other. However, seeing the issues for yourself can help you make changes that widen your potential audience.

If there are enough problems and you still have enough desire to reach the maximum number of people, consider making a generic HTML 2.0 version of your pages, minus any fancy layout or exotic *content-types*. That way, you'll reach the broadest possible audience. This is a great technique for welcome pages, even for Shockwave-intensive sites.

Follow That Link!

In the course of testing, you probably have followed many of the links on your site. More formal testing is required, however, and this testing must be sustained to keep your site working over the weeks, months, and years of its existence.

Intrasite links are probably the least likely to break, because you have control over where your files are located and will remember to update links whenever pages and content are moved. You *will* remember to make those changes, right?

Good! Links that lead to pages elsewhere on the Web must be tested on a regular basis. Content on the World Wide Web is so transient that new problems regularly crop up. If you link to other sites of interest or other resources for your users, test these links weekly. Better yet, find a robot that you can schedule to test them for you. (It won't forget or call in sick—ever!)

Monitoring e-mail sent to a site is also an excellent way to keep tabs on the shape of your pages. Users often find things you overlook simply because they're looking at your site with fresh eyes. Designate one or more people to be keepers of the *www@your.server* e-mail address and get them to regularly report on the types of messages your site receives.

If you want more structured feedback than freeform e-mail messages, consider creating a user survey for visitors to your site. You can structure it to get answers to specific questions or areas of concern. Make sure to keep the survey short so that people will want to complete it. Also, leave a large TEXTAREA for comments so users feel that they can comment the same way they could by sending an e-mail message.

Maintenance

Maintaining and sustaining your site can simply mean repeating the tests you've been discussing on a periodic basis, perhaps monthly. It's important that you plan for this level of continuing support as a bare minimum. Too often, sites decay. After a couple of months, they show all of the signs of having been posted and forgotten. It seems strange to speak about a collection of digital data in organic terms; but in truth, the average Web site is such a complex collection of text, graphics, sounds, movies, and links that entropy acts as strongly upon it as on any living system.

Even if you post your data to your own server and never touch it again, links to the outside world will likely degrade. Ultimately, all of them will be broken and out of date. More likely, your site will be one of many on a server and things on the server will frequently change, requiring your pages to change too. Changes in the server's configuration or the availability of CGIs, for example, could necessitate repairs. In the end, the specific event that requires maintenance cannot be anticipated, which is exactly why ongoing, routine support is so necessary.

Shockwave's Future

Now that your "shocked" Web site is up and running, you may have some time to sit back and wonder what you're going to do next with this technology. Adding true multimedia, with integrated inline animation and sound, entirely changes the way one experiences the World Wide Web.

Personally, we don't think we'll ever look at a Web page the same way again now that we've witnessed the early development efforts that incorporate Shockwave. As the technology matures and the Internet community continues to embrace and adopt it, we're sure it will play an increasing role in how users perceive the Net.

Sound

The most obvious area for improvement of Shockwave technology is its handling of audio data. When an audio-specific codec is developed, we hope to see more efficient compression of high-quality sounds. Sound woven into a Web page has a tremendous impact, and we'd like to see that power available at a lower download cost.

Macromedia has announced that Shockwave movies will soon support RealAudio connections using Lingo. This means that you'll be able to incorporate voice-quality audio into movies that play off a server rather than downloading sound to the client's machine before playback. This should bolster Shockwave's role in providing a customized interface for other Web data.

Instead of presenting users with a standard RealAudio plug-in interface, you can embed RealAudio connections into buttons or other Shockwave elements to enliven and explicate your content. In short, you'll control the audio as an integral part of your project.

Video

At the time of this writing, Shockwave's video capabilities are almost nil. It fails to support linked media in any form. This means that, to include QuickTime in your project, you must split the frames as we described in Chapter 6, "Shockwave Tips & Tricks."

By the time you read this, we hope that Macromedia will have made public announcements about when this may change. A good first step would be to allow embedding of QuickTime movies and of other media within Shockwave movies, perhaps to be passed off to another, appropriate plug-in for playback. This would still put an enormous strain on client download times, but it would be better than the current situation.

The ultimate goal with video should be to provide the same ability as RealAudio to stream content across the Internet. This would indeed be a welcome addition to Shockwave's video capabilities and would bring the dream of interactive television a big step closer to reality. Instead, if a Shockwave project could simply point at a URL for a movie and play it over the Net, the size of the base project need not be a barrier to the total content you offer. Rather, a small, initial Director movie could act as a gateway to an immense amount of content on various servers worldwide.

Linked Media

Another form of linking that is currently missing from Shockwave is the ability to include XObjects with a file. As external, compiled extensions to Director's capabilities, XObjects offer significant customization and differentiation among movie files. If Shockwave supported XObjects, developers could use XObjects to support nonstandard media types that would usually require an additional plug-in or system extension on the playing machine. At present, the difficulty is to guarantee security so a developer can create an XObject with the ability to manipulate the local file space.

Our latest visit to the Macromedia Developer support pages found the news that linked XObjects will be supported by the 1.0 release of Shockwave. Apparently, Macromedia plans to address some of the security issues by requiring that users place the XObject in the plug-in's Xtras folder themselves rather than embedding it in a movie file. This will be a good first step, but the real excitement will come when XObjects can be embedded, thereby allowing developers to extend functionality without requiring users to download new widgets to enable such functionality.

New Lingo

Director's development as an authoring platform has been paralleled by a constant stream of new Lingo functions and features. The upcoming release of Director 5.0 will include more than 100 new commands. We expect to see this progress matched in Shockwave projects as new commands are ported to the Internet context or created specifically for the new Shockwave technology.

Possible directions for these commands could include increased manipulation and interaction with other Web-borne content and integration with the CGI specification. This would enable Lingo to control the entire viewing environment and deliver enhanced interactivity.

Future Applications

If you are like us, seeing Shockwave in action spurs all kinds of creative thinking about its applications. Multimedia was defined by the things people did with it, and we expect a lot of additional crossover from existing platforms to the Internet. Specifically, we expect to see much, if not all, of the functionality now present in CD-ROM-based multimedia to be included in future releases of Shockwave. This will enable any of CD-ROM's myriad uses to be adopted and adapted by Internet multimedia.

Naturally, games are the first things that spring to many people's minds here. The inherent multiuser nature of the Internet has already made inroads into CD-ROM games that include the ability to link to other people's computers via the Net to play not just against the computer, but also against each other. If the game were in part or wholly based on Internet servers, this capability would only expand and mature. We also expect the rapid deployment of hybrid CD-ROM games in which larger content elements are distributed to individuals on CD-ROMs and interactive content is made accessible over the Internet. The two will link to create a homogeneous whole, with media-rich content loaded and displayed from the local CD-ROM in response to the interaction with Web-borne components.

Training and education are other areas that Shockwave technology has the potential to revolutionize. When we looked at Apple's proof-of-concept interactive training site in Chapter 7, "Integrating Shockwave with HTML," we were excited by what we saw. By providing the interactivity, feedback, and self-pacing previously supplied by HyperCard stacks or stand-alone help systems, slow and costly distribution can be replaced by an Internet-based alternative. As a distribution system, the Internet's essential qualities are nongeographical and one-to-many. That is, one server can provide content to a very large number of users located globally.

We expect the biggest short-term changes that Shockwave will enable are in the user interface area. With the torrent of commercial Web sites that are springing up, the demand for visual and experiential differentiation is becoming overwhelming. HTML is limited in this regard, with only a narrow range of possible layouts, formats, and behaviors. With Shockwave, these limits are virtually blown to bits. Already, a huge pool of seasoned Director developers can deliver an almost unlimited range of looks and feels to their projects. We expect to see virtually every commercial site on the Web "shocked" in the next 12 to 18 months. If you are among those developers capable of delivering effective, efficient, quality Shockwave content, prepare to be busy!

Keeping abreast of developments remains a day-in, day-out task. Staying on the wave, as it were, will be the key to staying busy. Developers who allow their knowledge to lapse will soon find their business going elsewhere. To help you stay current on the state of the technology, we have compiled the following collection of links, which also is included on the CD-ROM accompanying this book.

Shockwave Links

The home of Shockwave on the Macromedia Web site:

```
http://www.macromedia.com/Tools/Shockwave/index.html
```

contains the latest news from the company that created this technology. Check it out regularly for additions and changes. This URL also points to the Shockwave FAQ and a Shockwave discussion group. The latter is a lively forum for debate on the finer points of plug-in and content development.

Macromedia's QuickMarks page, a collection of sites that Macromedia considers hot spots for multimedia development, is located at:

```
http://www.macromedia.com/Guide/quickmarks.info.html
```

Please also visit the Shockwave developer's home page, which contains the Developer's Guide, and links to Afterburner and the plug-ins. Check out the Movie Lab page; it provides good illustrations of the techniques recommended by the Shockwave product development team. This page also has a link to the Made with Macromedia and the Shockwave for Director graphics that you may want to use on your site.

```
http://www.macromedia.com/Tools/Shockwave/sdc/Dev/index2.htm
```

Also on the Macromedia Web site, you find that the Multimedia & Digital Arts galleries have collections of early technology adopters. Check out the competition!

```
http://www.macromedia.com/Gallery/index.html
```

A growing number of independent Shockwave link pages can be found "out there" too. Two of our favorites are:

```
http://silver.nbnet.nb.ca:8080/
http://www.teleport.com/~arcana/shockwave/
```

The former is maintained by Gary Mason, the latter by MediaFlux. Both represent good, independent samplings of what's new and hot in the world of Shockwave.

Summary

Throughout this book, our intention has been to give you a comprehensive survey of all aspects of creating a Shockwave Web site. Besides introducing the technology itself, we attempted to dig a bit deeper and to explain the how and why behind those things that Shockwave does. In addition, we attempted to provide techniques you can use in your own Shockwave projects to give your content more impact on the Internet.

For those of you who are already familiar with Director and multimedia content, we included a great deal of information regarding the creation of a Web site, including selection of your connection, the necessary hardware and software, uploading of your data, integration of movies into HTML documents, and the testing and maintaining of your Web offerings.

At this point, with the tutorials and sample project behind you, you are ready to forge down the path to becoming a Shockwave developer. We wish you the best results from your adventures with this outstanding technology!

Shockwave URLs

*t*his Appendix contains all of the URLs found in the body of this book, in their order of first appearance. You'll also find these URLs on the CD-ROM, in the subdirectory named HTML, which also contains all of the Web documents associated with the book.

Macromedia's Web site:

```
http://www.macromedia.com
```

A discussion thread about Shockwave technology on Macromedia's Web site:

```
http://www.macromedia.com//Local/Bin/Threads/index.html
```

Our favorite WWW search engines:

```
http://www.yahoo.com
http://www.excite.com
http://www.lycos.com
http://www.webcrawler.com
http://www.opentext.com
http://www.infoseek.com
```

The *60 Minute Guide to Shockwave* Web site:

```
http://www2.outer.net/shock60/
```

A list of Shockwave examples:

http://www2.outer.net/shock60/examples.htm

An example of an animated film loop:

http://www3.outer.net/shock60/examples.htm

Ghost ink examples:

http://www3.outer.net/shock60/examples.htm

The Macromedia movie listing:

http://www.macromedia.com/Tools/Shockwave/sdc/Dev/Moviedocs/corpsite.htm

The Shockhead movie's URL:

http://www.macromedia.com/Tools/Shockwave/sdc/Dev/Moviedocs/shckhead.htm

For information on tables and their associated options, consult the Netscape documentation at:

http://home.netscape.com/assist/net_sites/tables.html

Statistics that describe the distribution of browsers on the Net today:

http://emporium.turnpike.net/J/jc/public_html/stats.html

DreamLight Multimedia's Web page showing an interesting pumpkin graphic:

http://www.dreamlight.com/dreamlt/gallery/pumpkin.htm

Information on leasing a server:

http://union.ncsa.uiuc.edu/HyperNews/get/www/leasing.html

Three providers that offer to locate others' servers on their backbones:

http://www.outer.net/prodserv.html
http://www.internex.net/
http://www.forest.net/

A server comparison chart:

http://www.proper.com/www/servers-chart.html

The Fetch ftp client for the Mac from Dartmouth University:

ftp://ftp.dartmouth.edu/pub/software/mac/

The home of Shockwave on the Macromedia Web site:

```
http://www.macromedia.com/Tools/Shockwave/index.html
```

Macromedia's QuickMarks home page:

```
http://www.macromedia.com/Guide/quickmarks.info.html
```

The Shockwave developers' home page:

```
http://www.macromedia.com/Tools/Shockwave/sdc/Dev/index2.htm
```

Multimedia & Digital Arts galleries:

```
http://www.macromedia.com/Gallery/index.html
```

Two of our favorite independent Shockwave link pages:

```
http://silver.nbnet.nb.ca:8080/
http://www.teleport.com/~arcana/shockwave/
```

Glossary

.dcr The common file extension for an Afterburner-compressed version of a Director file, ready for delivery over the Internet.

.dir The common file extension for a Director film strip or project file, which can be reopened and edited at will.

.dxr An experimental version of the Afterburner compression format for Director files used during the Shockwave beta testing phase. (This format is no longer supported in the current versions of Afterburner and the Shockwave plug-in.)

.gif (Graphics Interchange Format) A compressed graphics file format patented by Unisys and widely used in HTML documents for inline graphical elements.

.htaccess A so-called UNIX "dot file" used to control access to portions of a directory tree through the Internet. In conjunction with the Web, an .htaccess file may be used to establish recognized passwords and account names for access to a specific Web server.

.pcx A common PC bitmap graphics file format that supports only 256 colors. .pcx originated with the ZSoft PaintBrush application that Microsoft licensed and gave away with early versions of Windows (through 3.x).

.png (Portable Network Graphics) A worthy successor to the .gif format, .png is an efficient, compressed, bitmap graphics file format that supports up to 64 bits per pixel. It is most often used for 8- and 24-bit graphics. It's also unencumbered by any patent disputes and supports desirable characteristics such as graphics transparency and interlacing.

.tar An abbreviation for tape archival, tar is the eponymous UNIX compression command that creates .tar format files. *Untar* is the operation of decompressing a tarred file, even though you use the command, *tar -xvf junk.tar,* to decompress a file named junk.tar.

.Z A format designator associated with the UNIX *compress* program. Use the UNIX *uncompress* program to decompress .Z format files.

adaptive sampling A technique for representing graphics that change their information density (a.k.a. sampling rate) to match the level of detail in an image using higher sampling rates to capture high levels of detail, and so on.

Afterburner Macromedia's compression utility used to reduce the size of Director film strips and projects for delivery across the Internet.

algorithm A step-by-step, programmatic recipe for producing a certain set of results in a computer program.

alias A computer system name that points at another name instead of an underlying object. Most Web URLs are either wholly or partly aliases to protect the underlying file system on the Web server at which they point.

alpha A way of rating the completion status of a piece of software, alpha indicates that it's still in internal test and has not yet been released outside its development organization (except under special circumstances, such as for this book).

anchor An HTML term for the destination end of a link; it sometimes is used as a synonym for hypertext links of all kinds.

animation The use of computer graphics to prepare moving sequences of images; or, any graphic method in which the illusion of motion is created by rapid viewing of individual frames in sequence (at least 16 frames per second, usually 30).

ANSI (American National Standards Institute) One of the primary standards-setting bodies for computer technology in the United States.

API (Application Programming Interface) Usually, a set of interface subroutines or library calls that define the methods for programs to access external services (that is, to access somebody else's system or program).

application independent A format or facility is said to be application independent when it works in multiple environments and doesn't depend on a specific application to understand or use its contents.

arc of development The process of carrying a project from its initial design and analysis stages through implementation to completion and ongoing maintenance.

archie A program that catalogs files on more than a thousand *anonymous ftp* servers worldwide and lets users search this database using interactive queries, e-mail, or other programs such as *gopher* or a Web browser.

architecture The design of a software or hardware system as a connected set of logical building blocks with sufficient detail to allow each block to be completely designed and implemented, and to allow blocks that interact to successfully communicate with each other.

ASCII (American Standard Code for Information Interchange) A standard encoding for text and control characters in binary format that is widely used on most computers.

asynchronous Literally, "not at the same time," the term refers to computer communications in which sender and receiver do not communicate directly with each other, rather through accessing a common pick-up/drop-off point for information.

attribute In most object-oriented programming languages, including VRML, an attribute is a named component of an object or term with specific value typing, element definitions, requirements, and default status.

audience In general, the target group at whom a specific communication is aimed; for Director projects, the user community for whom a specific project has been created and tailored.

authentication A method for identifying a user prior to granting permission to access, change, or delete a system or network resource. Authentication usually depends on a password or some other method of proving that User A is really User A.

authoring tool or **authoring system** Software that generates formal code or movies (such as Lingo or film strips) based on how an author manipulates the tool's or system's interface.

Authorware Macromedia's simplified multimedia authoring toolset, intended as an entry-level tool to lead novice developers to Director.

back end Computer science jargon for a service that runs on a machine elsewhere on the network, usually driven by an interface or query facility from another machine elsewhere on the network (the *front end*).

background The base viewing area on Director's stage upon which other cast members are displayed.

batch processing The process of gathering a collection of data together and applying the same set of operations or transformations to each element in the collection, one after the other.

behavior A programmatic way of establishing how an object or node acts within a virtual reality, behavior describes characteristics that determine motion, response, or action when impinged on by actors or other objects.

beta A way of rating the completion status of a piece of software, beta indicates that the software has been released outside its development organization, but only to a hand-picked group of testers who will use it and abuse it to try to catch (and let its developers fix) remaining bugs prior to commercial release.

binary Literally, a file that is formatted as a collection of ones and zeros; in practice, this means that a file is formatted to be intelligible only to a certain application or that it is itself an executable file.

binary executables Files created by compiling (and/or linking) source code modules to create executable files.

bitmap A two-dimensional map of binary digits (*bits*) destined for use in a one-to-one mapping with a display device's pixels.

boot Used in computer-speak as a verb, boot means to start a computer from its turn-off state. As an adjective (for example, boot-time) it refers to the computer while it's in its start-up phase.

bottleneck A point in a computer or a network at which things become congested and slow down.

breakpoints A marked location in a program, usually set with a debugger or an equivalent tool, at which the program halts execution so that the programmer can examine its variables, parameters, settings, and so on.

browser An Internet application that lets users access World Wide Web servers and surf the Internet.

BSDI (Berkeley Software Distribution, Inc.) BSDI remains one of the major flavors of UNIX available today, though it is now distributed by a spin-off business rather than the University of California at Berkeley.

bug Programmer-speak for an error, glitch, gotcha, problem, or unsolved mystery in a computer program.

burn Used as a verb, it refers to applying Afterburner compression to a Director project file; used as an adjective, it describes a file that has been compressed using that technology.

C A programming language developed by two of the founders of UNIX, Brian Kernighan and Dennis Ritchie that is still very much in vogue among UNIX-heads, among others.

C++ A programming language developed by Bjarne Stroustrup, C++ is a successor to the C language. C++ is an object-oriented implementation of C.

caching The process of storing information delivered from a remote source locally so that any reference to that information, after obtained, can complete as quickly as the local system allows.

case sensitive This term means that upper- and lowercase letters are not equivalent (for example, UNIX filenames are case sensitive; *TEXT.TXT* is not the same as *text.txt*).

cast Following Director's theater-based metaphor, the cast is used to store items, or actors, for a multimedia project.

CD-ROM (Compact Disk–Read-Only Memory) A read-only computer medium that looks just like a music compact disk but contains computer data instead of music.

CERN (Centre European Researche Nucleare) The Center for High-Energy Physics in Geneva, Switzerland; the birthplace of the World Wide Web (whose stewardship has now been taken by the World Wide Web Consortium).

CGI (Common Gateway Interface) The parameter passing and invocation technique used to let Web clients pass input to Web servers (and on to specific programs written to the CGI specification).

channel Each cast member and various other aspects of Director's behavior (sound, score script, and so on) are associated with a separate channel in the program. Channels provide an ongoing mechanism to supply instructions and controls over individual multimedia elements over time, keyed to frame numbers and script commands.

chunk size Chunk size determine the granularity of a Director transition; that is, it affects how smoothly or choppily a transition completes its display.

clickable image A graphic in an HTML document that has been associated to a pixel-mapping CGI on the server; users can click on locations of the graphic to retrieve associated URLs and their contents.

client Used as (a) a synonym for Web browser (that is, Web client), or (b) as a requesting, front-end member for a client/server application such as the World Wide Web.

client pull A Netscape method through which a Web client instructs a server to send it a particular set of data (for example, client-initiated data transfer).

client/server A computing paradigm wherein processing is divided between a graphical front-end application running on a user's desktop machine and a back-end server that performs data- or storage-intensive processing tasks in response to client service requests.

close A formal communication term that refers to session tear-down and termination, usually at the end of a networked information transaction.

codec (COmpressor/DECompressor) A special set of algorithms for reducing the size of files for transmission or transport, then decompressing them into their original forms.

color depth The number of bits of information used to represent color values in an image; the higher the number of bits, the greater the number of colors (and shades) that can be represented. Common color depths include 2, 8, 16, 24, and 32 bits.

compiler A software program that reads the source code for a programming language and creates a binary, executable version of that code.

compliant Refers to conformance to some kind of defined standard.

compression The art and science of analyzing the contents of a data collection, and applying statistical and mathematical encoding techniques to that data to reduce it to a smaller but equivalent representation.

compression engine The compression software used to reduce the size of files that it manipulates.

connection A link between two computers for the purpose of some specific communication.

Content-Type The MIME designation for file types to be transported by electronic mail and HTTP.

content The usable information contained in a document. Users surf the Web looking for content.

continuous publishing A method for continuously delivering content over a communication link as an ongoing stream of information (for example, a 24-hour news service could be considered a text-only form of continuous publishing; future technology should support similar capabilities for multimedia).

Control Panel The Director interface for controlling playback and behavior of a project during the creation and editing processes.

data content model SGML-speak for the occurrence notation that describes what other markup is legal within the context of a specific markup element.

DBMS (DataBase Management System) Systematic programs and utilities that define, maintain, and manage access to large collections of data, which may be on-line or otherwise.

delimiter A specially designated text character that indicates a record or field boundary within a text stream rather than part of the actual text or other data itself.

development environment The collection of tools, compilers, debuggers, and source code management resources used as part of the software development process.

development platform The machine and operating system that a programmer uses to build a particular application or project.

Director Macromedia's outstanding multimedia authoring package that is widely regarded as one of the best such tools in the industry today.

directory structure The hierarchical organization of files in a directory tree.

distributed A program or service is said to be distributed when it is capable of operating across a network on multiple computers at the same time with part of its functionality executing on one machine and other parts executing on another machine or machines.

dithering A technique for approximating specific color values by mixing intermediate color values rather than by matching color values exactly.

DNS (Domain Name Service) An Internet service that maps symbolic names to IP addresses by distributing queries among the available pool of DNS servers.

document annotation The process of attaching comments, instructions, or additional information to a document (usually with annotation software).

document root The base of a Web server's document tree, the root defines the scope of all of the documents that Web users may access (that is, access is allowed to the root and all its children, but not to any of the root's peers or parents).

document tree A description of the collection of all of the directories underneath the document root, including all of the documents that each such directory contains.

downsampling Reducing the number of colors or bit depth, or otherwise lowering the amount of (often extraneous) information in a graphics file.

e-mail (electronic mail) A service that lets users exchange messages across a network; the major e-mail technology on the Internet is based on SMTP (Simple Mail Transfer Protocol). Also refers to those messages themselves.

editor A program used to edit a file; editors are available for specific programming languages, markup languages, and text formats.

element A basic unit of text or markup within a descriptive markup language.

element type The kind of value that an element can take (for example, text, number, or tag).

embed The technique used in HTML (through the <EMBED> tag) to include references to dynamic, interactive content such as Shockwave materials in Web documents.

encoding A technique for expressing values according to a particular notation (for example, binary, ASCII, or EBCDIC).

environment variables Like other UNIX programs, CGIs obtain and store their input rather than reading it in every time it's needed. This stored information—in the form of environment variables—is passed to the program by the HTTP server from the submitting client. An environment variable, therefore, is a value passed into a program or script by the runtime environment on the system on which it is running.

error checking The process of examining input data to make sure it is both appropriate (within specified value or scalar ranges) and accurate (correctly reflects the input).

exception handling If a program behaves abnormally, encounters an unexpected input, or detects an anomaly in its operation, it must react to such an event. This process of reacting is called exception handling.

extensibility Extensibility is a measure of how easy it is to write applications that build upon core mechanisms while adding functionality, new methods, or subclasses.

FAQ (Frequently Asked Questions) A list of common questions and answers maintained by most special interest groups on the Internet as a way of responding to basic questions.

field In a database, a field is a named component of a record and its associated values; in an HTML form, a field is a named input widget or text area and its associated value.

file mapping A method of supplying a filename to the outside world that does not reveal the complete internal file structures involved. (See also *alias*.)

film strip The formal name for a Director file saved in a format that can be reopened and edited within the Director application. These files commonly end in a .dir extension.

filtering The process of removing certain objects from a document. For example, removing processing instructions important to a specific scheme not used in a general markup scheme eliminates unintelligible materials.

flat color A way of assigning colors to an image that uses a single shade for each color instead of a complex collection of shades.

font substitution The process of reassigning fonts in a Director display when the fonts in the original version of the project are unavailable on the viewing machine. These reassignments follow regular rules and should be carefully checked in projects aimed at multiple platforms.

fork The Macintosh stores descriptive information about files (especially executable ones) in a series of partitions called forks, particularly a resource fork that contains special system resources and a name fork that contains filename and attribute information. The bulk of a Macintosh file, however, resides in the data fork, which contains the actual information or binary instructions.

frame A single Director scene is called a frame, which controls one set of coordinated acts (associated with a particular frame number) from the score upon the cast.

front end The user interface side of a client/server application, the front end is what users see and with which they interact.

ftp (File Transfer Protocol) An Internet protocol and service that provides network file transfer between any two network nodes for which a user has file access rights (especially a remote host and your local host or desktop machine).

GPL (GNU General Public License) A scheme for the mandatory distribution of source code with software, devised by Richard Stallman of the Free Software Foundation. (GNU tools are incredibly popular with the development community because source code is always available.)

guestbook A specific Web-based application that allows users to identify themselves and their interests, similar to its paper-based equivalent.

GUI (Graphical User Interface) A generic name for any computer interface that uses graphics, windows, and a pointing device such as a mouse or trackball instead of a purely character-mode interface. Windows, MacOS, and X11 are examples of GUI interfaces.

gzip (GNU zip) The program that produces .gz compressed file formats; primarily used in the UNIX world.

helper application An application invoked outside a Web browser to render, display, or play data that the browser cannot directly handle (for example, video or multimedia files).

hierarchical A form of document or file structure, also known as a tree structure, in which all elements except the root have parents, and all elements may or may not have children.

homed site A Web server and its associated Web sites that belong to a particular individual or organization, and that are installed at an ISP's location to partake of the ISP's high-bandwidth Internet connection.

host In Internet-speak, a host is a machine that provides services to users, usually through a unique name and an equivalent network address.

HTML (HyperText Markup Language) The text-based descriptive hypertext markup language derived from SGML and used to describe documents for the WWW.

HTTP (HyperText Transfer Protocol) The TCP/IP-based communications protocol developed for the World Wide Web, HTTP defines how clients and servers communicate.

httpd (HTTP daemon) The daemon, or listener, program on a Web server that listens for and is ready to respond to requests for Web documents or CGI-based services.

hypermedia Any of the methods of computer-based information delivery— including text, graphics, video, animation, and sound—that can be interlinked and treated as a single collection of information.

hypertext A method of organizing text, graphics, and other kinds of data for computer use that lets individual data elements point to one another; a nonlinear method of organizing information, especially text.

image map (also called clickable image, or clickable map) An HTML construct identified by the <ISMAP> tag, an image map is a graphical image that has an associated map file that lets users select links by clicking on certain portions of the image.

import A Director feature (and its associated window) used to bring graphics or other kinds of data into Director for incorporation into a movie or project.

infobahn A Teutonic synonym for the information superhighway, the digital infrastructure of information delivery that's best represented today by the Internet.

interactive television An experimental form of two-way television in which the audience interacts with the content supplier to control the behavior and outcome of the materials viewed.

interactivity The quality of supporting and reacting to input from users, as well as playback of predigested information.

interface The particular subroutines, parameter-passing mechanisms, and data that define the way in which two systems (which may be on the same or different machines) communicate with each other.

international standard In generic terms, an international standard is one that is honored by more than one country; in practice, this term usually refers to a standard controlled or honored by the International Standards Organization (ISO).

Internet The worldwide, TCP/IP-based, networked computing community with millions of users that links together government, business, research, industry, education, and individuals.

interpreter A software program that reads source code from a programming language every time the source code is run to interpret and execute the instructions it contains. (See also *compiler*.)

intranet An internal, TCP/IP-based network used within an organization that is based around the same services as the Internet (but not necessarily accessible to or through the Internet).

IP (Internet Protocol) The primary network layer protocol for the TCP/IP protocol suite, IP is probably the most widely used network protocol in the world today.

ISDN (Integrated Services Digital Network) A completely digital communication service delivered over the telephone network for higher-speed voice and data communications. ISDN is anywhere from 2.5 to 20 times faster than a modem.

ISP (Internet Service Provider) Any organization that provides Internet access to a consumer, usually for a fee.

Java Sun Microsystems' object-oriented programming language and environment, defined by the company as "a simple, object-oriented, distributed, interpreted, robust, secure, architecture-neutral, portable, high-performance, multithreaded, and dynamic language."

jpeg (also JPEG, Joint Photographic Experts Group) A highly compressible graphics format designed to handle computer images of high-resolution photographs as efficiently as possible.

keyword An essential or definitive term used for indexing data and for later search and retrieval. In programming languages, this term is sometimes used to describe a word that is part of the language itself. (See also *reserved word*.)

kiosk A stand-alone computer and display enclosed within a stand or workstation that is designed to play presentations, other multimedia, and interactive materials on demand.

kludge A programming term for a workaround or inelegant solution to a problem.

LAN (Local Area Network) A network linked together by physical cables or short-haul connections with a span of generally less than one mile.

library A collection of programs or code modules that programmers can link to their own code to provide standard, predefined functionality.

Lingo Director's built-in scripting language that provides programmatic control and behavior for cast members and that automates many aspects of a project's score.

link A basic element of hypertext that provides a method for jumping between points in one or more documents.

linked media A collection of graphics, sound, video, or animation files that together comprise the content of a multimedia presentation. Shockwave does not currently support linked media.

Lisp (LISt Processing language) A type of programming language for which all operations are defined through the evaluation of a list of functions.

log file Information about Web site access and use acquired by monitoring software integrated with a Web server and stored in files that usually adhere to standard formats.

loop In Director, a loop is a collection of frames that is repeated as specified by the script elements associated with those frames.

lossless compression A form of file compression in which the contents are reduced in size but can be restored to their original state.

lossy compression A form of file compression, usually applied to graphics information, in which the contents are compressed in a manner that does not permit them to be fully restored to their original form, but rather involves a loss of resolution, color information, or both.

MacOS An abbreviation for the Macintosh Operating System, currently version 7.5.

mail server Any member of a class of Internet programs (for example, *majordomo,* *listserv,* or *mailserv*) that allows users to participate in ongoing data exchanges or file retrieval via electronic mail.

mailing list A list of participants who regularly exchange electronic mail messages that usually focus on a particular topic or concern.

map files The boundary definitions for a clickable image, stored in a file format for a particular HTTP server implementation (usually NCSA or CERN), used to assign URLs to regions on an image for user navigation.

markup A special form of text embedded in a document that describes elements of document structure, layout, presentation, or delivery.

MIME (Multipurpose Internet Mail Extensions) Extensions to the RFC822 mail message format that permit more complex data and file types than plain text. Today, MIME types include sound, video, graphics, PostScript, HTML, and others.

mirrored servers Heavily used file archives, Web servers, or other network servers may be copied *en toto* and located around a network to lower the demand on any one server and to reduce long-distance network traffic. When one server acts as a full copy of another, the second server is said to be a mirror of the first.

modularity The concept that a program should be broken into components, each of which supplies a particular function or capability.

movie A synonym for a finished Director project or film strip that displays its scripted sequence of images, sounds, and interactions upon demand (and in response to programmed user interactions or events).

multimedia A computerized art form that permits the combination of graphics, animation, sound, interaction, and dynamic on-screen behavior.

multithreaded A computer runtime environment that uses a lightweight process control mechanism called threading to switch contexts among multiple tasks.

NCSA (National Center for Super-computing Applications) An arm of the University of Illinois that originally developed Mosaic, one of the best of the Web browsers.

net-pointers URLs, *ftp* addresses, or other locations on the Internet where you can go to get the "good stuff."

network services Access to shared files, printers, data, or other applications (for example, e-mail or scheduling) across a network.

network utilization The amount of network usage, usually expressed as the percentage of bandwidth consumed on the medium, for a specific period of time.

newsgroup On USENET, individual topic areas are called newsgroups. Such groups exchange regular message traffic and are a great source of information for diverse technical topics.

object oriented A programming paradigm that concentrates on defining data objects and the methods that may be applied to them.

outsource Literally, to find an outside source for information, services, or materials; in the context of this book, this term generally indicates involvement of a third party in the design, content creation, or production of a multimedia project.

palette In Director as in many other graphics programs, a palette is the collection of colors or shades used within a particular image. Whenever possible, it's wise to use standard, Microsoft Windows-compatible palettes for projects targeted for cross-platform use.

parameter A value passed into or out of a program or subroutine, or across an interface, when code components communicate with one another.

pattern matching A computerized search operation whereby input values are treated as patterns, and matches are sought in a search database. An exact match is called a hit; the results of a search produce a list of hits for further investigation.

Perl An interpreted programming language developed by Larry Wall, Perl offers superb string-handling and pattern-matching capabilities, and is a favorite among Web programmers for CGI use.

PICT A common Macintosh graphics file format that is one of many image file types that Director can import.

pixel A single addressable location on a computer display, a pixel, or picture element, is the most primitive individual element for controlling graphics. Pixels also are how image maps are measured and specified.

placeholder A parameter is an ideal example of a placeholder, because it is a symbolic representation that will be manipulated by a program, but only when it's running and an initial input value is defined. While the code is being written, all parameters are merely placeholders.

platform independence Indicates that a program or device will work on any computer, irrespective of make, model, or type.

playback head In Director, the playback head is a conceptual pointer that indicates the display's current position relative to a particular frame in a movie or project. During creation and editing, the playback head is moved to change the focus of activity; during playback, it's moved to control the flow of content on the user's display.

polygon A many-sided surface; polygons provide the basic visual units that VRML uses to define surfaces and to combine them to represent all kinds of visual objects.

port Short for transport (usually used as a verb), porting code refers to altering a program written for one system so that it run on another system.

port address In TCP/IP-speak, a port address refers to the socket identifier that a program or a service seeks to address for a specific type of communication. Most TCP/IP protocols have well-known port addresses associated to them (for example, HTTP's port address is 80), but system configurations allow other port addresses to be used (which can sometimes be a good idea for security reasons).

post-process To perform some translation or transformation on a collection of data (usually at the file level) after the information has been completely developed. Thus, Afterburner is a kind of post-processor for Director project files.

PostScript A page description language defined by Adobe Systems, PostScript files usually carry the extension .ps in the UNIX world and are a common format for exchanging nicely formatted print files.

processor intensive An application that consumes lots of CPU cycles (that is, runs for a long time) is said to be processor intensive. Good examples include heavy graphics rendering like ray tracing, animation, and CAD, which combine lots of number-crunching with intensive display requirements.

projector A self-running version of a Director project that doesn't require a copy of Director on the viewing machine. It's not possible to convert a projector file into a Shockwave .dcr file. On Microsoft Windows machines, projector files end with an .exe extension; on the Mac, because the projector's file type is APPL (application), no specific extension is required.

proprietary Technology that's owned or controlled by a company or organization and that may or may not be widely used is referred to as proprietary technology.

protocol suite A collection of networking protocols that together define a complete set of tools and communication facilities for network access and use (for example, TCP/IP, OSI, or IPX/SPX).

query string The parameters passed to a Web-based search engine, usually using the GET method. (Because search strings are nearly always short, this is quite safe.)

QuickDraw and **QuickDraw 3-D** Apple Computer's built-in two- and three-dimensional graphics packages included as part of the MacOS.

QuickTime Apple's video and animation-rendering library included with the MacOS but also available for other platforms (for example, Microsoft Windows).

RAM (Random Access Memory) The fastest and most volatile form of information storage used in a computer outside its central processing unit (CPU). The amount of RAM on a system greatly affects its performance and its ability to handle the large amounts of data typical of multimedia applications such as Director.

ray tracing A way of rendering virtual, three-dimensional graphical objects by calculating the way that rays of light travel and illuminate all of the objects in a viewing space. Although it is calculation intensive and time consuming to create such images, they deliver the most realistic computer graphics of any technique used today.

remote location A site or machine elsewhere on the network, remote location can also refer to a machine that is only intermittently connected to a network (usually via a dial-up connection).

render To interpret the contents of a document, image, or other file so that it can be displayed or played back on a computer.

replication The process of duplicating information on multiple servers, usually according to some strict synchronization protocol or scheme, so that a copy can be said to be an exact replica of the original.

repository A place where data is kept, such as a file archive, database server, or document management system.

request A network message from a client to a server that states the need for a particular item of information or service.

request header The preamble to a request, the header identifies the requester and provides authentication and, when applicable, formatting information. This lets the server know where to send a response,

whether or not that request should be honored, and what formats it may be allowed to take.

rescaling The operation of changing the dimensions of an image by reducing the height and width in proportion to its overall dimensions.

reserved word A specific term or keyword with a predetermined meaning. In a programming language, those terms that define operations or specific capabilities—for constructs like loops, conditionals, built-in functions, and more—are invariably reserved words; that is, users aren't allowed to define variables with the same names as these reserved words.

response A network message from a server to a client that contains a reply to a request for service.

response header The preamble of a response, the header identifies the sender and the application to which the response should be supplied.

response time The amount of time between the transmission of a request for service and the arrival of the corresponding response.

runtime environment The computer execution environment that performs the instructions specified in a particular collection of interpreted code and that plugs in the necessary environmental and dynamic variables to consummate the code's proper execution.

Save and Compact A Director File Save command for .dir files that reorders the cast and compacts the file to optimize playback behavior. Because this command produces more compact files to send to Afterburner, we recommend that you use it when saving a film strip for conversion to a Shockwave file.

score Following Director's theater-based metaphor, the score controls the actions of the members of your cast on the stage.

score script The Director script that controls the overall score for a movie or project (controlled through the script channel).

script channel A Director channel used to invoke and manage Lingo scripts associated with particular frames or sequences of frames.

script A synonym for program; programmers usually refer to their work as a script when it is written in an interpreted language because, like a script, it is read each time it is run.

search string The input passed for keyword search and pattern matching in an index to a search engine or database management system.

server A network computer that responds to requests from a client computer.

Shockwave Macromedia's compression and playback technology for specially formatted Director files, intended to provide efficient Internet delivery for playback within appropriately enabled Web browsers.

sound channel A Director channel used to control and manage audio information (See also *channel*).

source code The original text files containing instructions in a programming language that programmers write when creating software.

specification A document that describes the requirements, inputs and outputs, and capabilities of a protocol, service, language, or software program—a kind of blueprint for a computer system or service.

spline-based modeling A technique for rendering complex graphical surfaces and objects by approximating their true shapes with mathematical approximations called splines (or B-splines); a family of functions that approximate the curve between two points by fitting a curve (rather than a line) between them.

sprite In Director, a sprite is a graphical object that's animated or altered on the stage using a predefined transition or some other special effect.

stage Following Director's theater-based metaphor, the stage is where multimedia projects play for their viewers.

standard A program, system, protocol, or other computer component that has been declared to be standard may be the subject of an official published definition from some standards-setting body, or it may simply have acquired that status through widespread or long-term use. When talking about standards, find out if the designation is official or otherwise.

storyboard A technique for combining graphics and text when designing multimedia content in which pictures are used to describe visual elements and text instructions are used to describe emotions, intentions, dialog, and other aspects of images. Commonly used to build movies, commercials, and other forms of multimedia, storyboards also work well for designing Director projects.

streaming The process of double-buffering an ongoing stream of input data so that the front end of a data stream can be rendered and played in an application while new data arrives at the back end. Shockwave does not currently support streaming, but most pundits anticipate this support in a future release.

string In programmer-speak, a string consists of a sequence of character data, such as *William*.

subtype For MIME encodings, the subtype identifies the application or the particular instance of a general type (for example, *text/html* identifies a document as comprised of type text and subtype HTML—in other words, ASCII text to be interpreted as an HTML document).

symbolic link A mechanism whereby one name points to another name in a system rather than directly to an object. Symbolic names are common for Web servers, document roots, and other system objects. They provide a valuable technique to insulate users from long and unruly "real" names, but also protect servers from the kind of system access that knowing "real" names sometimes encourages.

synchronous A method of communication wherein all communicating parties interact simultaneously.

syntax The rules for placing and ordering terms, punctuation, and values when writing statements in a particular language (including programming languages, where the rules tend to be rather exacting).

system administrator An individual responsible for tasks such as maintaining a computer system, managing the network, setting up accounts, and installing applications.

system-level language A programming language that is suitable for implementing operating systems or equivalent code that gets "down and dirty" with the computer and its instruction set.

T1 A fully-digital telephone communication link capable of delivering bandwidth up to 1.544 megabits per second in the U.S., and 2.08 megabits per second in Europe and the Far East.

tar (Tape ARchival program) A UNIX utility used to compress and decompress files. Files compressed with this program normally have the extension of .tar.

TCP/IP (Transmission Control Protocol/Internet Protocol) The basic suite of protocols upon which the Internet runs.

Tempo control In Director, the Tempo control handles the speed at which one frame transitions to another within a project.

text to speech A facility for converting text from a variety of formats into speech, usually to provide telephone or other audio access to printed information stored on a computer.

tile A small, rectangular graphical element that usually contains a pattern or texture designed to replicate well. A single, small tile can cover a large area with an interesting pattern or texture, yet require only a small amount of data to represent it because the surface is covered by repetition

of that data rather than by unique graphical information.

toolset A collection of software tools useful for performing certain tasks (e.g., CGI input handling or image map creation).

transition A change of scene, back-ground, or special effects on Director's stage or its changing area as orches-trated by Director's Set Transition controls.

tree A hierarchical structure for organizing data or documents, common examples of which include file system directories, object hierarchies, and family trees.

UNIX The powerful operating system developed by Brian Kernighan and Dennis Ritchie as a form of recreation at Bell Labs in the late '60s that is still running strong today.

URI (Uniform Resource Identifier) Any of a class of objects that identify resources available to the Web; both URLs and URNs are instances of a URI.

URL (Uniform Resource Locator) The primary naming scheme used to identify Web resources, URLs define the protocols to be used, the domain name of the Web server where a resource resides, the port address to be used for communication, and the directory path to access a named Web document or resource.

URL encoding A method for passing information requests and URL specifications to Web servers from browsers, URL encoding replaces spaces with plus signs and substitutes hex codes for a range of otherwise irreproducible characters. This method is used to pass document queries via the GET method from browser to servers, and on to CGIs.

URN (Uniform Resource Name) A permanent, unchanging name for a Web resource. (Seldom used in today's Web environment.)

visitation rate The amount of activity or number of visitors on a Web server or on a specific Web site during a given time interval.

VRML (Virtual Reality Modeling Language) VRML is a language for describing multiparticipant, interactive simulations—virtual worlds networked via the global Internet and hyperlinked with the World Wide Web.

W3C (World Wide Web Consortium) An organization that seeks to guide standards related to the World Wide Web and that works in concert with the Internet Engineering Task Force on HTML, HTTP, and related protocols and services; funded by contributions from MIT, INRIA, CERN, and a host of other member organizations.

Wait option A Tempo control option in Director that causes playback of the score to pause at a particular frame for a specified number of seconds.

Web sites Individual Web document collections named by home pages or other unique URLs.

Web-space The total agglomeration of sites, resources, and documents available through the World Wide Web.

webification The act of turning complex electronic documents from some other format into HTML, usually programmatically rather than by hand.

webify The verb form of webification.

WebMaster The individual responsible for managing a specific Web site.

XCMD (eXternal ComManD) An API for developing additional, external commands to extend the Director application. These commands appear as files in an Xtras folder or directory.

XFCN (eXternal FunCtioN) An API for developing additional, external functions to extend the Director application. These functions appear as files in an Xtras folder or directory.

XObjects (eXternal Objects) An API used to extend Director's collection of definitions for graphic objects and elements, primarily to extend the capabilities of a particular project. These objects and elements appear as files in an Xtras folder or directory.

Xtras An API for developing extensions to the Director application that work like plug-ins to extend a specific project using XObjects or their equivalents to defined, external objects, functions, and capabilities. The Afterburner application has its own Xtras folder or directory to support the addition of other codecs to the codecs defined by Macromedia.

About the CD-ROM

*t*his book includes a CD-ROM that's crammed full of all kinds of interesting goodies. In fact, it's so full of material that you may notice that your CD-ROM player takes a while to locate materials, and to produce a directory listing. That's because there's so much stuff aboard this platter that it takes an appreciable while to get "there" from "here!"

We've built the CD-ROM using a hybrid format so it can be used on PCs and other ISO 9660 CD-ROM readers (such as UNIX, Windows NT, or other, similar operating systems) as well as the native Macintosh HFS CD-ROM format. The best part is that there's nothing special you need to do; just plop the CD into your drive, and go! Whichever platform you're using, the CD adheres to the same organization (though file names and extensions will vary).

The Big Picture

The *60 Minute Guide to Shockwave* CD includes three basic components:

1. Macromedia's Showcase
   Built around an interactive roadmap to the products and services offered by Macromedia, the Showcase includes functional working models of Macromedia's software that you can use with the materials prepared for this book.

2. The Shockwave Plug-In and Afterburner modules

   The Netscape Plug-In for Shockwave, and the Afterburner code needed to "shock" Macromedia Director presentations, are ready to install from the CD.

3. The *60 Minute Guide to Shockwave* materials

   The first of the two tutorials in Chapter 3, plus a number of examples developed specifically for use with this book. We give you illustrations of the exercises, and examples of "interesting" Director effects, ready for you to "shock" or otherwise play with.

In the sections that follow, we'll explore each of these areas in further detail.

The Macromedia Showcase

Macromedia's Multimedia Showcase provides an interactive roadmap to the products and services offered by Macromedia. The Showcase gives you detailed explanations of the Macromedia tools that power your ideas. Preview valuable information on Macromedia's product line; testimonials and example files from leading multimedia developers; fully functional working models that let you try out their software; and guided product demonstration files that take you step-by-step through Macromedia's most popular applications including Action!, Authorware, Director, Extreme 3D, FreeHand, Fontographer, SoundEdit 16, and xRes.

That's about all we can say about the Macromedia materials on this CD, except to add that there's over 635 MB of material to explore here. Although the Showcase CD's contents go well beyond the focus of this book—namely, Macromedia Director and the Shockwave modules—you'll find plenty of other stuff to while away the hours with here. Be sure to check out the hours of multimedia presentations and Director movies for some great examples of what this product can do! Refer to the "readme" file on the CD for installation instructions and other information.

The Shockwave Materials

If you look on the CD, you'll find one of the following two directory structures (directory names appear in bold):

1. Macintosh

    Shockwave:The Netscape Shockwave plug-in files

    Afterburner:A self-extracting archive containing the Afterburner modules

    Consult the Netscape Help system for information on how to install the plug-in; double-click the self-extracting archive in its own directory to create your Afterburner work area and toolset.

2. PC

    SHOCKWAV:The Netscape Shockwave plug-in files

    AFTRBURN:A self-extracting archive containing the Afterburner modules

    Consult the Netscape Help system for information on how to install the plug-in; double-click the self-extracting archive in its own directory to create your Afterburner work area and toolset.

With these components installed and in place, you'll be able to view Shockwave content within your Netscape browser. You'll also be able to "shock" Macromedia Director film strips (".DIR" files) to create your own Shockwave content.

The *60 Minute Guide* Materials

Within a top-level directory on the CD named "60minute" you'll find a collection of files and directories, as follows:

```
60minute        : the main directory for this book

  2d            : a two-dimensional Shockwave example
    twod.dir    : moving globes crisscross the stage

  3d            : a three-dimensional Shockwave example
    threed.dir  : animated, twisting 3-D cube with complex
                    color surfaces

  ch3ex         : Example 1 from Chapter 3, ready for use
    lesson.dir  : Pre-fabricated version of Example 1
```

```
flat              : A simple, two-dimensional animation
   flatclr.dir    : A red ball rolls up an incline, jumps the
                    gap, and rolls across the other side

inkfx             : An illustration of Director's "Ink effects"
   le.dir         : Text image cycles through a color sequence

rescale           : image scaling examples
   rescale1.dir   : small box static in center of stage
   rescale2.dir   : resize box, with complex color surface, to
                    fill the stage
```

By investigating these examples and illustrations as you read the book, you should be able to better understand the kind of effects and animation that Shockwave for Director can deliver. We expect that you'll find a lot of inspiration here, if not some pre-fabricated examples upon which to base your own work!

For More Information...

Because of the ever-changing nature of the Web and related technologies, we'd like to remind you that we've also established a Web site for this book. Follow the Shockwave links at this URL:

```
http://www.idgbooks.com
```

If you visit this site, not only will you gain access to some other special Shockwave materials from which we've created for it, you'll also be able to find out if there's any new or interesting information that's germane to the contents of this book. If we find any glitches on the CD, discover any new technologies or materials from which you might benefit, or simply want to point you at some additional information, you'll find it all here!

Index

IDG Books Worldwide, Inc. License Agreement

*i*mportant — read carefully before opening the software packet. This is a legal agreement between you (either an individual or an entity) and IDG Books Worldwide, Inc. (IDG). By opening the accompanying sealed packet containing the software disc, you acknowledge that you have read and accept the following IDG License Agreement. If you do not agree and do not want to be bound by the terms of this Agreement, promptly return the book and the unopened software packet(s) to the place you obtained them for a full refund.

1. **License.** This License Agreement (Agreement) permits you to use one copy of the enclosed Software program(s) on a single computer. The Software is in "use" on a computer when it is loaded into temporary memory (i.e., RAM) or installed into permanent memory (e.g., hard disk, CD-ROM, or other storage device) of that computer.

2. **Copyright.** The entire contents of this disc and the compilation of the Software are copyrighted and protected by both United States copyright laws and international treaty provisions. You may only (a) make one copy of the Software for backup or archival purposes, or (b) transfer the Software to a single hard disk, provided that you keep the original for backup or archival purposes. The individual programs on the disc are copyrighted by the authors of each program respectively. Each program has its own use permissions and limitations. To use each program, you must follow the individual requirements and restrictions detailed for each in the About the Disk section of this book. Do not use a program if you do not want to follow its Licensing Agreement. None of the material on this disc or listed in this Book may ever be distributed, in original or modified form, for commercial purposes.

251

3. **Other Restrictions.** You may not rent or lease the Software. You may transfer the Software and user documentation on a permanent basis provided you retain no copies and the recipient agrees to the terms of this Agreement. You may not reverse engineer, decompile, or disassemble the Software except to the extent that the foregoing restriction is expressly prohibited by applicable law. If the Software is an update or has been updated, any transfer must include the most recent update and all prior versions. Each shareware program has its own use permissions and limitations. These limitations are contained in the individual license agreements that are on the software discs. The restrictions include a requirement that after using the program for a period of time specified in its text, the user must pay a registration fee or discontinue use. By opening the package which contains the software disc, you will be agreeing to abide by the licenses and restrictions for these programs. Do not open the software package unless you agree to be bound by the license agreements.

4. **Limited Warranty.** IDG Warrants that the Software and disc are free from defects in materials and workmanship for a period of sixty (60) days from the date of purchase of this Book. If IDG receives notification within the warranty period of defects in material or workmanship, IDG will replace the defective disc. IDG's entire liability and your exclusive remedy shall be limited to replacement of the Software, which is returned to IDG with a copy of your receipt. This Limited Warranty is void if failure of the Software has resulted from accident, abuse, or misapplication. Any replacement Software will be warranted for the remainder of the original warranty period or thirty (30) days, whichever is longer.

5. **No Other Warranties.** To the maximum extent permitted by applicable law, IDG and the author disclaim all other warranties, express or implied, including but not limited to implied warranties of merchantability and fitness for a particular purpose, with respect to the Software, the programs, the source code contained therein and/or the techniques described in this Book. This limited warranty gives you specific legal rights. You may have others which vary from state/jurisdiction to state/jurisdiction.

6. **No Liability For Consequential Damages.** To the extent permitted by applicable law, in no event shall IDG or the author be liable for any damages whatsoever (including without limitation, damages for loss of business profits, business interruption, loss of business information, or any other pecuniary loss) arising out of the use of or inability to use the Book or the Software, even if IDG has been advised of the possibility of such damages. Because some states/jurisdictions do not allow the exclusion or limitation of liability for consequential or incidental damages, the above limitation may not apply to you.

7. **U.S.Government Restricted Rights.** Use, duplication, or disclosure of the Software by the U.S. Government is subject to restrictions stated in paragraph (c) (1) (ii) of the Rights in Technical Data and Computer Software clause of DFARS 252.227-7013, and in subparagraphs (a) through (d) of the Commercial Computer—Restricted Rights clause at FAR 52.227-19, and in similar clauses in the NASA FAR supplement, when applicable.

GET THE NET

GET ON.

Mecklermedia's Official Internet World 60-Minute Guide to the Internet Including the World-Wide Web

Get on the Net now! Internet World Editor Andrew Kantor gets you browsing the Internet in 60 minutes or less, downloading news, business data, games, sounds, and a whole lot more! BONUS disk includes browser software, connection utilities and lots of other cool stuff from Mecklermedia.

Mecklermedia's Official Internet World 60-Minute Guide to the Internet Including the World-Wide Web
By Andrew Kantor
ISBN: 1-56884-342-9
$19.99 USA / $26.99 Canada

GET PROTECTION.

Mecklermedia's Official Internet World Internet Security Handbook

Learn what works — and what doesn't. Author William Stallings has written more than a dozen books and several technical papers on data communications and security issues. His successful consulting business has managed top security projects for a variety of companies. Learn his best tips and techniques regarding firewalls, encryption, cybercash, and minimizing hacker risk.

Mecklermedia's Official Internet World Internet Security Handbook
By William Stallings
ISBN: 1-56884-700-9
$29.99 USA / $42.99 Canada

GET PAID.

Mecklermedia's Official Internet World net.profit: Expanding Your Business Using The Internet

Anyone can send e-mail, transfer files, and download software. But do you know how to use the Internet as a strategic business tool? There are more than 20 million potential clients on the Internet today — and lots more to come. Author Joel Maloff will teach you how to explore the Internet for opportunities in business innovation and cost reduction.

Mecklermedia's Official Internet World net.profit: ExpandingYour Business Using the Internet
By Joel Maloff
ISBN: 1-56884-701-7
$24.99 USA / $34.99 Canada

IDG BOOKS
WORLDWIDE

IDG BOOKS WORLDWIDE

Order Center: **(800) 762-2974** *(8 a.m.–6 p.m., EST, weekdays)*

5/8/95

Quantity	ISBN	Title	Price	Total

Shipping & Handling Charges

	Description	First book	Each additional book	Total
Domestic	Normal	$4.50	$1.50	$
	Two Day Air	$8.50	$2.50	$
	Overnight	$18.00	$3.00	$
International	Surface	$8.00	$8.00	$
	Airmail	$16.00	$16.00	$
	DHL Air	$17.00	$17.00	$

*For large quantities call for shipping & handling charges.
**Prices are subject to change without notice.

Ship to:

Name _____

Company _____

Address _____

City/State/Zip _____

Daytime Phone _____

Payment: ☐ Check to IDG Books (US Funds Only)

☐ VISA   ☐ MasterCard   ☐ American Express

Card # _____ Expires _____

Signature _____

Subtotal _____

CA residents add
applicable sales tax _____

IN, MA, and MD
residents add
5% sales tax _____

IL residents add
6.25% sales tax _____

RI residents add
7% sales tax _____

TX residents add
8.25% sales tax _____

Shipping _____

Total _____

Please send this order form to:
IDG Books Worldwide
7260 Shadeland Station, Suite 100
Indianapolis, IN 46256

Allow up to 3 weeks for delivery.
Thank you!

IDG BOOKS WORLDWIDE REGISTRATION CARD

RETURN THIS REGISTRATION CARD FOR FREE CATALOG

Title of this book: **60 Minute Guide to Shockwave**™

My overall rating of this book: ☐ Very good [1]   ☐ Good [2]   ☐ Satisfactory [3]   ☐ Fair [4]   ☐ Poor [5]

How I first heard about this book:

☐ Found in bookstore; name: [6]

☐ Advertisement: [8]

☐ Word of mouth; heard about book from friend, co-worker, etc.: [10]

☐ Book review: [7]

☐ Catalog: [9]

☐ Other: [11]

What I liked most about this book:

What I would change, add, delete, etc., in future editions of this book:

Other comments:

Number of computer books I purchase in a year: ☐ 1 [12]   ☐ 2-5 [13]   ☐ 6-10 [14]   ☐ More than 10 [15]

I would characterize my computer skills as: ☐ Beginner [16] ☐ Intermediate [17] ☐ Advanced [18] ☐ Professional [19]

I use ☐ DOS [20] ☐ Windows [21] ☐ OS/2 [22] ☐ Unix [23] ☐ Macintosh [24] ☐ Other: [25]_____
(please specify)

I would be interested in new books on the following subjects:
(please check all that apply, and use the spaces provided to identify specific software)

☐ Word processing: [26]

☐ Data bases: [28]

☐ File Utilities: [30]

☐ Networking: [32]

☐ Other: [34]

☐ Spreadsheets: [27]

☐ Desktop publishing: [29]

☐ Money management: [31]

☐ Programming languages: [33]

I use a PC at (please check all that apply): ☐ home [35] ☐ work [36] ☐ school [37] ☐ other: [38] _____

The disks I prefer to use are ☐ 5.25 [39] ☐ 3.5 [40] ☐ other: [41]_____

I have a CD ROM: ☐ yes [42]   ☐ no [43]

I plan to buy or upgrade computer hardware this year: ☐ yes [44]   ☐ no [45]

I plan to buy or upgrade computer software this year: ☐ yes [46]   ☐ no [47]

Name: _____   Business title: [48] _____   Type of Business: [49] _____

Address (☐ home [50] ☐ work [51]/Company name: _____)

Street/Suite# _____

City [52]/State [53]/Zipcode [54]: _____   Country [55] _____

☐ **I liked this book!** You may quote me by name in future
IDG Books Worldwide promotional materials.

My daytime phone number is _____

IDG BOOKS

THE WORLD OF
COMPUTER
KNOWLEDGE

❏ YES!

Please keep me informed about IDG's World of Computer Knowledge.
Send me the latest IDG Books catalog.

COMPUTER
BOOK SERIES
FROM IDG